RELIGION AND ECONOMIC JUSTICE

RELIGION AND ECONOMIC JUSTICE

Edited by Michael Zweig

TEMPLE UNIVERSITY PRESS

PHILADELPHIA

Temple University Press, Philadelphia 19122
Copyright © 1991 by Temple University
All rights reserved
Published 1991
Printed in the United States of America

Library of Congress Cataloging-in-Publication Data
Religion and economic justice / edited by Michael Zweig.
    p. cm.
    ISBN 0-87722-847-7 (alk. paper)
    1. Capitalism—Religious aspects—Christianity. 2. Capitalism—
Religious aspects—Judaism. 3. Capitalism—Religious aspects—
Controversial literature. 4. Economics—Religious aspects—
Christianity. 5. Economics—Religious aspects—Judaism.
6. Religion and justice. 7. Liberation theology. 8. Women and
religion. 9. Judaism—Doctrines. I. Zweig, Michael, 1942–
BR115.C3R44   1991
261.8'5—dc20   91-6755

CONTENTS

CONTENTS

PART IV

POLITICAL IMPLICATIONS

PREFACE

As Eastern European economies move to capitalism many in those countries hope that the changes will bring a better life. Some will not be disappointed. But those who know life in capitalist society know that for hundreds of millions of people there is no cornucopia here. Capitalism is no guarantee of prosperity. To the contrary, within capitalist economies people suffer from chronic unemployment, homelessness, inadequate medical care, extreme poverty, war, and social marginalization and powerlessness, to name only some of the deplorable conditions common around us.

These conditions are unjust in a world of enormous resources produced by many and taken by a few. These conditions also generate social movements seeking to correct them, movements that sometimes investigate the root causes of the problems and challenge the very structures of capitalist economy. Movements for economic justice are often based in religious communities. Their activists are motivated by religious conviction about the dignity of human beings and the need to nurture our humanity through personal empowerment and community involvement. Whether in Base Christian Communities in Latin America or peace and justice committees in North American churches and synagogues, religiously motivated activists are the core of many economic justice movements, often in alliance with labor unions, peace and antiintervention organizations, or community associations.

As activists confront the conditions and causes of economic injustice, conservative defenders of capitalism challenge their religious interpretations and their economic critiques. Yet there is much in theological reflection and in economic analysis that bolsters and helps to guide movements for the radical restructuring of capitalist society to promote economic justice and human dignity.

The essays in this book address two sets of issues central to the debates. We look at ethical questions associated with the moral critique of capitalism, which propels many people to be active in one or another social movement for economic justice. And it is important as well to consider issues of economic analysis as they bear on these concerns. It is my hope that this book will help people deepen their understanding of both sets of issues—and their interconnections. Despite the economic critique involved in the new theology, there has been little direct discussion between the community of theologians and the community of economists on matters of economic analysis. This book has been written to further that exchange.

Three interrelated themes are the basis of the dialogue concerning economic justice. First is a critique of the individualism that underlies mainstream economic analysis. There is a search here to understand "community" as something more, and more important, than the simple sum of all the individuals in the community.

Related to the notion of community is the understanding that an individual's economic well-being is in some important way determined by his or her place in the larger community with which that person is engaged in a mutually determining and mutually responsible relation. The social marginalization and economic deprivation suffered by individuals can then be understood in significant degree as the consequences of economic organization, not simply failings of the individuals involved. It thus becomes sensible to speak of economic injustice in terms of social relations and the operation of economic institutions. To address economic injustice within this framework, one must go beyond acts of individual charity and good will to change the institutional and structural characteristics of a community's organization of production and exchange.

There follows a third theme explored in several chapters of this book. The market, which motivates and integrates the economic activity of individuals in a capitalist economy, is not value-free. Its structure and outcomes embody and also contradict ethical norms and must be evaluated accordingly. Technological and economic efficiency, as measured by engineering and market tests, are insufficient guides to community decision-making where economic justice is concerned.

In Part I, I elaborate these themes as they appear in liberation theology and as they are treated in mainstream and Marxist economics. Part I provides a framework for the chapters that follow.

Part II presents diverse views of economic justice in religious thought. Norman K. Gottwald explores the connection between religious belief and conflicting economic interests in society, illuminating the origins and social content of liberation theology as well as early Jewish and Christian history. Gregory Baum presents modern Catholic social teachings on economic issues, particularly in the writings of Pope John Paul II. Pamela K. Brubaker provides a critique of Catholic and World Council of Churches economic teachings, showing how they systematically overlook or deny the place of women in society. She also demonstrates that women's reality is ignored or misrepresented in economic analysis and suggests ways in which feminist liberation theology can contribute to a more genuinely universal human liberation. Michael Lerner traces the emergence of liberation theology from Jewish belief and historical experience, bringing the lessons to bear on contemporary social movements, both religious and secular.

Part III focuses attention on two aspects of modern capitalism: its global character and its class composition. Ann Seidman analyzes the problem of famine in sub-Saharan Africa, showing that world hunger is in important ways the result of capitalist penetration into the Third World. Amata Miller then illuminates the global economics that binds the countries of the world into a single interdependent network and presents modern Catholic social teaching as it bears on the "sinful structures" of the global economy. In the final chapter of Part III, I look at the class structure of the U.S. economy and use it to help explain the extent and incidence of poverty in the United States, as well as the moral basis on which the poor may lay claim to the resources of the wealthy.

Part IV explores some political implications of the critique of individualism that runs as a common thread throughout the book. Samuel Bowles and Herbert Gintis evaluate the strengths and weaknesses of classical liberalism in light of the realities of capitalist economic relations and propose the extension of democratic norms into the economic arena. Frances Moore Lappé and J. Baird Callicott apply the insights of ecology to an understanding of the essential community of human existence, the better to enable the transformation of the economy and the creation of a society in keeping with the dynamics of the environment.

This collection is the product of many people. I am grateful especially to the contributors, who responded to my requests with diligence, intellectual depth, and clarity.

Although the book was three years in the making, in a certain way it originated in the Conference on Religion, the Economy, and Social Justice, held at the State University of New York, Stony Brook, in November 1984. Stephen Paysen and Janice Mullaney helped organize that conference, and my discussions with them helped shape my approach to the issues.

The first formulation of this project came in response to the urgings of the Reverend Bob Lepley, who saw the possibilities of bringing together the voices here included. He also introduced me to the work of many proponents of liberation theology and helped me to understand their philosophical and practical meanings. His continued interest has been an important source of strength for me throughout the development of this book. Kathy Chamberlain also provided consistent support from the earliest days through final editing.

The early stages of such a project are the most delicate, and I am grateful for the encouragement I received when the book was still only an idea. Colin Day, David Emblidge, and Egon Neuberger helped give form to what was at first a vague notion. Philip Newell, Jack Price, and the Reverend Rob Perry gave me confidence that people would be interested, as did Emily Thomas, who also helped me think through the best structure and read early drafts of several chapters.

Once I had written a draft of what appears here as Chapter 1, I had several helpful discussions with Norman Gottwald, Robert Lekachman, and Cornel West, each of whom generously shared his time and experience. In the course of discussion as the collection was taking shape, other people also provided important insights and encouragement, particularly Rabbi Marshall Meyer and the Reverend William Sloan Coffin.

Many people read and commented on chapter drafts. My appreciation for particularly detailed appraisals goes to Michael Frohlich, Beverly Harrison, Timothy Lytton, Ruth Misheloff, Doug Orr, and Warren Sanderson. Carl Swidorski made important contributions in the preparation of the manuscript. Staughton Lynd, Leonard Miller, Milagros Peña, and Charles Staley also provided useful responses.

Doris Braendel, my editor at Temple University Press, had helpful suggestions for each chapter of the book and solved some difficult problems. Her prompt, enthusiastic, and practical assistance in the final stages kept me going apace. Carole Roland prepared the manuscript for submission, solving the myriad word-processing glitches so common in the modern era. Patricia Sterling, the copyeditor, gave especially careful attention to the manuscript and was a pleasure to work with.

The writing and editing of this book were made possible by financial support from several sources: the United University Professions, Local 2190 of the American Federation of Teachers, AFL-CIO, the union representing faculty and professional staff throughout the State University of New York; the United Church Board of Homeland Ministries; and the

Gerson Frohlich Trust. I am also grateful to the School of Social Welfare at the University of California, Berkeley, for Visiting Scholar appointments in the summers of 1989 and 1990, during which time I had a quiet and congenial place to work and a spectacular library at my disposal.

I work best when I have someone to talk with as questions or mental blocks arise. In this regard I owe a special debt to Dennis O'Neil, whose skill as an editor and writer and whose sharp intellect and knowledge of the broad subject matter here presented made him a most welcome colleague.

I

TERMS FOR A DIALOGUE

1

ECONOMICS AND
LIBERATION THEOLOGY

Michael Zweig

One day, when I was a boy growing up in Detroit, I ran home crying to ask my mother, "Who is this guy Jesus? They say I killed him, but I don't know anything about it." From those early confrontations with Catholic children and their parents, still influenced by the pro-Nazi broadcasts of Father Charles Coughlin and the thousand-year tradition of anti-Semitism, I learned that Christianity opposed me.

I was not surprised to learn in later years that the institutional church had oppressed the common people throughout feudal times. It was natural to me that Christianity, whether in the form of Roman Catholicism or any of the Protestant denominations, remained a conservative or outright reactionary force wherever it exercised power in the modern era. In fact, religious belief of any sort seemed to me a hindrance to people's ability to deal with one another directly as people, an atavistic thread of ignorance, superstition, and divisiveness in an age when science and rational thought promised an alternative course to the irrationality and hatred I saw all round.

During the 1960s I began to see a different aspect in religion. Black churches and religious leaders were at the center of the civil rights movement. Religious pacifists played a visible and militant role in the movement against the draft and U.S. military aggression in Southeast Asia.

Still, I was surprised when Michael Quinn, then the Catholic chaplain at the State University of New York at Stony Brook, came to my office in 1981 and asked permission to sit in on my course in Marxist economics, and also in my class on the economics of socialism. Quinn was a peace activist trying to prevent further U.S. military intervention in Central America, and he had no trouble contemplating the importance of Marxist analysis, or the experience of socialism, as they might serve to guide his own beliefs and actions concerning Central America, despite his deep commitment to Catholic theology. It was Michael Quinn who introduced me to the writings of Pope John Paul II and the debates through which liberation theology is developing today.

I have been drawn to these debates because they address issues of central importance to the organization, functioning, and development of society. They are the issues that drew me to social science, and to economics in particular, when I was a college student absorbed with the civil rights and Vietnam War movements of the 1960s.

We experience and observe around us many forms of injustice and human degradation: unemployment, racism, the oppression of women, hunger, war, exploitation, and the waste of lives lost to the diseases and ignorance of poverty. In whatever form, injustice is an outrage that calls for, and in time always receives, strong response. But despite the moral disgust engendered by these conditions, little is accomplished if response is limited to moral condemnation, nor can individual acts of charity and good will deal effectively with the problems. A truly moral response entails an effective response, which must be constructed with due consideration to the functioning of people within social institutions.

Liberation theology interprets religious teachings as a call to social action toward the goal of social justice. It is theology that prods religious institutions to serve as active agents for social change, on behalf of and in connection with the poor, the oppressed, and working people who experience injustice as a daily fact of life. It is theology that seeks to address and change social institutions, not just individuals. It is, therefore, theology that extends the bounds of traditional religious discourse by seeking dialogue with social science, the better to understand society and the role of religion in it.

Although for convenience I speak of liberation theology as a single phenomenon, there is no single liberation theology. Rather, in each religious tradition there is an attempt to guide the faithful toward progressive social participation, mainly based on an interpretation of humans' responsibilities to one another and to God in light of religious texts, but with some degree of direct social analysis as well. Taken as a whole, liberation theology is today a minority presence in all religions, but its influence is growing, as people look for ways to define and advance social justice. Not surprisingly, this is especially so in the inner cities and in depressed agricultural areas. But liberation theology also affects foreign policy issues, as exemplified by the work of the Maryknolls and others

4

concerned with ending United States intervention in Central America, by the sanctuary movement, and by other peace actions.

Contact with the work of liberation theologians in Latin America has provided a major source of inspiration and leadership for North American religious activists, who have been challenged to reassess the role of religion in society. As expressed by the Brazilian priest and Franciscan seminarian Leonardo Boff, "There are structural evils that transcend individual ones. The church is, whether it likes it or not, involved in a context that transcends it. What shall be its function? Shall it be oil or sand within the social mechanism? . . . It ought to participate, *critically*, in the global upsurge of liberation."[1]

What Boff observes about the church can equally well be said for social science. We economists develop our scholarship "in a context that transcends" us, too, the same context that embraces the church. We too perform a function in the social mechanism, whether we are conscious of it or not. For the individual social scientist, as for the individual theologian, knowledge and activity are not simply a means of self-expression but inescapably a contribution to the larger context and activity of the social mechanism, for which we as individuals must take our share of responsibility.

This context is of course the complex dynamic structure of human activity we call "society." As theologians and social scientists, each with a particular method and intellectual history, deliberately confront society with the aim of understanding it in order to change it, we find we have things to say to each other. This is especially the case when we take as a common objective the freeing of ordinary people from the many profound injustices they still suffer in modern society.

Deliberate dedication to such service is rejected by most social science, whose practitioners seek to remain aloof from the value-laden conflicts of everyday life, at least insofar as their "objective science" is concerned. Those who develop and shape social investigation for the *express purpose* of human liberation are typically dismissed as ideologues whose work is tainted by subjectivity.

Similarly within theological circles, there is a deep division over the appropriateness of deliberate action by religious leaders to change society. Unlike the social sciences, religion has always presented itself as a vehicle for the alleviation of human misery. But except for the briefest historical interludes, religion has also sought to remain aloof from direct social relations, at least as a matter of official doctrine, preferring instead to concentrate attention on religious doctrine and ritual.[2] It was the otherworldliness of religion that prompted Marx to articulate his famous (partial) characterization of religion as the "opium of the people." And it is this very otherworldliness that is being challenged by liberation theology today.

Despite the shared desire to be understood as aloof from the conflicting demands of society—social science in the name of objectivity, religion in the name of transcendence—neither social science nor religion can in fact escape from active participation in social conflict. As Bob Dylan titles a song in his first gospel album, "Gotta Serve Somebody."[3]

Issues of social justice have neither gone away nor been resolved. Whatever degree of complacency or "benign neglect" may characterize the overall approach to society within religion and social science, there remain many in each camp who urgently seek humane solutions to injustice. In one way or another we seek to mobilize our own constituencies as a progressive social force, whatever specific content we might give to such an aspiration, by whatever means we find appropriate.

It seems to be true that where there is oppression, there is resistance to oppression—if not immediately, then after a time. Although the social dynamics that trigger and shape such resistance are poorly understood, we know that oppressed and exploited people do rise to free themselves, driven by the harsh realities of life. We also know that others in society, who may live at a remove from daily injustice, are drawn into the freedom struggle, either because they, or institutions they associate with, become targets of the struggle or because their ethical norms call them to act on behalf of others. The more intense the liberatory activity of the oppressed themselves, the more broadly and persistently do their claims penetrate society.

It is exactly in such circumstances that Boff calls for the church to "participate in the global upsurge of liberation." This upsurge, like all broad social movements, is chaotic and bewildering, ill-defined and unsure of itself. Still, running through its core are unmistakable claims for justice, claims that call equally to social science and to religion. Although Boff is responding specifically to conditions in Latin America, the same fundamental issues are at stake in a hundred other battles in a hundred other places, not least in North America. In each case, the ripples arrive equally at the doors of religious institutions and places of higher education.

To do justice requires us to overcome enormous obstacles. Now especially do we work in adverse circumstances, caught in the midst of a reactionary countercurrent that eats away at every past gain and seeks to reimpose domination through sheer force where it cannot prevail by arrogance and deceit. Those in power proclaim that we must develop constructive proposals and not "merely" criticize, even as they dismiss as wrong and naive the thinking and values on which we seek to base our program.

There are confusions, retreats, and isolation among the social justice movements, especially in North America. Yet we are not thrown back to the 1950s on some seesaw of history. Even though in many ways earlier progress has been undone, important aspects of society have changed irrevocably. And because of the social justice movements themselves, in North America and throughout the world, both religion and social science have changed.

Within each, learning has taken place, based on the experiences each has had in contact with contemporary demands for justice. Within each, those committed to social justice are pondering recent defeats as well as past gains, the better to bring religion and social science into play as history continues to unfold. It is clear that our past understanding and practice have been insufficient for the tasks at hand. Those committed to social justice need to carry one another beyond past inadequacies. Fortunately, the possibility exists for such an advance.

When I was asked for the first time to address an audience of devout Roman Catholic social activists on the subject "Marxism and Christianity," I entered into a kind of dialogue with which no one in the room had had any direct experience. As I prepared my remarks, I thought about all that the church had meant to me and considered all that Marxism must conjure up for people who attend Mass every day. Discussion could not proceed without some initial clearing of the air. And so, recognizing that their invitation to me, and my acceptance, both reflected new learning, I made this offer: "I will not hold you responsible for the Inquisition, Father Coughlin, or Franco's Spain, and hope you will not hold me responsible for Stalin and Pol Pot. Let us come together to learn from each other how best to advance our common goal, a world of human dignity." A lively and fruitful exchange followed.

There is nothing simple in working out new understandings and putting them into new practice. There is, however, real prospect now for unity between strands of religion and strands of social science. Each can bring important insights to bear in the movements for social justice.

Unity does not mean sameness. Religion will not become science; social science need not accept religious faith. Rather, through common action, each will discover how better to grow to complement the other, as each subjects itself to the objective discipline of effecting social change.

Just as this process is not simple, neither is it automatic. Theologians and social scientists, taking up the urgent business of social justice together with the people in motion, must deliberately apply themselves to the task. We must consciously identify the issues involved and the learnings we can contribute. It is to this process that this book is dedicated.

THEMES OF LIBERATION THEOLOGY

As with every important social institution, religion both helps to shape and is shaped by the larger society in which it operates. The recent growth of liberation theology exemplifies the complex dialectic through which religion and society continue to unfold, in a rich context of doctrinal history and practical human struggle.

Within the various expressions of liberation theology there are some essential points common to all the teachings that give coherence to the general term. Four unifying themes are especially important. First, liberation theology calls on each person to be socially active in the process of human history, for it is in our temporal works that the work of God is done. Second, in history it is correct to side with the poor and the oppressed. Third, it is necessary to go beyond acts of individual charity and good works to identify and then change the institutions through which poverty is created and the poor are oppressed. Finally, it is necessary to have a social analysis of poverty and oppression, wherein religion and social science must converse. A bit later we shall look at these four common themes in more detail.

Although liberation theology is most often associated with Roman Catholicism, especially in Latin America, parallel teachings are also playing an increasing role among Protestant denominations and within the Jewish community. Many African-American theologians are reinterpreting the long history of the Black churches as social institutions in the United States, while continuing to develop a theology and religious practice devoted to ending racial oppression.

In each case, we see an attempt to bring religion to bear on worldly activity, in particular in connection with political movements for social justice. As has always been true, people today seek guidance from their ethical principles and spiritual leaders as they confront the hardships of life. Liberation theology arises as one attempt to make religion relevant to the lives of religious people seeking justice, and to the lives of those in desperate need of justice, in the modern, secular world.

In each religious tradition, liberation theology is a minority, embattled doctrine, actively asserting a new outlook and religious agenda. The controversies involve a complicated amalgam of theological dispute and socioeconomic policy disagreement, issues that we will consider in greater detail.

Liberation theology, associated with radical critiques of the capitalist economic system, is not the only religious trend leading to social activism. In the United States, for example, the Reverend Jesse Jackson and the Reverend Pat Robertson each presented himself as a candidate for president in the 1988 primaries. Each led a sophisticated political movement with deep religious roots. Both sought to transform society, yet their theologies and social programs could hardly have been more different.[4]

Beyond programmatic political differences is an even more fundamental debate over the propriety of any secular political activity whatever on the part of religious leaders. Significant sections of Protestant religious leadership think it inappropriate for the church to be deeply involved in secular matters of state. Similar disagreements extend through Catholic and Jewish circles as well, in the United States and throughout the Western world. Shortly after his installation, Pope John Paul II forbade anyone in Holy Orders to fill any government post and required many priests to resign positions of state.

The disputes by which religious doctrines are developing today are a reflection of deep conflicts in the surrounding secular society. Such connections have always existed. Today, however, some religious leaders are seeking to reinterpret theology and religious practice in light of the realities of the secular world, in a conscious attempt to make religion serve sociopolitical ends in that world. As the Peruvian theologian Gustavo Gutierrez has written, "Rather than define the world in relation to the religious phenomenon, it would seem that religion should be redefined in relation to the profane."[5]

This "profane" world contains conflict, through which human society develops dialectically. The call to redefine the religious life in terms of temporal needs necessarily confronts religion with class conflict and requires of religion a position on that conflict and the issues through which it is manifested. Not surprisingly, this has generated considerable turmoil in the Christian churches and among Jewish, Islamic, and other religious bodies as well.[6]

The political and economic activism now shaking Latin American Catholicism has its immediate doctrinal origins in the documents of Vatican Council II, in which the Roman Catholic leadership took bold and still controversial steps to orient the church toward the modern world. As one example, in the Pastoral Constitution adopted in 1965, there is an emphasis early in the document on "the duty of scrutinizing the signs of the times and of interpreting them in the light of the gospel."[7]

In Latin American countries where liberation theology has its strongest proponents and organization, "the signs of the times" over the past twenty years have been filled with oppression and sometimes tumultuous resistance to it. The Argentinian Protestant theologian José Miguez Bonino has called for close analysis of society as a condition for an appropriate church role: "Are we really for the poor and oppressed if we fail to see them as a class, as members of oppressed societies? If we fail to say *how*, are we 'for them' in their concrete historical situation? Can we claim a solidarity which has nothing to say about the actual historical forms in which their struggle to overcome oppression is carried forward?"[8]

Why the emphasis on "the signs of the times" and social analysis? Because in a secular world the churches must compete with every other institution and way of thought for the allegiance and respect of people. The modern world confronts people with a host of practical and ethical problems. As people turn to religious institutions, among others, for guidance, the pastoral duties of the clergy and the hierarchy require a search for the meaning of religion and its institutions in the world of everyday experience.

From earliest times, the history of religious doctrine has always been tightly connected with social conditions. Norman Gottwald, analyzing in detail the creation of Jewish belief in the context of the life of Israelite tribes in Canaan over three thousand years ago, proposes that religion is "the symbolic side of social struggle."[9] In the same vein, Elaine Pagels has explored the connections between worldly politics and the battle over early Christian orthodoxy, finding that religion and politics "reciprocally influenced one another."[10]

It was in this tradition that modern Christian social teaching emerged in direct and explicit competition with Marxism and socialist thought, which underlay the increasingly militant secular labor movements of Europe in the last quarter of the nineteenth century. In the first paragraph of his 1891 *Rerum Novarum* (The condition of labor), the first modern statement of Catholic teaching on labor, Pope Leo XIII notes:

> It is not surprising that the spirit of revolutionary change, which has long been predominant in the nations of the world, should have passed beyond politics and made its influence felt in the cognate field of practical economy . . . wise men discuss it; practical men propose schemes; popular meetings, legislatures, and sovereign princes, all are occupied with it—and there is nothing which has a deeper hold on public attention."[11]

Having thus focused on economic matters, Leo warns of the "danger . . . that crafty agitators constantly make use of these disputes to pervert men's judgments and to stir up the people to sedition."[12]

In *Rerum Novarum* Leo XIII devotes himself to the task of exposing the "evils" of socialism and to setting the basis for an alternative, Christian labor and political movement that will respect private property. In a more obscure but no less interesting book written shortly before World War I, an English minister addresses the realities of society with much the same fear and purpose.

> The labor problem lies at the very heart of the still wider problem of Collectivism or Socialism, which has grown to such dimensions in recent years; and believing, as I do, that it is not only more complicated than ever, but that it has in it all the elements of revolution and even of disaster, unless Christ is made our guide, I venture to make my contribution to its solution.[13]

More recently, Pope John Paul II made his contribution to Catholic teaching on the economy with a far-reaching analysis of the rights and essential dignity of labor. In the encyclical *Laborem Exercens* (On human work), issued on the ninetieth anniversary of *Rerum Novarum*, John Paul spoke of the "priority of labor over capital" in terms reminiscent of Marxist doctrine.[14] Yet John Paul writes explicitly to condemn Marxism and to urge the Church to deepen its defense of labor "so that she can truly be 'the Church of the poor,' " the better to challenge Marxism, "which professes to act as the spokesman for the working class and the worldwide proletariat."[15]

The Vatican is not engaged in battling Marxism as some abstract doctrine with which it disagrees. Marxism is a target because it is important not simply as a force in the broader society but as a specific resource toward which liberation theology is itself drawn to give effect to the moral teachings of the Church.

To understand this attraction, it is useful to consider the content of liberation theology not as theology per se but as an intellectual framework with a secular message and a worldly mandate. To do so, let us consider more deeply each of the four central elements common to liberation theologies, identified briefly above.

As a basic point of orientation, liberation theology directs people to be active in the world, to participate in the unfolding of human history as creative agents. Proponents of liberation theology reject the view that the Church should turn away from temporal concerns and lead its flock solely in a spiritual preparation for the coming Kingdom, a Kingdom completely removed in time and place from the profane world of humanity. As Bonino has put it: "God builds his Kingdom from and within human history in its entirety; his action is a constant call and challenge to man. Man's response is realized in the concrete arena of history with its economic, political, ideological options. Faith is not a different history but a dynamic, a motivation, and, in its eschatological horizon, a transforming invitation."[16]

Gustavo Gutierrez, one of the leading Catholic contributors to liberation theology, analyzes and rejects the "two planes model," in which a clear dichotomy is drawn between Church and world. He too proposes that "to participate in the process of liberation is already, in a certain sense, a salvific work. . . . The growth of the Kingdom is a process which occurs historically *in* liberation, insofar as liberation means a greater fulfillment of man." Most clearly put, "there are not two histories, one profane and one sacred, 'juxtaposed' or 'closely linked.' Rather, there is only one human destiny. . . . The history of salvation is the very heart of human history."[17]

Recent Christian attention to the importance of human action in history is consistent with the millennia-old Jewish religious tradition on which liberation theology is founded. As Albert Vorspan, executive director of the Union of American Hebrew Congregations, explained this heritage to young Jewish activists in the 1960s:

To be a Jew is to see the world from a particular angle of vision.
To be a Jew is to be mobilized for life in the task of perfecting the

world. . . . To be unreconciled to the world as it is—that is your charge. Judaism is a this-worldly religion. In our tradition, man is the co-partner with God in improving the world. To be a Jew is to say no when men murmur yes to wrong-doing. . . . To be a Jew is to get your hands bruised in the arena of action, because a cloistered virtue is un-Jewish, and Jewish belief is tested by deed.[18]

Rabbi Abraham Heschel, an influential scholar and teacher whose work has guided a section of progressive Jewish thought and action in recent decades, stresses:

History is a nightmare. . . . It would be blasphemous to believe that what we witness is the end of God's creation. It is an act of evil to accept the state of evil as either inevitable or final. . . . [Yet] human history is not sufficient unto itself. . . . A battle is raging: man in his presumption undertakes to fashion history in disregard and defiance of God. The prophets witness the misery that man endures as well as man's wickedness that God endures, and even tolerates. But God is wrestling with man. History is where God is defied, where His judgment is enacted, and where His kingship is to be established.[19]

In calling on people to be active social agents, the proponents of liberation theology seek to give some guidance to that action so that a temporal outcome consistent with God's design may result. Contemporary Catholic teaching expresses one aspect of its guide to social practice in the "preferential option for the poor," a central tenet of liberation theology that was propounded by the Conference of Latin American Bishops meeting in Puebla, Mexico, in 1979. As explained by sympathetic Canadian commentators:

The option for the poor in this instance means solidarity with the oppressed and the willingness to look at one's own society from their viewpoint. . . . [It is] based on God's words in the Scriptures. Solidarity with the oppressed has been revealed in Exodus in the liberation of the people of Israel from the power of Pharaoh; it was emphasized in the Torah, the Law of Moses, which expressed God's special care for the poor, the helpless and the unprotected; it was reinforced by the Hebrew prophets who condemned exploitation and announced that to know God was to seek justice for the disinherited and oppressed; it was confirmed through the coming of Jesus Christ, who stood in solidarity with the poor of his day, who announced God's blessing on those who hunger and thirst after justice, and who was himself persecuted as a troublemaker by the religious establishment and later condemned to be crucified by the imperial authorities, the punishment reserved for rebels and insurgents. The option for the poor was endorsed by Christ's resurrection, the divine pledge that all the humiliated people of the world will be vindicated. The murderers shall not remain victorious over their innocent victims.[20]

If the starting point of *liberation* theology is the proposition that people must be active in history in the continuing process of unfolding and perfecting the work of God on earth, then the second principle holds that to do justice, such human action in history must side with the oppressed. As the Hebrew prophets made clear:

> The world is full of iniquity, of injustice and idolatry. The people offer animals; the priests offer incense. But God needs mercy, righteousness; his needs cannot be satisfied in the temples, in space, but only in history, in time. It is within the realm of history that man is charged with God's mission.
>
> Justice is not an ancient custom, a human convention, a value, but a transcendent demand, freighted with divine concern. . . . Justice is as much a necessity as breathing is, and a constant occupation.[21]

The Black churches have historically been central in African-American resistance to oppression and racism. In his pioneering work on the role of Black theology in the American context, James Cone contended:

> Christianity is essentially a religion of liberation. The function of theology is that of analyzing the meaning of that liberation for the oppressed community so that they know that their struggle for political, social, and economic justice is consistent with the gospel of Jesus Christ. Any message that is not related to the liberation of the poor in the society is not Christ's message.[22]

The urgency of Cone's analysis is completely consistent with the message emanating from Latin America today, fully in the tradition of Exodus and the prophets.

Jewish and Christian traditions have from their beginnings encouraged acts of charity toward the poor. Liberation theology distinguishes itself within this tradition, however, by stressing the need to go beyond acts of *individual* charity and good works to confront what we have seen Leonardo Boff describe as the "structural evils that transcend individual ones." Shortly before his murder, Martin Luther King, Jr., made the point quite clearly: "We are called upon to help the discouraged beggars in life's marketplace. But one day we must come to see that an edifice which produces beggars needs restructuring."[23]

Liberation theology focuses attention on what Leonardo Boff has called "social and structural sinfulness," consistent with the call by Pope John Paul II "to seek out the structural reasons which foster or cause the different forms of poverty in the world."[24] But institutional sin involves far more than poverty.

One of the most dynamic strands of liberation theology is being developed by women in connection with the broader feminist movements that challenge patriarchy and male chauvinism in all their forms.[25] Extending their critiques beyond economic issues, women are among the most active in exposing the interplay between traditional theological methods and broader social ideologies of control and domination. Feminist theology examines the role of culture in the structures of oppression, looking with special care at the representation of women (and men) in religious thought and institutional practice.

Feminist theology confronts the structures of organized religion as well as those of the broader society. In this it deepens and generalizes the work of Leonardo Boff, Gustavo Gutierrez, and other Latin American liberation theologians who have been sharply critical of hierarchical Church structures.[26] It is interesting to note that of all the Latin American liberation theologians who have been involved in controversy with the Vatican on matters of doctrine, only Leonardo Boff, the most outspoken critic of hierarchical and antidemocratic Church structures, was the only one to have been silenced, albeit temporarily.

Liberation theologians present a sharp critique of past church policy and practice in their analysis of the ways in which social institutions contribute to the generation of injustice. Many have traced the close ties between church leadership and oppressive ruling elites, from contemporary societies back to the adoption by Constantine of Christianity as the official religion of Rome.

> The dominant classes, in their strategy for power, try to incorporate the church in the widening, consolidation, and legitimation of their dominion. . . . However, it is not preordained that the church ac-

commodate itself to the ruling classes. The subordinated classes also solicit the church to aid them in their search for greater power and autonomy in the face of the domination they suffer.[27]

Liberation theology seeks to redirect the historic links of church with society, replacing oppressive ones with ties that bind the church to the lives and needs of the oppressed and exploited.

Without in any way dismissing the importance of personal choice and individual moral action, liberation theology calls for active participation in history through the process of radical *social* change, often based on a critique of the deepest structures of capitalist society. As Gustavo Gutierrez wrote in one of the founding works of liberation theology:

> It is also necessary to avoid the pitfalls of an individualistic charity. . . . The term refers also to [people] considered in the fabric of social relationships. . . . It means the transformation of a society structured to benefit a few who appropriate to themselves the value of the work of others. This transformation ought to be directed toward a radical change in the foundation of society, that is, the private ownership of the means of production.[28]

It is not enough to be a "do-gooder" or person of moral intent. One must act effectively in the world to bring about social change, else one's morality is empty. Gayraud Wilmore recognized the importance of this point in his analysis of the reasons why liberation theology and support for political action are not more widespread. Although he was analyzing the Black churches in particular, his remarks are all the more appropriate for white churches, where liberation theology has a much more tenuous hold. "Because their [the majority of Black preachers'] sense of sin is personal and individualistic," Wilmore wrote, "they have an understanding of redemption that cannot admit the sanctification of secular conflict and struggle."[29]

The call to confront institutional sin brings theology fully into the secular world as an active, conscious agent and requires of theology some familiarity with the doctrines of social science. This of course greatly complicates the theological task, which now must address the controversies of social science as well as the doctrinal disputes internal to the religious institutions themselves. Such complications are understandably difficult and contribute to the resistance that liberation theology finds among religious leaders.

Consider, for example, the processes of history so vital to liberation theology. Gutierrez tells us that history is the unfolding of the covenant God made with Abraham,[30] but this is no more helpful than a statement that the law of gravity expresses the will of God. To understand how history actually works, and how people can be active agents of their own history, Gutierrez and other liberation theologians turn to Marx.

To be sure, they approach Marxism with a range of critiques and disclaimers, putting distance between themselves and the mechanical materialism and economic determinism so often exhibited by Marxist writings (if not by Marx and Engels themselves). Still, the Uruguayan Jesuit Juan Luis Segundo speaks for the main force of the trend: "With this theory of historical materialism . . . we now have a theory that enables us to discover the authentic face of reality in line with our own historical commitment."[31]

The connection between liberation theology and Marxism is a point of controversy in theological circles, as well as among social scientists, where Marx is hardly more respected than in the traditional religions. But the connection is not surprising when we consider that Marx developed one of the few theories of history in social science, and the most insightful of those whose focus is the liberation of humanity from oppression. I return in the final pages of this chapter to the connections between liberation theology and Marxism.

Liberation theology is only one path among many by which religion seeks to come to grips with the problems people and religious institutions face in modern society. All involve some explicit treatment of economic analysis. Whether one follows the right-wing prescriptions of Pat Robertson and the Christian fundamentalist defense of capitalism, or the left-liberal leadership of Jesse Jackson, or the vaguely social democratic reforms espoused by the United States Catholic bishops, or the revolutionary thrust of Latin American liberation theology, one sees a close and conscious link between theology and economics.

MAINSTREAM ECONOMICS

When the United States Catholic bishops first proposed the adoption of a national priority to eradicate unemployment, they noted that consensus on the issue was blocked in part as "a consequence of conflicting interpretations of what causes unemployment and of what policy steps will actually improve the situation."[32] The bishops had come up against a troubling and significant characteristic of modern economics: intellectual disarray leading to a range of opinions on practical policy questions appallingly diverse for a discipline that aspires to the status of a science.

There are a great many schools of thought contending among economists, some of them with names that occasionally appear in the popular and business press. Within the broad camp of mainstream economics, one finds monetarists, supply-siders, Keynesians, post-Keynesians, laissez-faire libertarians, rational-expectations advocates, and efficient-market theorists, to name a few.[33] Each group is in turn divided among varying interpretations of more or less fine points, sometimes with significant policy implications.

Mainstream economics is the dominant arena of economic discourse in the United States. It has an elaborate theoretical structure founded on a few simple assumptions about human behavior. Although the mathematical properties of economic theory are often elaborated for their own intellectual interest without regard to practicality, we shall see below that some results of economic analysis may be useful in guiding some short-term decisions by individuals and businesses seeking to gain maximum advantage with limited available resources.

Mainstream economics, however, is notoriously incapable of accurately forecasting economic developments. No school of thought within this camp has been able to present an understanding of the economy that yields reliable predictions, but this does not stop economists from making predictions anyway. How often do we read that some "economic analyst" in business, government, or a university predicts that the economy will grow at a rate of 2 percent, only to read another analyst predicting 4 percent growth or no growth at all? Inflation will get worse, or is it licked? The stock market will go up, or down, or make a "sidewise correction." American manufacturing is doomed because of foreign competition, or will it surge because of new export markets?

The economic analysts making these predictions all have opinions, and they all have a story to tell to justify their opinion, but the fact is that there is no consensus among economists because no one really knows how the economy works or how it will move. The version a person adopts often fits well with the desires he or she has for the future to start with. Or, as Nobel Laureate in Economics Paul Samuelson has put it: "Each person shades his objective [sic] . . . estimate in the direction most likely to call forth policy decisions that will maximize the expected value of the utility of the outcomes *as he ethically evaluates the utility of those outcomes.*"[34]

The dismal state of predictive power in economics, often noted in popular media, is frankly acknowledged by economists themselves. Victor Zarnowitz, a professor at the Graduate School of Business of the University of Chicago and a specialist in economic forecasting, has found that over the thirty-year period following the mid-1950s "there are no indications that U.S. forecasts have grown systematically worse. . . . Neither do any definitive trends in a positive direction emerge."[35] Despite the enormous financial and intellectual resources the economics profession has poured into elaborating forecasting techniques for three decades, there has been no gain in effective knowledge.

The U.S. economy is so complicated that one might well be forgiven for being unable to predict its course. Yet something profoundly wrong must lie at the heart of a profession that has, as Samuelson once observed, "predicted nine out of the last five recessions" and has been unable to learn how to do better despite prolonged, concerted effort.

What would we think of medicine as a science if doctors were no better able to diagnose and cure disease today than was the case in 1955? For all the diversity of opinion and controversy at the frontiers of a science such as physics, there is a body of settled understanding at the core of the field. Yet in economics, nothing is settled; even the most basic questions are controversial.

Zarnowitz explains that economic models perform poorly "because of paucity of generally agreed upon and successfully tested economic theories that would provide strict guidance for [building models of the economy]." How are we to advance our theory? Zarnowitz provides a clue when he says that "forecasters tend to rely heavily on the persistence of trends. . . . More attention to data and techniques that are sensitive to business cycle movements and turning points could help improve their record."[36]

In other words, the problem is that economists predict that the future will continue as the present: if there are good times, good times will continue; if there is recession, recession will continue. Whatever is, will be.

Yet good times turn to bad, and recessions yield to recoveries; and economists, like everyone else, know these things perfectly well. So economists will sometimes predict a change just because one must come eventually. If the economy has expanded for a time, it must be due for a recession. After a dismal stretch, improvement must surely be at hand. Still, we cannot predict when or how the changes will happen. Except to acknowledge their certain existence, mainstream economics knows almost nothing about the "movements and turning points" Zarnowitz and so many other economists have shown to be the nub of the forecasting problem.

Change and development are central characteristics of modern capitalist economies. In addition to the business cycle of boom and bust, individual markets change, technologies and desirable work skills change, industrial structures and the relative importance of and connections among different industries change, the place of the domestic economy in the international economic network changes. An examination of some fundamental features of the method of mainstream economics will help to explain why it is ill suited to address such changes and is thus of greatly restricted scientific value and of limited use to anyone interested in social change and economic development.

The basic analytic unit of economic theory is the individual. Beginning with certain assumptions about the desires and behavior of individual consumers and producers, economists reach conclusions about how markets form and react to prices, production, and the employment of labor and other resources. On the basis of these stylized assumptions, economists conclude in particular that given markets, and even the entire economy, can reach an equilibrium at which the desires of all consumers to buy and to save, and the plans of all producers to sell and to invest, are precisely satisfied at the market prices.

Since the forces of demand and supply just balance, so that all are able to accomplish their market goals at equilibrium, this equilibrium becomes a basic point of reference against which to compare market activity. If, to take a characteristic example from microeconomics, automobile prices are above their equilibrium value, consumers will demand fewer cars than the equilibrium number, while producers will increase their output because of the higher price they can receive. Too many cars will be brought to market in relation to demand; the market will respond to the excess by reducing auto prices, simultaneously causing increased demand for cars and reduced supply, until the two balance at equilibrium with a market price that equates demand with supply. Once established, if nothing else changes, the equilibrium tends to perpetuate itself, because all producers and consumers are satisfied and so have no reason to adjust their actions.

Now, if technology should change, for example, and production costs decline so that producers become willing to offer more cars at a given market price, a new equilibrium can be determined. By comparing the demand, supply, and price of cars, and the amount of labor and of other resources used to produce them at the new equilibrium with those amounts at the old equilibrium, economists establish the effect of changes in technology on market outcomes.

The technique of assessing the economic impact of an event by comparing market equilibrium before and after the event is called "comparative statics." It is the principal means by which economists explore the effects of changes in income, consumer tastes, the price of gasoline, or anything else figuring into the equilibrium determination.

This simple story of supply and demand is quite powerful and at the same time extremely limited as a guide to complex modern economies. I would like to focus attention on three characteristics of mainstream economics which render it ineffective for social analysis (as opposed to the analysis of a single business or consumer). First, it is static rather than dynamic. Second, it is ahistoric. Further, it is based on an extreme form of individualism that obliterates community in all but the most formal sense.

Even a brief look at these characteristics will help to reveal why economics is essentially conservative and cannot provide the guidance needed to advance economic justice. Just as liberation theologians have found it necessary to critique mainstream theology in fundamental ways, so too "liberation economics," as it comes into being, must identify and surmount the obstacles that prevent mainstream economics from capturing and illuminating important economic realities, and so keep it from contributing to the project of economic justice and social change.

First, consider the static nature of mainstream economics. In a world of rapid changes in market conditions and constant dynamic adjustments by business, consumers, and governments, the comparative-statics method of economic theory is hopelessly inadequate. A most important expression in the economist's lexicon is the Latin *ceteris paribus*, "other things being equal." In the economic method, one changes a single element in the economic picture—the price of a car, for example—and, *ceteris paribus*, one concludes that more cars will be demanded at a lower price, fewer at a higher one.

But in reality, other things are not equal. Such important elements of the problem as consumer income, styling and consumer taste, the quality of the cars, the nationality of their origin and the foreign policy stance of the United States government, the price of gasoline, government policy on mass transportation (both public and private)—to name but some of the considerations—also change, and the task of integrating all the interactions among these changes, presuming one could forecast them, overwhelms the machinery of mainstream economics.

The method of comparative statics presumes that the basic structure of the economy stays fixed, while a single change percolates through that structure to a modest change in some market, represented by a new equilibrium. The problem of forecasting by trend, previously identified by Victor Zarnowitz, is deeper and more subtle than one might imagine. We forecast the future by looking at the past to learn from experience. But past relationships will continue into the future only to the degree that the past economic structures remain in place. Using historical data to discover relationships on the basis of which to predict the future is historical method only in the most formal sense. In fact, it is ahistoric because it requires *no* change, no difference between past, present, and future, at least as far as the underlying economic structures are concerned. Since those structures do in fact change all the time, the economy is a kind of moving target that cannot be anticipated by static and ahistoric methods.

This is why no one really knows what unemployment will be, or how changes in the amount of money in the economy will influence inflation, or what the market for domestically produced automobiles will be, or what the effect of a change in the minimum wage will be. Economists have long recognized that effective forecasting requires an understanding of dynamic structural changes, and there have been some attempts to address the problem; but no real progress has been made, and economic dynamics remains a fringe activity among economists.

Because the method of comparative statics demands a stable economic structure, it is incapable of analyzing structural change. Like a Newtonian mechanical system, the economy is at rest, at equilibrium, until some external shock changes one of the conditions of the market, and then the structure adjusts to a new equilibrium, a new stasis.

Once equilibrium is achieved, no actor internal to the economy has any reason to change behavior. Any change must originate from outside the system, from the impact of an "exogenous" force such as new technology, sunspots, government policy, market structure, or some assumed and unexplained change in prices, incomes, or other component of the economy.

Because mainstream economics takes economic structures as given, then, modern economic analysis is completely ahistoric, the second of the characteristics that render it ineffective for social analysis. One might think that economic theory would be enriched by consideration of economic history, but this is not the case. As Professor Robert Solow points out: "For better or worse . . . economics has gone down a different path . . . economic theory learns nothing from economic history, and economic history is as much corrupted as enriched by economic theory."[37]

Unable to analyze structural change, mainstream economics limits itself to the operations of economic actors within the existing structure. These actors, whether consuming or producing (the two broad categories of human activity proposed for analysis by mainstream economics), base their actions on a few simple rules, which are declared to be "rational." All producers want to gain the greatest possible profit; all consumers seek to derive the greatest personal pleasure. Each person is limited only by the resources available for spending in relation to the prices that must be paid. Faced with the need to make choices among alternatives in the face of scarcity, which keeps all desires from being satisfied simultaneously, each person chooses so as to maximize his or her own personal pleasure and gain.

Mainstream economics embraces this notion of rationality as an elementary part of human nature. People are naturally out for themselves, have always been so, and will always be. In this connection, capitalism is the most rational, the most effective economic system, because it most conforms to and harnesses the strengths of basic human nature. If prior economic systems were not organized like our own, still the people in them were similarly motivated.

Capitalism arises, in this view, as the ultimate historical form of society, beyond which it is irrational and even inhuman to go. Here is the second sense in which mainstream economics is ahistoric. Having reached modern capitalist life, history stops, at least insofar as basic social structures are concerned. Humanity has reached the peak of its organizational form, through which the maximum possible human potential can be realized.

Obviously, an approach to social study that is static and ahistoric is an approach that fosters and is consistent with a conservative cast of mind and a conservative social policy. To call mainstream economics (even its "liberal" strands) conservative, however, cannot by itself lead to any evaluative conclusion. The problem is that society and the economy are dynamic, and rapidly changing at that. Further, there *is* history beyond capitalism. The distance between these social realities and the methods of mainstream economics is what renders mainstream economics of such little value for those interested in economic justice.

A third aspect of mainstream economic method that limits its value as a tool for understanding the economy around us is its extreme individualism. Economics begins with the individual and proposes to analyze the economy as a whole and its various markets by simply adding together the behaviors of all the individuals participating in those markets or in the entire economy. The whole is treated strictly as the sum of its parts.

Mainstream economics has developed some important insights into individual behavior in the presence of scarcity. Given the financial and institutional constraints within which each consumer, worker, or business operates, economics provides powerful ways of thinking to guide the individual's actions, presuming of course that the individual wants to maximize his or her personal gain in the situation. Since this is often the case, mainstream economics has something important to offer.

A problem arises, however, when one tries to make sense out of the economy as a whole by simply adding together the actions of all individuals. One example of the problem well recognized by economists is the "fallacy of composition" (the belief that the whole is simply the sum of its parts) in a naive analysis of people's decisions to save money. Any one person can save more money just by deciding to spend a little less each week out of his or her income. But can there be greater savings in the entire economy if everyone in it makes that simple personal decision? If all that is involved is a simple addition of individual behaviors, the answer is clearly "yes." But the world isn't so simple. If *everyone* spends less, then there will be significantly less demand for products, and companies will cut back on the number of people they employ and the number of hours their employees work. So people's incomes will fall, and they will be able to save less, not more. Adding up individual behaviors can lead to the opposite behavior for the economy as a whole, and for the individuals in it as well.

Mainstream economics contains such contradictions in many guises. What is true for the individual cannot readily be generalized to the economy as a whole; rules for social policy cannot be derived by the simple aggregation of individual preferences. In work that became the basis for his Nobel Prize in Economics, Kenneth Arrow addressed the problem of "moving from the preferences of individuals to social values on the basis of which public choices are to be made." He concluded: "If consumers' values can be represented by a wide range of individual orderings, the doctrine of voters' sovereignty is incompatible with that of collective rationality." [38]

In other words, starting with individuals, each with his or her own preferences and each acting rationally as economists understand the term, it is not possible to find a guide to social policy (sometimes called a "social welfare function") that will also display such rationality simply by allowing each person to vote on the basis of personal preference. As economist Amartya Sen explains, "Arrow proved that a set of very mild looking conditions [defining rational behavior] are so restrictive that they rule out not some but *every possible* social welfare function." [39] That is, Arrow found that there is simply no way to make sense out of social policy by limiting one's view to the interests of the individuals in society, each taken alone.

Another example of the limited results achieved by considering the economy as the simple resultant of individual behavior is the failure of classic supply-and-demand analysis to anticipate the Great Depression of the 1930s. Before it occurred, economic theory held that a broad depression with chronic unemployment was not possible in a market economy. Using the techniques of comparative statics described above, economists concluded that if each person were free to pursue his or her own interests within the market, there could at most be temporary and local imbalances, which would soon be corrected and full employment restored. There was no need to have concern for the economy as a whole, since "the invisible hand," in Adam Smith's classic expression, of interpersonal competition would guarantee an efficient social outcome without conscious human attention beyond each person's own self-interest. The historical fact of the Great Depression demolished this theoretic complacency in all but its most die-hard proponents. The whole *is* more than the sum of its parts.

It is of course true that society arises from the acts of the individuals composing it. But society in turn constrains and shapes us as individuals, so that we arise as individuals from society as much as society arises out of the collectivity of its members. Mainstream economics cannot illuminate the joint determination of individual and society.

The individualism of mainstream economics is completely consistent with the mechanistic approach to science and nature current in the eighteenth and nineteenth centuries, when modern economics was created parallel with the development of capitalism. Important insights into rational economic behavior can be derived from the theory to guide the most short-run decisions of individuals who are out for themselves in a capitalist world. The theory has proved utterly incapable, however, of explaining or predicting how individual behaviors will combine to determine the aggregate economy. And since the aggregate economy is an essential component to consider in any individual economic decision, the theory is ultimately ill suited to guide individual behavior as well.

When we turn to economics to understand what is going on around us and to formulate policy in our own interest, we find the confusion and disarray reported by the United States Catholic bishops, as noted above. We have seen that this sad state of affairs can be traced to three interrelated characteristics of mainstream economics. It is static. It is ahistoric. And it is based on an extreme individualism that denies community in all but the most formal sense.

All these features are serious deficiencies from the point of view of liberation theology, which seeks to play a dynamic, transformative role in history as part of a human community in motion. One further weakness in mainstream economics, a product of its individualism, sets it at odds with liberation theology and with the corpus of humanist thought in general: mainstream economics has no genuine ethics and can have none—an important distinction between mainstream and Marxist economics.

Mainstream economics imagines a world of individuals isolated from one another, each individual an island of self-consideration who enters into contact with others only to advance his or her own interests. As Adam Smith so clearly stated in a justly famous passage: "It is not from the benevolence of the butcher, the brewer, or the baker, that we expect our dinner, but from their regard to their own interest. We address ourselves not to their humanity but to their self-love, and never talk to them of our own necessities but of their advantages."[40]

It is interesting that Smith counterposes humanity with self-love, for in some basic sense there is no humanity in unrelieved self-assertion, in an outlook of total disregard for others. By presenting economic actors as solely self-interested, economics strips them of humanity, hardly an auspicious starting point for a social science.

If one takes as a starting and ending point one's own interests, and treats all others as though they too have only internal points of reference to guide their actions, morality can play no role. Without addressing questions of personal responsibility toward others, ethics turns into some kind of solipsistic triviality. Morality, of whatever stripe or ethical content, must describe and bound *relations* between people, mutual responsibilities.

Where there is no obligation beyond self-interest, all one has are relations of exchange at arm's length, not the close interpersonal relations of mutual responsibility which are the very subject matter and essence of ethical questions. Because ethics is relational while mainstream economics is not, the idea of humane economic ethics is an oxymoron.

This is not to say that economists are people without ethics or moral norms. Economists certainly have values *as individuals*, but they typically present their field of study and learning as a science free from value judgments, a method and body of conclusions perfectly general and applicable by all who grasp them, whatever their personal desires.

The conservative economist Milton Friedman makes a principle out of amorality in economics. He has proposed that economic science be developed with a keen regard for the distinction between "positive" and "normative" economics first suggested by John Neville Keynes in 1891. Positive economics is the study of "what is," whereas normative economics deals with "what ought to be." Normative economics is speculative and personal, a matter of values and preferences that are beyond science. Economics as a science, as a tool for understanding and prediction, must be based solely on positive economics, which "is in principle independent of any particular ethical position or normative judgments." [41]

In this view, which is dominant in the economics profession, economic analysis is designed to describe and predict the operations of the market economy as it is and as it functions, without regard to the ethical considerations one might pose concerning whether market outcomes are "good" or "bad." The normative issues involved are "differences in basic values, differences about which man can ultimately only fight." [42]

Any economist is presumably able to use the scientific techniques of positive economics to assess the potential effects of various economic policies or actions, to test whether undertaking them would, or would not, advance the goals the economist prefers from a normative standpoint. In this way one can *apply* economics to ethical purpose, whatever one's ethics might be. Economics, in this view, is equally a tool for progressives or conservatives, and indeed, liberals and conservatives alike avail themselves of the same tools of economic analysis to promote entirely conflicting policies.

This standard claim for value-free science has a certain appeal, but there are problems with it. First, the positive economics of the mainstream tradition is, as we have seen, inadequate to the purpose it claims. It cannot predict, and it does not explain. It is a poor guide to the consequences of economic policy, of whatever political orientation, because it is founded on propositions that cannot comprehend the dynamic, historical communities that economies are.

Further, the very process of separating the "positive" aspects of economic theory from its "normative" aspects denies the important truth that economic analysis embodies a definite set of values concerning human behavior and the relationship between individual and society. Adam Smith was, after all, a professor of moral philosophy when he wrote his economics. Mainstream economics is based on the philosophic principles of hedonism and utilitarianism. As Arrow expresses it:

> To the nominalist temperament of the modern period, the assumption of the existence of the social ideal in some Platonic realm of being was meaningless. The utilitarian philosophy of Jeremy Bentham and his followers sought instead to ground the social good on the good of individuals. The hedonist psychology associated with utilitarian philosophy was further used to imply that each individual's good was identical with his desires. Hence, the social good was in some sense to be a composite of the desires of individuals. A viewpoint of this type serves as a justification of both political democracy and laissez-faire economics.[43]

From the outset, economic doctrine was constructed to show that an economy based on these values and assessments of human nature could be productive, and to show how such an economy might function.

In sum, mainstream economics cannot embrace a genuine human ethics because it is based on the values of stark individualism. Although mainstream economics presents itself as value-free, it is not. Rather, it supports, apologizes for, and trumpets the virtues of individualism and the private accumulation of capital. In doing so, it is blind to the social relations established in economic processes and can only promote the blame-the-victim conclusion that those who suffer economic privation do so voluntarily or in some way through their own fault.

Because economics is a *social* science, it cannot be pursued outside of the political and ideological differences operating in society. We should therefore not be surprised that economic theory carries ideology and values in it, claims to positiveness notwithstanding. This fact takes on special importance as economic processes divide the population into antagonistically conflicted groups with sharply different interests and problems. By denying and masking these aspects of the economy, mainstream economics promotes the interests of capital, as it was designed to do, with profound ethical implications contrary to the goals of liberation theology and the interests of the poor and working people who are the subjects of liberatory practice in capitalist society. For them, a different approach to economic issues must be found.

MARXIST ECONOMICS

Marxist economics stands counterposed to mainstream economics and is in many ways more suitable for the tasks of economic justice. Instead of individualism, one finds an exploration of social relations. Instead of static methods, one finds dynamic change and a richly textured appreciation of history. It is no accident that liberation theologians have been attracted to Marxist social science.

Yet after the collapse of Eastern European state economies and the adoption of market economies there and in the Soviet Union, Marxism seems to most people a failed experiment at best. Mainstream media proclaim capitalism triumphant; Marxist thinking, vehemently denounced in countries where once it was promoted as dogma, is on the defensive and appears unsuited for any positive purpose.

Some general observations will help us gain perspective at the outset of our discussion of Marxism. First, Marxist economics is overwhelmingly an investigation of the way *capitalist* economies work, not a prescription for organizing society after capitalism. Marx wrote many decades before the first attempt to create a socialist economy. What little he did write about socialist economies was necessarily speculative and quite general. Weaknesses and errors in Marx's anticipations of socialism do not negate the powerful insights he had into the functioning of capitalist society, which was fully functioning when he wrote and the subject of his detailed investigation.

The failure of Eastern European economies is therefore not a failure of Marxism. A great deal of work remains to be done before the experiences of those countries can be understood.[44] Ironically, the failure of Soviet-styled economies provides an opportunity for a renaissance in Marxist thinking. For decades, Marxist economic analysis has been stunted and distorted by enormous pressure to justify or rationalize the actual practices of Soviet economic policy. This has been true among Marxists in the United States and other capitalist countries, as well as in the so-called socialist bloc. Perhaps as the failure of Soviet-styled economies frees Marxist analysts from the constraints imposed by the operation of those systems, a stronger and more subtle Marxism may rise from the ruins.

In all events, the interest of liberation theologians in Marx has not been driven by support for any socialist country whose leaders have justified their actions with reference to Marx. Rather, these theologians have been drawn to Marx because they find in his method and orientation a social science with the analytic and moral strength to advance the cause of social and economic justice.

Marxism is not a part of the standard curriculum of most academic economics departments.[45] I studied economics as an undergraduate at the University of Michigan in the early 1960s because I was searching for understanding to guide my activities in the civil rights and antiwar movements of the times. Marxism was presented as a curiosity of intellectual history, long since discarded in favor of the more modern, "scientific," mainstream approaches we were taught. I went on to graduate study in economics, thinking that perhaps I had missed what I was looking for only because of the elementary presentation of the subject at the undergraduate level.

But it turned out that I, along with many other economics graduate students in the mid-1960s, found nothing in mainstream economic theory that gave us the tools to grapple with the economic aspects of racism or foreign domination. For example, throughout the decade not a single article appeared in mainstream professional economics journals analyzing the Vietnam War. Nor was racism seen as anything more than the personal preference of the racist individual.

As activist-intellectuals, we developed a critique of mainstream economic theory and sought an alternative way of understanding the economy, one that would give better guidance to the justice movements in which we were working and to which we hoped to bring an understanding worthy of the moral impetus that motivated our efforts. In 1968 graduate students from a number of U.S. universities formed the Union for Radical Political Economics (URPE) as an organization dedicated to promoting economic understanding in close connection with the movements of the time, what we might have called "liberation economics."

Marxism was not a central part of the thinking of this group of economic activists arising from the New Left. We thought of ourselves only as "radicals": that is, people searching for root causes, critical of received doctrine, politically committed to empowering people to gain social justice through mass movements, and intellectually convinced that no adequate social science could develop removed from the experience and questions thrown up by those movements.

It was only over a period of years that Marxism came to be widely accepted among "radicals" as an important framework for the elaboration of economics. Although there had been Marxist voices in the discussion from the beginning, especially those of Paul Sweezy, Paul Baran, Victor Perlo, and Ernest Mandel, the new generation of activist-intellectuals was leery of Marxism. We had been taught that Marxism was old and wrong, that it was only dogma; and the Soviet invasion of Czechoslovakia in 1968 only reinforced the idea that Marxism in practice led directly to oppression and represented the very antithesis of all our aspirations. Yet as we pursued our purpose, Marxism emerged, for all its problems, as in fact an essential point of departure for any economics that hoped to contribute to economic justice.

I review this history to indicate that the growth of Marxism's influence among economists, especially in North America, has been just as difficult and problematic and controversial as has been the spread of interest in Marxism within religious circles. In each community, people have come to an appreciation of Marx only over great resistance. Yet that appreciation and interest continue to grow, as the need for economic justice becomes ever more clear and urgent in the world.

Just as mainstream economics has many currents, so Marxist economics is no single doctrine. It is a collection of often conflicting and highly contentious theories and views: underconsumption, overproduction, falling rate of profit, political business cycle, gender oppression, and a number of theories of imperialism, dependency, and national liberation. Still, certain themes and methods are common to all the approaches contained under the Marxist umbrella. A look at these common elements will show something of why Marxism has had such an enduring influence, and why it is attractive to those committed to economic justice.

Not surprisingly, Marxism is in method and outlook the opposite of mainstream economics, even though both share a common ancestry in the work of Adam Smith and other early English political economists. Let us consider some of the features of Marxism that commend it to our attention. By building on these strengths, we can hope to overcome earlier weaknesses in Marxist theory and practice, while helping to advance the liberatory goals for which they are intended.

Perhaps the most important starting point is Marx's observation and conviction that the individual person is a profoundly social creation: "It is not the consciousness of men that determines their being, but, on the contrary, their social being that determines their consciousness."[46] The human being is determined and defined only in a structure of relationships with other people.

For Marx, the relationships among people established in the processes of production are among the most important in determining the content of human existence, human nature. Individuality is not negated by social relations; it is brought into existence by them. Marx began his economic writings in the mid-1840s with reflections on the way capitalist production, based on private property, atomizes the worker, dehumanizes the worker, by enforcing the alienation of each worker from all other workers and from the product of the worker's own labor.[47]

Whereas mainstream economics defines the individual in terms of his or her own resources and subjective preferences, Marxism asserts that one can find one's individuality only in community, only in relation with other people. The individualism of capitalist society obliterates the individual; it is the social connectedness among people that gives each one individuality.

It is therefore one of the great ironies and distortions of intellectual history that people have come to believe that Marxism denies the individual in favor of the collective society or the State. Rather, Marx began to develop the dialectical-materialist approach to human society as a tool to appreciate and enhance the complex *interdependence* between the individual and society, their mutual determination. His affirmation of the individual and his outrage at the conditions of life for common humanity were what carried Marx into his deep critiques of philosophy and economics.

Instead of the comparative-statics method of today's mainstream economics, Marx elaborated a dynamic theory of the capitalist economy. He found the basis of economic growth in the tensions and contradictions of the production process, wherein capital is produced by labor but appropriated by the employers of labor, the owners of capital. By analyzing the *social* basis of production, profit, and capital, Marx developed a foundation for an understanding of how capitalist production is undertaken and how economic activity fluctuates and expands over time.

Marx's dynamics extend beyond the workings of capitalism itself. In contrast with mainstream economics, he analyzed capitalism as a system within a historical process of social development, showing its origins in the decay of feudalism and foreseeing its historical future beyond itself, when "the expropriators will be expropriated"[48] and capitalism replaced by socialism.

Even though Marxism predicts revolution and is rightly considered to be a revolutionist's doctrine, it would be an error to reduce Marxist economics to the question of revolution alone. Rather, it seeks to explain the social dynamics of capitalist accumulation itself. This process is central to the lives of all people touched by capitalism, and the insights into it which have been developed by Marxists are of interest and importance.

To summarize, three aspects of Marxist economics commend it to the attention of liberation theology. It locates the individual in a social network of substantial human relationships and seeks to penetrate the complexities of these relations in order to understand the mutual determination of the individual person and society as a whole. Further, it is dynamic, providing the basis for understanding social change, which characterizes capitalist society. And, related to the dynamic character of the analysis, Marxism is historical in its approach, tracing the intimate connections between economic processes and historical development.

In all these aspects, Marxism presents a sharp contrast with mainstream economics. And so it does, too, in the matter of ethics. Rather than seeing each individual isolated and solely self-interested, Marx provides a rich mosaic of human interconnection from which to draw ethical judgments. By showing how people are related to one another in the course of production, not isolated from one another only to meet at arm's length in market exchange, Marx's economics provides the basis for understanding the networks of community and conflict in society. One can see in these networks the basis for mutual responsibility, not simply as an a priori moral imperative but as a reality and necessity of economic life, an objective basis for ethical norms.

Since ethics addresses the terms on which people relate to one another, Marx's insights into social relations arising in production are central to his moral judgments. At the heart of the matter stands the Marxist conception of class. This complex issue is the subject of Chapter 8 in this volume, and so I confine myself here to a couple of schematic points.

An individual is in one class or another according to the ways in which that person is related socially to other people in society. Class is not a taxonomic category into which a person is put solely on the basis of her or his own characteristics (the class of all redheaded people, or the class of all poor people, or the class of people graduating from high school in a given year). Class is a relational category, including all people who share some important aspect of relationship with another class of people.

Production is a central aspect of human society and a key (but not simple) determinant of class. Let us begin with the observation that human labor creates all wealth in society. As Adam Smith put it in the opening sentence of his famous book *The Wealth of Nations* (whose more revealing full title is *An Inquiry into the Nature and Causes of the Wealth of Nations*), "The annual labor of every nation is the fund which originally supplies it with all the necessaries and conveniences of life." [49]

As laboring people produce wealth, they enter into relations with other people: other people who labor and—another class of people entirely— those for whom they work and into whose possession comes the entire wealth created by labor. Although those who create the wealth are pro- vided a part of it for their own consumption through the payment of wages, which allow workers to buy back some of what they have already created, a substantial part of the wealth remains in the hands of em- ployers, simply because they own the means of production—capital— which workers need in order to produce.

The wealth that remains to the class of employers is the surplus wealth created by labor, surplus beyond what they are provided for their own use. A part of this surplus is turned into capital, means of production in the hands of employers, with which workers must create still more wealth and surplus as they do their jobs.

It is important to note that the wealth of the capitalist is the product of the worker and that the conditions of life for workers are intimately bound up with their relations to capitalist employers. These relations of exploitation are part and parcel of the production process and provide it the dynamics that are the heart of Marxist economics and history. Exploi- tation, a word freighted with emotion, is a social fact of the production process, whatever one may conclude about it from a moral standpoint.

Some of Marx's approach to exploitation is incorporated in Pope John Paul II's encyclical *Laborem Exercens*. Although the Pope is certainly not a Marxist, when he proclaimed "the principle of the priority of labor over capital," he justified it in part by pointing out that "all these means [of production] are the result of the historical heritage of human labor." [50]

John Paul II, however, tries to accommodate the conflict between labor and capital by seeking their equality and joint destiny in a common transcendent relation with God, whereas Marx sees the conflict contained entirely within human history. For him, no ultimate common ground exists between these two antagonistic classes. The fact and process of exploitation is for Marx the engine of economic development. Seeing into the structure of exploitation provides him the basis of his moral outrage at the conditions of life for working people and fuels his contemptuous dismissal of bourgeois morality, as in this passage from *The Communist Manifesto*: "The bourgeois clap-trap about the family and education, about the hallowed co-relation of parent and child, becomes all the more disgusting, the more, by the action of Modern Industry, all family ties among the proletarians are torn asunder, and their children transformed into simple articles of commerce and instruments of labor."[51]

Capitalist economic relations extend beyond national boundaries. It is no accident that in the twentieth century, Marxism has played a central role in guiding so many national liberation struggles that have sought to extricate their people from the structures of domination characteristic of modern international capitalism.

One of the most important contributions of the Marxist approach is its ability to trace the international links of solidarity between peoples of different countries, exploited and oppressed in common by a common system. Able to penetrate the superficial calls to "national interest" and talk of "the white man's burden" which have justified imperial and colonial dominations, the Marxist approach helps people in the advanced capitalist countries to formulate and carry out projects of solidarity with movements for national independence.

The structure of exploitation informs not only Marx's analysis of capitalist dynamics but his view of history as well: "The history of all hitherto existing society is the history of class struggles."[52] History and economics are enmeshed. The process of human history is bound up with the human drive for liberation from want and backwardness, and with the quest for economic justice in the end of exploitation.

There is of course a political dimension to the making of human history. A social structure is organized, codified, and ruled through political institutions that change as society changes, sometimes slowly, sometimes precipitously. In a society riven by deep class antagonisms (whether these are clearly articulated and understood or not), history has a differential impact on classes. History is not a neutral process but in substantial measure the outcome of a contentious battle over the organization of production, in which different classes have different interests.

Marx approaches economy, history, and politics all from the vantage point of the interests of working people, those who are exploited and oppressed. Marxism has a class stand, or orientation, which is why it is so often dismissed as unscientific and branded propaganda by defenders of the class interests that Marxism opposes. But the ahistoricism and individualism of mainstream economics also has a class stand, one consistent with the interests of the capitalist class whose problems that economics was constructed to address.

One might of course object that the problem of the capitalist is the same as that of the worker—how to get maximum self-satisfaction and gain from limited resources. I have often heard students say that workers and capitalists are the same because they both want to live well and make as much money as possible. This identification of a common human nature in selfishness defines human beings by their subjective state of mind rather than their objective relations with one another.

While it may be granted that all people want to be as well off as possible, in a class-conflicted world of exploitation the social practices required to achieve that best state of being will differ radically, depending on where one finds oneself in those production relationships. By guiding our attention to the dynamic mechanisms of exploitation, Marx provides an indispensable guide not only to economics per se but to history and political practice as well.

It must also be immediately admitted that although Marxism may be an important foundation of social knowledge, it is in many aspects undeveloped and preliminary. Weaknesses in theory have contributed to calamitous errors in practice. To say that Marxism is an arena for progress is to say not that everything with Marx's name attached has been positive but only that the Marxist tradition provides a framework for further study and social action, through which existing weaknesses and errors can be overcome by applying and extending the methods and basic insights Marx pioneered. Collaboration between Marxist economists and social theorists of liberation theology may contribute to such an extension.

TERMS FOR A DIALOGUE

We have seen that the principal themes of liberation theology resonate with the approach of Marxist social science. In many ways, the issues so controversial in theology have their counterpart disputes in economics. In fact, the range of theological approaches to social issues closely parallels the range of opinion, approach, and policy conclusion found in social science.

Much theological writing of course has nothing directly to do with social issues, and large segments of leadership in organized religion deliberately eschew social activism as a matter of religious conviction. Similarly, most social science proceeds without reference to religious institutions and beliefs, often as a matter of secular principle. Still, as social conflicts and dislocations thrust themselves upon the scene with greater intensity, elements of both segments of society, the religious and the social-scientific, are drawn into the disputes and seek to influence the path and outcome of these conflicts. At the same time, unavoidably, all who enter into social conflict are deeply shaped by it in turn.

It is in the very arena of conflicted social practice that liberation theology and Marxism have been born and shaped, and have recognized the opportunity for joint discourse. For all their differences, these two spheres of thought and action both stem from what Juan Luis Segundo has said "a theology worthy of attention" must have: "a *pretheological* human commitment to change and improve the world,"[53] related to what we earlier called a "class stand" in the Marxist framework.

It is a commonplace that all manner of actions, values, and beliefs, however diametrically opposed, can be defended by appeal to the Bible. So it is with appeals to economic theory in general and even within the narrower range of Marx's work. In choosing a particular theology or economics, one always makes, implicitly or explicitly, a prior choice of values, the criteria by which one evaluates good and evil, just and unjust, or, in Segundo's terms, whether a given change does "improve the world."

Marxism and liberation theology have both discovered that the social world is conflicted in significant part along class lines. Both have frankly taken sides in this conflict. They have chosen to stand with workers, poor farmers, peasants, and other oppressed and exploited people as they confront a ruling class of owners of the means of production who are served by an elite of political, cultural, and religious leaders. It is this common class stand, this particular prior human commitment, that provides the opportunity for common work and discourse between such seemingly opposed spheres as theology and Marxism.

Liberation theology can be distinguished from liberal theology in that the former recognizes class conflict as a primary characteristic of society and positions itself consciously as an ally of one class against the other; whereas liberal theology, which also seeks to ameliorate the conditions of capitalism and sees the need for structural change, denies the class-conflictual nature of society and proposes instead a plan for social harmony among all classes. In analogous ways, Marxism distinguishes itself from the many politically liberal and pluralist conceptions of economic relations which challenge the extreme individualism of laissez-faire economic formulations and seek to reform capitalism along harmonious paths.

Religious fundamentalism in the United States is another example of an element of the religious community drawn into the arena of public policy, albeit with a very different agenda from that proposed by liberation theology. Typically aligned more clearly with business interests and the conservative to reactionary end of the political spectrum, fundamentalist leaders also choose among the array of economic analyses available. They tend to prefer the free-market approach and to condemn any opening to Marxism or even liberal humanist social thought.

Some fundamentalist preachers embrace a more populist stance, proclaiming the needs and aspirations of the poor and sometimes calling for economic priorities consistent with a leftist agenda. Whether one starts from one of the main-line Protestant denominations, or from a fundamentalist outlook, or from Catholic or Jewish teachings, attention to the worldly interests of the poor leads to evaluation of various social theories and policies, once one recognizes the need to go beyond acts of individual charity as the foundation of ethical social practice. Then the limits of individualism come into focus, as moral outcomes seem to require collective action.

The prospect for cooperative work between any strand of religion and Marxism appears to contradict Marx's famous condemnation of religion as "the opium of the people." Marx actually had a more nuanced understanding of the issue.

Religious suffering is at the same time an expression of real suffering. Religion is the sigh of the oppressed creature, the sentiment of a heartless world, and the soul of soulless conditions. It is the opium of the people.

The abolition of religion as the illusory happiness of men is a demand for their real happiness. The call to abandon their illusions about their condition is a call to abandon a condition which requires illusions. The criticism of religion is therefore the embryonic criticism of this vale of tears of which religion is the halo.[54]

Liberation theology is an attempt to make religion consistent with the "call to abandon conditions which require illusions." It is an attempt to make religion an instrument of progressive class struggle. Not surprisingly, the attempt is vehemently opposed both inside and outside the churches on theological as well as practical grounds, evidence that class struggle percolates through every institution of society, including religion, as Leonardo Boff has so bravely pointed out.[55] Liberation theology turns to Marxism as the most promising basis for the understanding needed to achieve liberation in this conflicted world.

The partnership between Marxism and religion is an uneasy one, emerging from a history of deep mutual antagonism. The Jesuit Juan Luis Segundo makes the important observation that "instead of viewing it [religion] as a specific sector of the culture, and disregarding the variety, richness, and universality of its forms, Marx seems to view it as *nothing but* an error. In Marx's view, philosophy can *make* errors . . . but religion *is* an error, a unique and universal illusion, a barrier to any and all significant social change."[56] Indeed, Marxists have been overwhelmingly dismissive of religion and suspicious of religiously motivated action. Until quite recently, where Marxists have held state power, religious institutions and practices have been severely restricted and often harshly punished. In part, this antagonism has been a direct political response to the open and implacable opposition that religious institutions have often displayed toward socialism and revolution.

Underlying this history of opposition is the fact that religious leadership has so often been politically and economically allied with the ruling elite against which socialist revolution has been aimed, guided by Marx's social theory. This history of reactionary church practice has been acknowledged and come under intense criticism in the writings of liberation theologians.

Religious opposition to Marx at the ideological level has been organized around three points of contention. The first, and most closely related to the economic interests at play in capitalist society, is that Marxism is faulted for proposing an antagonistically conflictual view of the world. This problem is often incorrectly conflated with issues of violence. Rather, the heart of the matter is the Marxist contention that capitalism entails class antagonisms, and that the contradictions of capitalism can be resolved only through the victory of one class over the other and the eradication of the capitalist class as a socially significant force. Counterposed to this revolutionary vision (which may be combined with nonviolent means) is the more conciliatory view historically championed in church doctrine. While not denying the existence of conflicts of interest, it proposes to solve those conflicts through some form of mediation, negotiation, or other dialogue consistent with the conception that all people are united in a common relation to God.

Beyond issues of conflict resolution but still related to them are two other deeply divisive features of Marxist thought: atheism, and the materialist philosophy on which it is based. Marx's analytic method, dialectical and historical materialism, rejects any claim that a god or spirit precedes or orders either the material universe or the social structures and values of human history. Atheism is an especially important issue among fundamentalists, to whom Marxists appear as tools of Satan. Catholic social doctrine since Leo XIII has condemned the atheistic nature of Marxism, but since Vatican II less emphasis has been placed on the point as the Church has sought out more cordial working relations with people of other faiths. Rather than dwell on the issue of atheism, Catholic and main-line Protestant churches focus on the materialist philosophy embedded in Marxism.

For liberation theology, Marx's attention to class struggle presents no obstacle. In fact, as we have seen, Marx's theory of history and social change is a major attraction. The fact that Marxists are atheists likewise presents little problem to liberation theologians, who are secure in their own faith even as they work cooperatively with all who can contribute to the liberatory work of God in history. And Marxists, for their part, are increasingly aware that practicing theists can be revolutionaries.

Liberation theology and Marxism contend most on questions of materialism. But while traditional church opposition to Marxism and Marxist materialism has been destructive, reducing the possibility of dialogue, the criticisms posed by liberation theologians are more positive, seeking to work out differences or at least to explore them constructively for a mutual understanding that allows for common pursuits. As a Marxist economist, I find their criticisms important and often on the mark, calling for careful thought and deeper understanding in response.

Cornel West has given us a clear statement of the problem: "The orthodox Marxist analysis refuses to acknowledge the positive, liberating aspects of popular culture and religion, and their potential for fostering structural social change."[57] This criticism is related to the difficulty that much of Marxist social analysis suffers from economic determinism, or a logical reductionism in which all the political, cultural, and other social phenomena understood by Marxists to compose the "superstructure" of society find their origin, driving force, and historical content solely in the interplay of economic interests defined in the course of production and exchange, the "base" of society.

There is much in the writings of Marx and Engels and many of their political disciples which warns against such reductionism and attempts a more rounded analysis. Still, it is too often true, as Juan Luis Segundo has said, that "Marxist sociology has not accepted the relative autonomy of the superstructural levels in its methodology."[58]

In analyzing modern capitalism from a socialist perspective, economists Samuel Bowles and Herbert Gintis also criticize the reductionism of Marxist thought:

> Although the Marxian analysis of exploitation and other forms of domination has immeasurably advanced democratic understandings, we remain deeply skeptical of the proposition that exploitation, particularly class exploitation, provides a sufficient conceptual foundation for a rigorous and critical treatment of the variety of forms of political domination and cultural supremacy commonly observed in social life.[59]

A number of important Marxist theoreticians have paid special attention to superstructural questions, most notably Antonio Gramsci, Georg Lukács, and Mao Zedong. But by and large their insights have not been integrated into Marxian *economic* analysis, and the two realms of inquiry have remained largely separate, to the substantial disadvantage of both.

Economists believe that they develop their theories in the scientific spirit of testable hypotheses and empirical verification, a guiding light to all the social sciences. Marxism is also presented by its adherents as a scientific body of thought, based on the materialist and dialectical approach to society embodied in Marxism. Engels went to considerable length to explain the difference between "scientific" socialism based on a Marxist analysis and the many "utopian" critiques of capitalist society rooted in one or another idealist conception.[60] In a certain way, the modern controversy between the churches and Marxism is a continuation of the centuries-old conflict between religion and science.

The rejection of Copernican astronomy as heresy and the silencing of Galileo by the Catholic Church in the early seventeenth century are among the best-known examples of church hostility to science. Now, of course, the church has come to some accommodation with the natural and physical sciences, although the debates about evolution show that even in these realms science and religion have not established altogether easy working relations. Social science has come along much later than the physical sciences, and the process of finding suitable working relations between it and religion is accordingly even more retarded than in the physical sciences. A look back at the Galileo controversy provides some guidance to its modern analogue.

The Catholic Church now, after more than 350 years, does acknowledge that silencing Galileo was an error. But at the same time, as Father Jerome Langford puts it:

> Galileo is not completely blameless. . . . Had there been more proof, I think the qualifications would have been considerably less severe. . . . Everyone knew that Bellarmine had challenged Galileo to come forth with solid proof. The Jesuit astronomers of the Roman College were quite certain that Galileo had gone beyond his evidence in asserting Copernicanism to be a fact. Father Grienberger, the leading Jesuit astronomer, said frankly that Galileo would do better to produce more convincing proofs for his theory before trying to adjust Scripture to fit it.[61]

True, Galileo's understanding was primitive by later standards, and some of the justification he provided for his views turned out to be wrong. Still, it is important to conclude that with respect to his adversaries in Rome, Galileo was completely correct. For when it came to improving our understanding of the solar system and the universe beyond, Galileo's methods and conclusions were the basis of progress, whereas Father Grienberger's Procrustean bed of scripture as a limit on scientific inquiry could *only* stunt and deform the growth of knowledge.

The Church generally condemns Marxism as wrong and lacking conformity with scripture. To be sure, much in Marxist social teaching is wrong and incomplete. As one indication of this, we know that there are severe practical and ethical deficiencies in the social experience of countries where Marxists have led revolutions against capitalism and established new orders in the name of socialism. But Marxism is newly emerging and still quite primitive, although seemingly an extraordinarily powerful and partially successful tool. Rather than dismiss it for its continuing errors and "lack of proof" (proof that can come only after a long period of trial and error through which successive approximations to a correct understanding emerge, but always in the presence of at least some continuing error), it would seem more productive to develop and refine it in the course of transforming society.

But the application of Marxism to social change must be guided by ethical norms. While it may be true, as philosopher Kai Nielsen argues, that a coherent ethics can be elaborated without reference to religion or God, and that therefore in some sense religion is irrelevant to ethics,[62] it remains undeniable that it is religion which has carried the Western sense of ethics down through history. It is therefore important for religion to be able to contribute that heritage to the scientific world, which so desperately needs the guidance of ethical norms in its work. For Marxists it is not enough to aver the *possibility* of an atheistic ethic and then to preside over social systems that in their everyday practices degrade the dignity and humanity of their citizens. If, in principle, ethics can come to social science and society independent of religion, as a practical matter this does not seem to be the case. Dialogue with religion is in order.

As theology and economics undertake their joint project of advancing human dignity and liberation, some common themes emerge and are examined from various angles in the chapters of this book. First, and in a way most fundamental, is an investigation of the relations that connect us as individuals with the larger communities in which we live and work. The simple individualism of classical liberalism, on which laissez-faire economic and political analysis is based, must be set aside, and a more nuanced, dialectical appreciation must be found to describe the processes by which individuals and communities are jointly determined. At the same time, the naive collectivism of Marxist experience, in which the fact that people are socially determined has been used to deny the individuality of each person in society, must be understood and surmounted. In this connection it will be important to consider the practical and ethical implications of the conflicted character of social relations prevailing in today's world.

A second theme for joint reflection is the proposition that injustice is structural in character and not simply a matter of individual action. In the theological setting this question appears as a debate over the character of sin and the need (or not) to participate in movements for social structural change in the redemptive process. For economists the problem is whether it makes sense (or not) to ascribe meaningful existence, let alone purpose or moral responsibility, to collections of individuals, and whether there is any meaningful way to hold institutional structures to any moral standard.

The third subject of common elucidation is the manner in which values are embedded in market function. Standard notions of economic efficiency appear to present objective truths about resource allocation, free from normative considerations. Yet issues of fairness and power are always present in market operations, whether in matters of the distributions of income and wealth, or in the authority structure of the labor process, or in the very purpose of production itself.

It is certainly true that where scarce resources must be allocated among competing potential uses, microeconomics as an element of positive economic science can contribute to an efficient solution to the problem. And it is clear from the experience of socialist countries that any waste of scarce resources is increasingly viewed as an intolerable affront to the dignity and well-being of the people.

Yet we know from the experience of capitalist society that no simple application of microeconomic principles can secure a just society. Serious attention must be paid to the reasons for this fact, in the search for a practical and ethically acceptable interplay of efficiency and equity in economic affairs. It is to this end that the dialogue between religion and economics can be most fruitful, and it is with this focus that liberation theology and Marxism can each contribute their best understanding to human progress.

Shortly before he was assassinated, the Reverend Martin Luther King, Jr., called attention to the potential for collaboration across ideological and political lines. In his last presidential address to the Southern Christian Leadership Conference, titled "Where Do We Go from Here?" he said: "Communism forgets that life is individual. Capitalism forgets that life is social, and the kingdom of brotherhood is found neither in the thesis of communism nor the antithesis of capitalism but in a higher synthesis . . . that combines the truths of both. . . . The problem of racism, the problem of economic exploitation, and the problem of war are all tied together."[63]

To reach the synthesis needed to understand and eradicate the "triple evils" King identified involves a process quite different from the one he suggested. It is not just a matter of considering two social systems, discarding the unwanted aspects of each, and combining the remaining truths and positive features into a new system that is some weighted average of the two from which it is drawn. The process of social change brings one social system into existence out of the dynamics of its historical predecessor and continues its development through the playing-out of its own internal dynamics.

Still, there is in King's remarks something suggestive for the dialogue between liberation theology and Marxism. It is tempting to approach the discussion by expecting to find and adopt what is correct or acceptable in the other's view while being prepared to give up what one can be persuaded is incorrect or unhelpful in one's own view. This is what one might anticipate in a respectful give-and-take. Yet it misses what is required and mistakes how such a dialogue can be most fruitful.

An analogy illustrates the point. The elements sodium and chlorine are each, taken alone, poison to humans. Yet their chemical combination, ordinary salt, is an essential ingredient of life. Salt is in no way an average of the two elements it comprises. In some dialectical fashion, the joining of the two components results in their qualitative transformation into something altogether new.

There is ample evidence that religion alone in power is dangerous to human beings. Wherever state power has been exercised in the name of religious authority (and not simply by people of religious faith), human dignity has suffered, and social progress has been retarded. This lesson of the Middle Ages has been repeated in modern times in Franco's Spain, in Islamic Iran, and in the assertion of Jewish religious authority for control over Israel and Palestine.

Similarly, where science is applied untempered by ethical norms, human catastrophe easily follows. Perhaps in their common pursuit of human liberation, social science and theology can come to some synthesis that infuses ethics into social analysis and gives practical moment to ethical norms.

To contribute to human progress, social science—Marxism in particular—must gain greater sophistication as it develops through trial and error along with the various stages of capitalist and socialist societies that it observes. Liberation theology must go through the same process. At best, with clear understanding and conscious effort on both sides, religion and Marxism may develop together to serve a common purpose of securing a life of dignity and plenty for all people.

Notes

1. Leonardo Boff, *Jesus Christ Liberator* (Maryknoll, N.Y.: Orbis Books, 1978), p. 46 (original emphasis).

2. Religious institutions have of course always operated within the larger social world and have had powerful social impact for thousands of years, usually as a conservative force linked to ruling powers but sometimes interpreted in a revolutionary fashion. Church leaders have long held to one or another social doctrine as a guide to church social practice. In this sense, liberation theology is not a departure from past practice. Still, by challenging the dominant modes of church participation in contemporary society, and by challenging the dominance of a transcendent spirituality that so often covers over the oppressive content of church practice within society, liberation theology seeks to place the church within history in a new way.

3. Bob Dylan, "Gotta Serve Somebody," New York, ASCAP, 1979, from the album *Slow Train Comin'*.

4. The Jackson campaign is analyzed in Sheila D. Collins, *The Rainbow Challenge: The Jackson Campaign and the Future of U.S. Politics* (New York: Monthly Review Press, 1986). For a review and analysis of conservative religious political activity in the United States, see Sarah Diamond, *Spiritual Warfare: The Politics of the Christian Right* (Boston: South End Press, 1989). Right-wing political activity has also been mobilized through religious institutions in Latin America. In addition to conservative sectors of the Catholic Church, Protestant conservatism is a growing social factor. See David Stoll, *Is Latin America Turning Protestant? The Politics of Evangelical Growth* (Berkeley: University of California Press, 1990).

5. Gustavo Gutierrez, *A Theology of Liberation* (Maryknoll, N.Y.: Orbis Books, 1973), p. 67.

6. While the focus here is on Jewish and Christian traditions, the same questions arise also in other religious traditions. Islam has shown itself repeatedly to be a powerful political force, with differing programs based on differing interpretations of the Koran. Buddhism, too, has been embroiled in a variety of political stances, from the anti-Communist Tibetan lamas to the revolutionary bonzes in Vietnam and Kampuchea and more recently in Myanmar.

7. Second Vatican Ecumenical Council, Pastoral Constitution on the Church in the Modern World, *Gaudium et Spes* (1965), in *Renewing the Earth: Catholic Documents on Peace, Justice, and Liberation*, ed. David J. O'Brien and Thomas Shannon (Garden City, N.Y.: Doubleday, 1977), p. 180, n. 4.

8. José Miguez Bonino, *Doing Theology in a Revolutionary Situation* (Philadelphia: Fortress Press, 1975), p. 148.

9. Norman K. Gottwald, *The Tribes of Yahweh* (Maryknoll, N.Y.: Orbis Books, 1979), p. 647.

10. Elaine Pagels, *The Gnostic Gospels* (New York: Vintage Books, 1981), p. 55.

11. Leo XIII, *Rerum Novarum*, in *Five Great Encyclicals* (New York: Paulist Press, 1939), p. 1.

12. Ibid., p. 2.

13. William Muir, *Christianity and Labor* (New York: Hodder & Stoughton, n.d.), p. vii.

14. John Paul II, *Laborem Exercens* (Washington, D.C.: United States Catholic Conference, 1981), p. 25, n. 12. Pope John Paul II has had close contact with a brand of Marxist thought and social policy in Poland. He does not uphold capitalism as a system superior to socialism, nor does he make a principle out of support for private property. His critique of "collectivist" societies parallels his critique of capitalism. His views on the relations between labor and capital are more closely aligned with Marx than were those of any of his predecessors. Although the Pope is fiercely conservative on church organization and rules, his economic views in many ways reinforce those of liberation theology. For an analysis of *Laborem Exercens*, see Michael Zweig, "The Economics of Pope John Paul II" (paper delivered at the Allied Social Science Association convention, December 1983, State University of New York at Stony Brook); and Gregory Baum, *The Priority of Labor: A Commentary on Laborem Exercens* (New York: Paulist Press, 1982).

15. John Paul II, *Laborem Exercens*, p. 19; n. 8; p. 24, n. 11.

16. Bonino, *Doing Theology*, p. 138. Bonino and others quoted in this essay unfortunately continue the use of the term "man" when speaking of all humanity, regardless of gender.

17. Gutierrez, *A Theology of Liberation*, pp. 53–77, 72, 177, 153.

18. Albert Vorspan, *Jewish Values and Social Crisis* (New York: Union of American Hebrew Congregations, 1968), p. 297.

19. Abraham Heschel, *The Prophets* (New York: Harper & Row, 1962), 1:181, 184, 190. Rabbi Heschel is a guiding voice to such Jewish currents as New Jewish Agenda and the magazine *Tikkun*, as well as the reconstructionist branch of Jewish practice. In 1965 he was cofounder, with Protestant and Catholic theologians, of Clergy and Laity Concerned (CALC), which opposed American participation in the Vietnam War and which continues as one of the leading North American religion-based organizations devoted to economic and social justice.

20. Gregory Baum and Duncan Cameron, eds., *Ethics and Economics* (Toronto: Lorimer, 1984), pp. 41–42.

21. Heschel, *The Prophets*, pp. 198–99.

22. James Cone, *A Black Theology of Liberation* (Philadelphia: Lippincott, 1970), p. 11.

23. *A Testament of Hope: The Essential Writings of Martin Luther King, Jr.*, ed. James Washington (New York: Harper & Row, 1986), p. 250.

24. Boff, *Jesus Christ Liberator*, p. 272; John Paul II, speech at Yankee Stadium, New York City, quoted in Baum, *The Priority of Labor*, p. 90.

25. For an introduction to the issues, see Pamela Brubaker, Chapter 4 in this volume. See also, e.g., Elisabeth Schuessler Fiorenza, "Feminist Theory as a Critical Theology of Liberation," in *Churches in Struggle: Liberation Theologies and Social Change in North America*, ed. William Tabb (New York: Monthly Review Press, 1986), pp. 46–66; Susannah Heschel, ed., *On Being a Jewish Feminist* (New York:

Schocken Books, 1983); and the essays of Beverly Harrison in *Making the Connections: Essays in Feminist Social Ethics*, ed. Carol Robb (New York: Beacon Press, 1985).

26. Leonardo Boff, *Church: Charism and Power* (New York: Crossroad, 1985), provides the fullest treatment.

27. Ibid., p. 112.

28. Gutierrez, *A Theology of Liberation*, p. 202.

29. Gayraud Wilmore and James Cone, eds., *Black Theology: A Documentary History, 1966–1979* (Maryknoll, N.Y.: Orbis Books, 1979), p. 246.

30. Gutierrez, *A Theology of Liberation*, p. 161.

31. Juan Luis Segundo, *The Liberation of Theology* (Maryknoll, N.Y.: Orbis Books, 1976), p. 14.

32. National Conference of Catholic Bishops, *Catholic Social Teaching and the U.S. Economy*, first draft, par. 167, published in *Origins* 14, nos. 22–23 (1984): 360.

33. Mainstream economics studies are generally divided into two areas: the microeconomic study of individual behavior and the operation of markets; and the macroeconomic study of economic aggregates such as the rate of inflation or unemployment for the economy as a whole. E.g., Keynesians approach the economy from a macroeconomic angle, whereas laissez-faire libertarians stress microeconomic thinking. Both macro- and microeconomics suffer from the methodological weaknesses discussed in this chapter, and I have drawn examples from each.

34. Paul Samuelson, "Policy Advertising in Economics," *Challenge* 21, no. 1 (1978): 38 (original emphasis).

35. Victor Zarnowitz, "The Record and Improvability of Economic Forecasting," National Bureau of Economic Research, Cambridge, Mass., Working Paper 2099, December 1986, abstract.

36. Ibid., p. 15 and abstract.

37. Robert M. Solow, "Economic History and Economics," *American Economic Review* 75, no. 2 (1985): 328.

38. Kenneth Arrow, *Social Choice and Individual Values*, 2d ed. (New Haven, Conn.: Yale University Press, 1963), p. 60.

39. Amartya K. Sen, *Collective Choice and Social Welfare* (San Francisco: Holden-Day, and Oliver & Boyd, 1970), p. 36 (original emphasis).

40. Adam Smith, *The Wealth of Nations* (1776; New York: Modern Library, 1937), p. 14.

41. Milton Friedman, *Essays in Positive Economics* (Chicago: University of Chicago Press, 1953), p. 4.

42. Ibid., p. 5.

43. Arrow, *Social Choice*, pp. 22–23.

44. For an early but insightful collection of essays on the collapse of Eastern European economies, see *Monthly Review* 42, no. 3 (1990).

45. The pressures to conform with mainstream methods are strong within the economics profession. Graduate study and standards for publication marginalize heterodox ways of thinking, with the result that "of all the intellectuals whose perspective should provide a critical understanding of capitalism as a whole, economists are the most complacent"; see W.H.L. Anderson, "Apologizing for Capitalism," *Monthly*

Review 38, no. 10 (1987): 37–48. From the beginnings of professional association among economists, those holding heterodox views have been systematically disadvantaged and excluded. See Mary Furner, *Advocacy and Objectivity* (Lexington: University Press of Kentucky, 1975).

46. Karl Marx, preface to *Contribution to the Critique of Political Economy* (1859), in *The Marx-Engels Reader*, ed. Robert Tucker, 2d ed. (New York: Norton, 1978), p. 4.

47. See, e.g., Karl Marx, *Economic and Philosophic Manuscripts of 1844* (New York: International Publishers, 1964), esp. pp. 106–27. See also Bertell Ollman, *Alienation: Marx's Conception of Man in Capitalist Society* (Cambridge: Cambridge University Press, 1971).

48. Karl Marx, *Capital* (1867; New York: International Publishers, 1967), 1:763; also in Tucker, *The Marx-Engels Reader*, p. 438.

49. Adam Smith, *The Wealth of Nations*, p. vii.

50. John Paul II, *Laborem Exercens*, pp. 25, 27.

51. Karl Marx and Friedrich Engels, *The Communist Manifesto* (1848), in Tucker, *The Marx-Engels Reader*, pp. 489–90.

52. Ibid., p. 473.

53. Juan Luis Segundo, *The Liberation of Theology*, p. 39 (emphasis added).

54. Karl Marx, *Contribution to the Critique of Hegel's Philosophy of Right* (1843), in Tucker, *The Marx-Engels Reader*, p. 54.

55. Boff, *Church*, esp. chap. 8, "Characteristics of the Church in a Class Society."

56. Juan Luis Segundo, *The Liberation of Theology*, p. 59 (original emphasis).

57. Cornel West, *Prophesy Deliverance!* (Philadelphia: Westminster Press, 1982), p. 117.

58. Juan Luis Segundo, *The Liberation of Theology*, p. 60.

59. Samuel Bowles and Herbert Gintis, *Democracy and Capitalism: Property, Community, and the Contradictions of Modern Social Thought* (New York: Basic Books, 1986), p. 19.

60. Frederick Engels, *Socialism: Utopian and Scientific* (New York: International Publishers, 1972), and *Anti-Dühring* (New York: International Publishers, 1977), from which it is excerpted.

61. Jerome J. Langford, *Galileo, Science, and the Church*, rev. ed. (Ann Arbor: University of Michigan Press, 1971), p. 91.

62. Kai Nielsen, *Ethics without God* (London: Prometheus Books, 1973).

63. King, *A Testament of Hope*, p. 250.

II

RELIGIOUS PERSPECTIVES ON
ECONOMIC JUSTICE

2

VALUES AND ECONOMIC
STRUCTURES

Norman K. Gottwald

The advent and spread of liberation theologies following the middle 1960s is the most important development in Christian theology and practice since the Protestant Reformation. In their approaches to religious doctrine, social action, and church organization, these theologies present a profound challenge to existing orders, both civil and religious. They constitute a radical rupture with the modern theological traditions of the capitalist era.

Liberation theologies have emerged in the context of the specific social and material conditions of the latter half of the twentieth century. They arose first in poorer countries of the Third World, but their influence and the intense controversies surrounding them have reached into the advanced capitalist societies of North American and elsewhere. Liberation theologies have claimed roots in the most ancient Jewish and Christian religious traditions. These traditional beliefs, no less than the newly emerging ones, were the products of the social and material conditions of the times in which they originated.

A thorough evaluation of liberation theologies must therefore consider social conditions as well as beliefs, beginning in ancient times and continuing down to the present. This chapter seeks to probe the historical, theological, economic, and social foundations of liberation theologies and to evaluate the theoretical and practical challenges they pose to global capitalism. This complex task is best served by a materialist method, which traces the far-reaching connections between religions and their socioeconomic contexts.

ECONOMIC GOOD IN JEWISH-CHRISTIAN TRADITION

Jewish and Christian ethics have been theological ethics from their origin. In both, the human good was perceived to derive from a divine source. Because a transcendent God was seen as Creator, the human good was constituted as a communal good, for which all particular humans were jointly accountable, since to be a human being was to exist in solidarity with other human creatures under the aegis of the one God. The good of each could be fulfilled only in the context of the fulfillment of the good of all. Moreover, the human good validated by God embraced an unbroken web of "goods," extending from physical provisions through all the social and spiritual necessities of life. Thus, human welfare was not restricted to religious beliefs or ritual practices, nor were "material" and "spiritual" goods sharply separated.

The significance of this comprehensiveness of scope in the working ethic of early Jews and Christians is this: whereas mainstream capitalist economic theory allows of no "higher ethic" to pass judgment on the practice of economics, Jewish and Christian ethics both overarched and "interfered" with economic activity. In fact, this primitive biblical socioeconomic ethic arose within the context of a particular political economy that corresponded closely to the ethic.

On the basis of painful experience, it was evident to Jews and Christians from earliest times that there were many natural and human threats to the premise of a harmonious creation. The necessary good things of life often had to be wrested from a resistant and threatening natural environment. Even more troubling was the divisiveness and strife within the human community itself, the greed and hate that drove people to violate the covenantal grounds of mutual regard for the welfare of their partners in community.

The theological rejoinder to this disruption of human community was to see God not only as Creator but as Redeemer. In fact, it was in the mode of Redeemer that Jews first experienced their God, for Israel was born by "redemption" out of a hostile world empire. And as the premised new community of equals before God was internally tarnished— and sometimes ravaged—by injustice and oppression, God the Redeemer was invoked as the rectifier of sins against community and was the model to be emulated by all those who wished to keep the community healthy: that is, holy, righteous, and just.

Although this formulation of the basic Jewish-Christian ethic sounds excessively abstract, that ethic was in fact the most immediate concern of everyday existence and often a life-and-death matter, insofar as it was no mere teaching but the ethos of actual communities where both the goodness and the brokenness of human life were experienced. As inhabitants of the ancient Near Eastern and Greco-Roman worlds, the Jewish and Christian communities had to come to terms with the reality that their own social and economic structures existed within larger international settings from which they could not be entirely independent and which, unfortunately, frequently overrode their preferences and values.

If we wish to make a viable Jewish-Christian ethical critique of economic structures today, it is essential that we analyze the ways in which our Jewish and Christian forebears performed economically, both of their free will and under compulsion. Furthermore, we must examine their evaluation of economic life as facilitating or impeding the human good they understood their God as actively willing through creation and redemption.

The "first wave" of Jewish faith and ethics appeared in a tribal society that practiced a communitarian mode of production in agriculture and organized itself in a loose confederacy with limited powers and circumscribed leadership roles. This community resisted the surrounding dominant state politics and the tributary mode of production, which taxed peasants in order to maintain a privileged political elite. It is important for our purposes to recognize that the initial "ethical monotheism" of Israel went hand in glove with a free agrarian political economy that featured cooperative forms of labor, mutual aid measures, and safeguards against gross inequality and political aggrandizement. Communitarian laws served to foster an approximation of economic equality among households organized into larger protective groupings. The Exodus story symbolizes this symbiosis of religious and socioeconomic self-determination in defiance of state domination.

The "second wave" of Jewish faith and practice swept in when Israel became a single state and then, before long, two states: Israel and Judah. Their own rulers eventually imposed the tributary mode of production upon Israelite peasants, thereby requiring of them taxes, rents, and conscripted labor.

The clash within Israel between the older communitarian economics and the newer tributary economics was reflected in a contest of significantly opposed theologies and ethics. Some viewed the Creator and Redeemer God as authentically at work in the rule of the Israelite kings who were pledged to pursue justice and abundance for all (Davidic covenant or royal theology). Others found the disproportion of wealth and privilege between the rulers and the ruled to be profoundly contrary to the founding charter and guiding ethos of Israel (Mosaic covenant and prophetic theology).

Heavy state taxation and loans to hard-pressed peasants at onerous interest rates led to debt servitude, expropriation of land, the formation of large estates, and an increasing disempowerment of the landed majority. These pauperizing trends were in violation of the old communitarian customary laws. From time to time these laws were compiled into "codes" as the basis of reform movements that sought to reverse or mitigate the harsh economic conditions exacerbated by war, foreign tribute, and famine. David and Solomon, on the one hand, and the prophets of Israel, on the other, epitomize the tension and conflict that this second wave of Jewish experience introduced into the life of the people. As Michael Lerner explains in Chapter 5, the contested interpretation of Jewish ethical norms continues to this day in the divisions among Jews concerning the Israeli-Palestinian conflict and many other matters.

The interplay of economics and ethics was further complicated by a "third wave" of Jewish faith and ethics, the so-called Exile and Dispersion. The destruction of both Jewish states momentarily interrupted the clash of native tributary and communitarian modes of production. The Jews were now thrown on the mercy of foreign tributary rule, and they undertook protracted experiments to learn how to survive in scattered communities throughout the ancient world. But when Jews rebuilt Jerusalem and its environs as the religious and cultural center of their faith, issues of political economy reemerged in the struggle over leadership in the restored community.

In fact, the economics of this third-wave era were predominantly controlled by the tributary mode of production. Wherever they lived in the ancient world, Jews were subject to the political economy of foreign states. The limited home rule of restored Jerusalem was under Persian supervision, and its leadership formed a native Jewish elite that exacted taxes and tribute through a temple-based economy.

When Greece and Rome seized control of Palestine, they introduced the slave mode of production and private property. Jewish resistance to this foreign rule involved a mix of nationalist aspiration and a strong streak of communitarian economic sentiment. Frequently, the native Jewish elites were as much resented and opposed as were the foreign rulers, for both promoted economic bondage of the great majority of Jewish peasants. The people did not relinquish their belief in God as Creator, but the sense of the disjointedness and injustice of human society was so sharpened that God as Redeemer was ever more urgently cherished and implored to restore Israel as a just community.

The redemption anticipated was quite consistently a collective one rather than the sparing from misery of a pious few. What the oppressed desired was not the rescue of "pure consciences" and "saved souls" but the reestablishment of a just human order as the necessary ground for good conscience and health of soul.

The emergence of Christian faith and ethics, at first only one of several forms of Judaism, belongs to the era of the third wave. The Jesus movement, precursor to the Christian church, sought a renewal of communitarian faith, ethics, and socioeconomic practice. It was not an individually oriented, spiritualizing sect, for it aimed at the renewal of the Jewish people in all aspects of their existence. The life of its leader was cut short, and it did not make major inroads among Jews in Palestine. Rome's final defeat of the Jewish rebellion in 135 C.E. ended both the distinctly national life of Israel in Palestine and the enclosure of Christians within Judaism. There followed Rabbinic Judaism on the one hand and, on the other, an autonomous Christian Church composed increasingly of Gentiles.

With Jews a marginal group in a wider Gentile world, Christians became the chief bearers of the Jewish economic ethic to the West. As Christianity rose from ignominy to become the dominant religion in the Gentile West, it also developed a transnational church hierarchy. On the one hand, this enmeshed the Church itself in politics and economics; on the other hand, it provided the platform to project an ethic that tried to ameliorate the worst economic abuses without directly challenging slavery or private property.

This moderately critical accommodationist stance continued on into the feudal and capitalist eras. By virtue of its own extensive property holdings and the outspoken interests of its wealthiest members, the Church as an institution was integrated into the ongoing economies of feudalism and eventually of capitalism. The gulf between the lofty social ethic preached by the Church and its cumulative socioeconomic behavior was highlighted both by many within its fold and by those who came to oppose its influence or to look for other institutional channels to social change.

Throughout, an economic ethic of the common good was maintained in principle, even though for the most part it lacked any means of binding implementation by the Church as an institution. Among rank-and-file Christians there were many who held to communitarian hopes and sometimes introduced small-scale communitarian practices, especially among the monastic orders, the pre-Reformation sects, and the left wing of the Protestant Reformation. In nearly all periods of Christian history, as in nearly all periods of Jewish history, there have been voices criticizing social and economic injustice as distortions of God's creation, which should be "redeemed" by whatever means were at hand, whether prophetic denunciation, charity, voluntary poverty, intentional community-building, reform, or revolution.

This subversive practice of the Jewish-Christian ethic was, taken as a whole, ineffectual in promoting enduring structural economic change, but it was insistent and tenacious. It forms an unbroken continuum of testimony and example that links biblical Jews and Christians with contemporary Jews and Christians who take up the call to liberation.

With the recurrence of secular philosophy unfettered by theology, the rise of science, the birth of parliamentary democracies, and the onrush of capitalism as the mechanism for intensive economic development, the grip of the Jewish-Christian ethic in the West was loosened. Its faltering was as much due to internal division and uncertainty as to external attack, and the results were highly complex—with ramifying consequences for good and ill.

One happy consequence was that Jews at last began to emerge as vocal participants in wider society after centuries of enforced marginalization. Less happy was the restriction of ethics to the private sphere, a particularly virulent tendency in North America with its freewheeling colonial conditions.

Individualism, whether errantly prideful or sadly alienated, went in tandem with the runaway social and economic consequences of applying rapidly developing technology to privately controlled and enjoyed moneymaking. The sense of the common good that Jewish and Christian ethics had always claimed, in spite of very inconsistent practice, was now more and more difficult to conceive and to formulate in a manner that could call autonomous economics into question.

The strain and fracturing within Christian ethical tradition erupted in the Protestant Reformation. Protestantism displayed a large measure of consonance with the capitalist spirit of private judgment and self-control.

It was not a difficult step from the right of people to possess and develop their own souls unfettered by the church to the right of people to possess the means of production and enjoy their fruits unfettered by civil institutions. But this "right to possession" was envisioned for individual owners, not for the community of believers in common, much less for the populace at large.

In contrast, Catholicism retained a much stronger sense of a transnational and transcommunal ethic of the common good, but it was severely hampered by its conservative "backward look," dependent on and nostalgic toward feudal and monarchic arrangements and uncomprehending of the new possibilities for good in expanded economic enterprise and political democracy.

Still, the workings of the Jewish-Christian ethical impulse were evident in reform movements that applied stopgap measures to aid those most severely hurt by the inexorable advance of capitalist enterprise. In the end, however, no Jewish or Christian ethical initiative was able to find a social form powerful enough to reinvigorate the sense of the public good to the point where it could confront and alter the increasingly prevalent assumptions of capitalist individualism.

CHRISTIAN VALUES AND MODERN ECONOMIC STRUCTURES

Rather than lament this situation, it is probably wiser to recognize that it could scarcely have been otherwise. It must be remembered that Jewish and Christian theologies and ethics arose in ancient precapitalist circumstances. In those settings there were disputes and struggles over the proper economics, and both Jewish and Christian believers were often in the forefront as advocates of communitarian economics against the dominant tributary economics.

While Jews and Christians were able to establish communitarian economic orders of varying scope for limited periods of time, their decided economic preference to value justice over privilege did not prevail in antiquity. Moreover, while the theologies, ethics, and liturgies of those faiths lived on in tradition, social and economic practices suitable for ancient agrarian conditions could not be simply reproduced in new conditions, especially under high-intensity capitalism, save in the form of small-scale experiments.

Thus, although Jews and Christians had little difficulty cherishing and perpetuating their traditional religious beliefs and rituals, in larger social and economic terms the specific socioeconomic directives from their religious heritage gave them no concrete or comprehensive answers to the way the capitalist society and economy confronted them. Jews and Christians were at the mercy of fast-breaking developments in economics which seemed to defy piecemeal analysis and correction.

As many liberation theologians and ethicists have correctly noted, neither Judaism nor Christianity in and of itself contains a method of social analysis. Instead, Jewish and Christian historical records present us with a series of socioeconomic situations about which judgments were made and actions taken. In retrospect, we can reconstruct the social analysis implied in those judgments and actions. Nonetheless, our ancestors did not bequeath us a method of social analysis to employ today; they left us instead a strong predisposition toward communitarian values and commitments.

In short, Judaism and Christianity received their classic shapes in "pre-analytic" times: before the development of the natural sciences and advanced technology, before full-blown historiography, in large part before or outside the pale of philosophy, before the theoretical formulation of political economy. Consequently, these religions cannot directly judge the accuracy of the method and content of more recent human achievements. Nevertheless, the heritage and consciousness of Jews and Christians do come vitally into play in any assessment of the meaning and import of these achievements for people's lives.

How do modern "secular" forces shape a particular notion and practice of the common good? What do they say about the place of moral and spiritual experience and values when economic considerations increasingly constrain and shape those experiences and values? If we cannot look to our major religious traditions for a method of social analysis, where do we look? Necessarily, we must look to the two major traditions of capitalism and socialism, for it is these modes of analysis and forms of public life that shape economics and social reality throughout the world today. Jews and Christians must accept that if their commitment to the common good is to find embodiment, it will necessarily be in a society shaped by one or the other of these dominant modes of production with its attendant visions of the human good. How can the social, critical, and ethical heritage of Judaism and Christianity be brought to bear in a fundamental assessment of economic structures that will make a practical difference in the way we look on our world and act within it?

THE SOCIAL CONFLICT OVER THEOLOGIES OF LIBERATION

Over the last two decades or so, a closely related family of theologies classed as theologies of liberation has emerged within the Jewish and Christian traditions. This extended family embraces Latin American liberation theology and its Hispanic cognates in North America; the feminist theology emergent in North America and increasingly influential worldwide; Black theology both in the United States and abroad, notably in South Africa; and various so-called "Third World" theologies, such as Korean *minjung* ("underdog") theology.

The grassroot bases and feeders of these more or less formally developed theological positions are found in action-reflection groups within and on the edges of the churches, variously engaged with biblical, theological, and social questions. These "liberation cells" are locked in struggles over church practice (for example, forms of liturgy, sanctuary for political refugees, ordination of women) and over social issues (such as ecology, disarmament, human rights, homelessness, unemployment, drugs, abortion, and health care).

Collaborative with theological and ecclesial expressions of liberation are new schools of biblical interpretation, such as materialist exegesis in Europe and social-critical hermeneutics in North America. These provide a class-oriented and power-conscious, often explicitly feminist, reading of the churches' biblical heritage. The new modes of biblical interpretation correspond closely to Latin American liberation theology's summons to "hermeneutical suspicion" toward traditional apolitical ways of construing both the present social situation and the biblical text. The socioeconomic, mode-of-production analysis of ancient Israel and the early Church presented in the first part of this chapter is one significant fruit of this kind of social-critical biblical research. Through its findings, we are able to link the theological battles of our age to the theological struggles reflected in the Bible, to view the two connectedly as ideological dimensions of social-material reality.

Taken together, the theologies, ecclesial and social practices, and biblical hermeneutics of liberation constitute a major new reality in the Catholic and Protestant churches. This novel development has with good reason aroused a profound unease and a vehement opposition among those who adhere to the more traditional, supposedly apolitical understandings of religion and church, notably among the hierarchies of the established churches. Unfortunately, the issues at stake between "liberation" and "orthodox" theological and ethical stances are often debated on narrow religious grounds, with insufficient reference to the social reality that has precipitated the quarrel. Too often the theological and social topics debated by liberationists and traditionalists simply do not reveal the respective comprehensive social interests and agendas that underlie and pervade the debate.

This won't do. The materialist perspective I have employed to survey the history of Jewish and Christian ethics is the method best suited to an examination of the conflicts over liberation theology and practice. It will help us to identify the social factors that condition the participants and the issues at stake in the struggle for control of thought and practice within the institutional churches today.

It is not difficult to recognize that the eruption of liberation theologies coincides with the exacerbation of sharp contradictions in capitalist society in the last half of the twentieth century. These intensifying contradictions are the logical development of forces we saw at work in the collapse of feudal and monarchic society. In the consequent unfettered pursuit of economic gain, the triumphant European and North American bourgeoisie carried their dominion throughout the globe, severely disadvantaging in the process sizable underclasses in their own lands as well as the great majority of people in colonial regions.

The system-generated deprivation and murder of people on the basis of class, race, and gender became brutally evident in the colonial world after World War II. It also came increasingly to public light within the capitalist bastions themselves during the 1960s because of the war in Vietnam and the exposure of endemic poverty amid all the wealth of first-class societies, poverty that went hand in glove with stubborn racial and sexual injustice. Sectors of the so-called "middle class," prone to apathy as a result of the material comfort they enjoyed in the capitalist economy, began to experience economic and cultural loss accompanied by moral disquiet. Maldistributions of power and wealth were seen to affect the quality of public life and the standard of living for everyone. The needless cruelty of oppression that seemed built into the very structure of the capitalist "good life" began to gnaw at—even to outrage— the conscience of many.

These social contradictions spawned not only criticisms of capitalist society but also equally determined defenses. Because capitalist society, despite serious strains, held together and continued to work economic miracles for some, while offering possibilities of personal development and indulgence for its prospering members, many people simply denied the gravity of capitalism's failure to meet human needs. Others contended that capitalism, if given more time, would eventually make good on its promise to eliminate poverty and injustice by means of intensified capitalist development and honest electoral politics.

Often, adherents of the capitalist way of life saw most of the problems not as the result of a failure of capitalism but as a consequence of inordinate demands by people who either had no substantive grounds for complaint or who should be more patient in awaiting social improvements and more industrious in working their way up the socioeconomic ladder of success. Others took this rationalization a step further, attributing the grievances to bad faith, the work of committed troublemakers influenced by Communist conspiracies or misled by Marxist rhetoric, and ideology perceived as foreign, unpatriotic, and atheistic. It must be recognized that far and away the great majority of official church pronouncements on these social contradictions, including papal documents, however much they deplore massive social suffering, adopt one or more of these intellectual and moral stances, which in the last analysis operate in defense of the capitalist world order.

In sum, the guardians of capitalism display a social-psychological temperament that rests securely on the status quo, at most allowing for cosmetic changes in society to make conditions of life look better or to make minor concessions that are not too costly. Needed large-scale reforms, espoused by radical liberals and praised in the moral teaching of the churches, are diplomatically left to the discretion of the capitalist leaders and thereby postponed into an indefinite future.

In practice, the capitalist apologists use heavy doses of pacifying ideology, buttressed by most official church teaching. The defenders of the status quo condescend to their critics until sufficiently threatened, when they resort to suppression by law and police power. Such acts of forceful repression may be mildly—even on occasion vehemently—condemned by church authorities, but usually with "balancing" condemnations of the protesters and always with the tacit understanding that the capitalist world order is the only one within which to think and make moral assessments about the "real" world, as sharply distinguished from the "spiritual" realm. And it is precisely because theologies of liberation refuse to play by these rules and conventions of capitalist hegemony that they are so threatening to traditionalists within the churches and to economic and political authorities.

RELIGION, SOCIAL CONFLICT, AND SOCIAL CLASS

It is not at all surprising that neither the critics nor the defenders of capitalist society have been able to silence or to convince one another by logical argument. Each party sees certain undoubted truths, but how do all the "truths" fit together in a proper construal of the overall ethical evaluation of capitalist society? Since the parties to the debate are personally gaining or losing as members of the society, what they see and how they evaluate it depends greatly on their location within the economic system. Likewise, their view of how their religious faith bears on society-rending contradictions will be based heavily on their respective locations in the social system. Therefore, it is necessary to look at how social actors at the top, in the middle, and at the bottom of society respond to social contradictions and how their religious identity is linked to their social experience and interpretation.

People of material means and commanding position in the capitalist order have every reason to minimize and "paper over" the social deprivations that others feel keenly. Those at the top do not as a rule experience socially caused human suffering at first hand. Moreover, they do not want to see any changes in society that will risk their own economic status and exercise of power. They may be willing to entertain or even initiate changes, but only those that advance their overriding interest in staying at the summit of the socioeconomic system that rewards them so well.

Those at the top also want to believe that the system rewards everyone, at least everyone deserving of reward, perhaps not in every respect or at every moment but certainly over the long haul. Both in their continuing prosperity and in their good will and high hopes as social leaders, the upper classes see convincing evidence that the social contradictions confronting them are only minor disorders.

These same socially dominant persons normally experience religion as a validation of their psychic and socioeconomic security and as a bulwark against external challenges and inner doubts. Religion symbolically adorns and ritually reenacts their view of themselves as beneficiaries of and leaders within a thriving, well-functioning society that is basically good for people. They interpret much that is given positive evaluation in the Bible, theology, and liturgy—such as the righteous ones, faithful believers, those Jews and Christians through the ages who followed God and upheld the moral law in the world—as validating the prevailing structures, role hierarchies, and differential rewards of capitalist society. Furthermore, the social honor and emotional comfort they feel in their "church home" corroborates and reinforces their sense of mission to uphold a system they see to be under unreasonable attack.

Upper-class church members use the same sensibility to interpret all that is negatively symbolized in the Bible, theology, and liturgy: the godless, sinners, idolaters, troublemakers, Canaanites, Pharisees, and so on. They apply such terms either to earlier times and distant places or to those who are currently troubling society because they are unwilling to work hard enough, or are impatient and insolent, or have been infected by evil influences and forces that God opposes and calls on his righteous servants to eliminate.

Ironically, within this symbolic structure, the disprivileged can be the object of sentiment and good will in public prayers and even in prophetic sermons. Those of the disadvantaged who are "worthy" are helped by the churches' organized benevolence projects. The "worthy" disadvantaged are those who can't help their plight and especially those who remain passive and unpolitical about their circumstances; disadvantaged people who resist their conditions and seek power thereby become unworthy, morally suspect.

Despite all defenses, a few of the socially privileged believers are pricked so deeply in conscience by aspects of their religious beliefs and by unexpected exposures to social suffering that they may be moved to make adjustments in their investment patterns, places of employment, or life-style and may become involved in social causes they once despised or ignored. When this happens, it is usually a lonely struggle. Such a reversal or shift in social perception is generally viewed by fellow believers as "religious" rather than "social" conversion, so that the larger social systemic implications may not be grasped either by convert or by congregation. Individuals go through these changes in belief and orientation without assistance from their churches in confronting social contradictions and their causes or in exploring the grave options society faces.

Those in the middle echelons of society typically have more ambivalent and contradictory reactions to social conflict than do those at the top. As Michael Zweig shows in Chapter 8, the middle class does not fall clearly on either side of economic contradictions. Consequently, when middle-class people internalize social contradictions, they tend to form split and contradictory psychosocial, intellectual, and moral responses.

People "in the middle" appear typically to straddle the social issues, seeing merit and demerit on all sides of a conflict, in a social vacillation born of mutually conflicting experiences and interests. On the one hand, those in the social middle, including most church leaders and academicians, tend to side with those in command because their own relative privilege and possibility of advancement are dependent on the system and on trusting the top leadership. On the other hand, they are more likely than their superiors to have seen or experienced social suffering. Further, they often entertain grievances of their own toward a system that does not accord them much control over their working and living conditions.

These middle sectors typically waffle between criticizing and defending the social system, until some critical juncture of conflict "smokes them out" and they are pushed to take a position through deliberate action or inaction. By keeping a separation between their public and private lives, a fair number of the discontented middle people carry on "subversive" social-critical activities. In countries where Marxist and radical theory and organization are strong, they may have fairly well-developed social analyses. In the United States, where radical alternatives to dominant social views are not highly visible, they are more often moved by conscience and duty alone.

Middle-range social actors tend to be as ambivalent about their religion as they are about social conflict. Their usual starting point and fallback position, as with the upper social levels, is a sense of comfort and security in the face of the pressures of everyday life. Lacking the more monolithic self-confidence of their socioeconomic superiors, however, their religious perspective is less dependably coherent and stable. Alongside the system-affirming elixir of religion, they often feel reservations about the basic goodness of the life they live. The security they derive from religion is often less a celebration of capitalist achievement than a shoring-up of their personal resources for doing the best they can in difficult or boring jobs, making financial ends meet, and coping with the deterioration of their physical and social environments.

The considerable references to the poor and needy in the Bible, theology, and liturgy often awaken qualms in the conscience of the middle class. Because of their personal awareness of daily structural injustice, its members may more or less consciously recognize that a social dynamic of systemic cause and effect is at work to foster individual poverty and crime. The sensitized social conscience, when mixed with social hostility, is a volatile combination. It may turn leftward into "liberal guilt" or rightward into "reactionary hostility," or it may oscillate between the two from moment to moment and from issue to issue.

As a consequence, the positively and negatively charged religious symbols, which possess relatively stabilized contemporary associations for the upper classes, will contain confused and shifting meanings for many persons in the middle. Theological and social "good guys" and "bad guys" may swap places erratically in the religious texts and rituals they attend to and in the social scene they are a part of. They may associate themselves with the religious symbols in oddly capricious ways, regarding themselves as God's instruments or martyrs when they are feeling "up" and God's obstacles or enemies when they are "down." In defense against social guilt and social hostility, middle-sector churchgoers will often opt for social apathy, turning their energies to spirituality, liturgy, or tasks of church administration and budget.

Yet a sizable sector of the midpositioned people will find ways to "work out" guilt and hostility, coupled with genuine altruism and religious feeling, through church-based or church-related activities directed to social welfare or social change. Usually, however, they will not receive much help from their churches in deepening their social analysis or broadening their understanding of criteria and options for social change. The institutional church will "fuel" them socially mainly at the level of diffuse sentiment and generalized moral challenge.

The people at the bottom of society are those with the most severe and bitter experiences of the social contradictions of capitalism. Those experiences have been life-determining for them, and they are likely to be aware, as was the biblical Job, that their crippling social circumstances are not due for the most part to personal flaws in themselves. Their success in fashioning a large picture of how the system works to inflict deprivation, and what it might take to change matters, cannot be taken for granted, however. Their vision may extend no further than blaming particular employers or politicians, or even other oppressed social groups. Engrossed in surviving from day to day, they may well see critical thought and social action as luxuries they have no time or energy to pursue.

The communities they live in may have little organized social or political activity, and the organizations devoted to social change, peopled heavily by middle-level "activists," often have little appeal to persons at the bottom because of differing social, ethnic, and cultural sensibilities. If these "lowest" take visible action, they are vulnerable to reprisals that may prove costly to their survival. Some people, especially under the influence of authoritarian status quo organizations—notably churches—may internalize a message of personal guilt, contrary to all the facts and their own best interests. As the capitalist crisis deepens, with generation on generation damned to unemployment and poverty, others may turn in hopelessness to sex, drugs, and crime. This course of action multiplies misery throughout poor communities and supplies defenders of capitalism with further justification for dismissing their complaints as the ravings of social barbarians or ingrates.

The false turns that the socially weakest can and do take demonstrate that any notion of the downcast "spontaneously" overthrowing the capitalist order is mistaken. Nonetheless, the confidence of capitalist leaders that these people at the bottom are constitutionally passive, and the fear of middle-class social activists that they are inherently unreliable, are equally wide of the mark. In their own way, and in unexpected times and places (to name only Nicaragua and South Africa), the poor can awaken as a potent force for social change. Although nearly everything in capitalist society works against them, those in the lower strata do manage to keep alive their self-interests and are capable of entering alliances when they are assured that they are partners and not mere pawns in somebody else's power play.

Religion in the lower classes is stamped with as much contradiction and ambivalence as it is in the middle classes but in significantly different ways. Since the lower levels of society tend to be "voiceless" and are interpreted by others more often than they interpret themselves to outsiders, these remarks about "the poor" are necessarily more probative and speculative than I prefer. Given that liberation theologies are seeking to lend a social voice to these "poor," however, it is incumbent on us to try to hear what they are saying, for only by including them do we get a full picture of the social contradictions and of the sources and impulses of liberation within theological discourse and religious practice.

In considering what religion means to the lowest members of society, we probably need first to recognize that in comparison with their upper- and middle-class counterparts, the lower classes are less "churched." There are many exceptions and variations from country to country in this overall pattern, but it does mean that for many of society's weakest, organized religion has little or no attraction. In the main, this is a virtually instinctual social reflex to the reality that most churches have been oriented "upward" on the social scale, even when they are based among those toward the bottom. As a result, many of the poor do not find that their life experiences and struggles are recognized or assisted by religion.

The social orientation of organized religion appears in the tendency of churches serving the poor to cultivate the values and customs of the middle classes, thereby supplying a kind of compensatory religious mobility in place of the social mobility that the vast majority of the poor cannot reasonably hope to attain. To the extent that this tendency prevails, for example in some Black churches in the United States in the wake of three decades of civil rights struggles, differing class-imbued perceptions of the faith may coexist in the same congregations. The older "deliverance from oppression" themes are often celebrated by people who have become middle class in many respects but are still vulnerable to ethnic injustice. In such contexts, the coexistence of differing class values and perceptions may have positive and negative effects, both serving to connect the better-off members with their still disadvantaged fellows and fostering a too complacent attitude toward what has been accomplished in the actual advancement of the group as a whole.

The churches of the poor thus tend to exhibit a profound ambiguity or contradiction, with great potential either for evading or facing up to the social inequities all around them and in their midst. The ethos of upward social mobility in these churches, if seen as a way of equipping members for improved social analysis and action toward social change, may be a powerful instrument for organizing among the poor in the absence of or in alliance with other community mechanisms. However, an ideology of upward mobility may instead merely facilitate and praise the advance of a small minority of the ethnic poor into the middle class, without challenging the whole social system or attending to the conditions of those who are left behind. In so doing, a church may give the deceptive appearance of social advance for the community as a whole when in fact it is chiefly promoting a few members from one class station to another and presenting that very limited achievement as the proper social goal for all the poor.

With these important qualifiers, some things can be said that are distinctive about the religious orientation of the lower classes in respect to social contradictions. First, people at the bottom of society are largely free of the pervasive social guilt that infects so many morally sensitive members of the middle ranks of society. This is objectively realistic, since these poor have not gained what little they have at the expense of others and are not responsible as a class for the injustice in society. Second, the lower classes who do participate actively in the churches are likely to regard the church as their primary social affiliation beyond the family. This too has an objective foundation, since in their churches they find a sense of solidary community that is in short supply elsewhere in society and not readily available to them in voluntary social and cultural organizations of the sort that attract the religiously motivated middle classes.

For socially disadvantaged people, the Bible, theology, and liturgy carry a strong message of divine support for those on the social and economic margin. Religious symbols and rites provide them with meaning and motivation to carry on their daily struggles. They tend to have an immediate and vivid sense of the presence of God as a resource for life in the world. Two factors condition how such people relate their faith to their social existence: the degree to which they think of their religious faith along either individualistic or communal/systemic lines; and the scope of communal solidarity they feel across ethnic, gender, regional, and other lines of demarcation that set them apart from others.

As the lower classes face outward to their world, their lack of social guilt and sense of church solidarity equip them to confront their social contradictions without "liberal illusions." Nonetheless, the poor encounter serious obstacles to translating their experience of church community into a gripping sense of social solidarity beyond the church walls.

The theology and polity of the churches peopled by the poor are frequently pietistic and individualistic, negatively dismissive of "the world" and emphasizing authoritarian obedience to ecclesial and political authorities. While their church ideology does not directly foster social guilt, it does devalue social action in many instances. Thus it can open the door to the harboring of personal guilt for not being "good" enough morally or skillful enough personally to advance in society and to provide for their families.

Along with a vivid sense of God may go a contrary fatalism about social improvement and sometimes a strong sense that this unjust society must be "God's will," since it seems explicable in no other way. This religious "frosting" reinforces a sense of social powerlessness that has a very concrete basis: the religious poor have seen many promises and efforts to improve their lives falter and come to nothing.

The conditions that convert the social-critical potential of religious belief into social action usually develop from local concerns in the immediate lives of the poor or from blatant oppression directed against a large sector of the lower classes, oppression based most obviously on race or region. The religious impulses in the Nicaraguan revolution and in the fight against apartheid in South Africa are instances of such activation of religious energy for social change on a broad front. The energizing conditions usually arise when the social contradictions are most sharply posed and the social enemy is clear. Where the lower classes are more integrated into bourgeois class ideologies and church formations, it is far more difficult for them to reach even an implicit class analysis and to unite with others possessing similar interests across church denominational lines and across the social and cultural divisions reinforced by capitalist ideology.

The difficulties in translating the religious drive for social justice into concrete effects can be observed in the churches of the poor in the stagnated inner cities of developed countries and the burgeoning slums of Third World cities. In those bleak, often nearly anarchic conditions, the most religious segments of the lower classes are daily face to face with others of their class whose antisocial behavior is frowned on by church teaching and directly threatens their own precarious security. The church-connected poor naturally tend to moral condemnation of this antisocial behavior, without appropriate recognition of the social roots of such "acting out."

The result is a feeling of highly restricted "class solidarity" toward fellow church members, coupled with "class dissociation" from those outside the church. Although with respect to critical social contradictions, all these inner-city lower classes are "in the same boat," religion may function perversely to obscure this fact and to give the church folk a false sense of social superiority that can even make their views as reactionary as those of the upper classes and the right-leaning members of the middle class.

Often decisive in these situations is the perspective of the church leaders, who have a choice between stressing the solidary compassion and justice of core biblical and theological traditions, and opting for moralistic individualism and the narrow in-group defensiveness that caters to the "divide and conquer" strategy of capitalist ideology. In this social context the dispute over liberation theology among church leaders and rank-and-file members takes on a lively significance quite beyond the doctrinal issues involved.

ORTHODOX AND POSTORTHODOX THEOLOGIES
AND SOCIAL CONFLICT

The foregoing phenomenological sketch of the social meaning of religion for the various classes in society allows us to look more specifically at the ideological and social class content of the debate over liberation theologies. The dominant theologies in the churches, if not in the ecclesial academy, are the traditional orthodox theologies. Catholic and Protestant versions premise a universal course of salvation for the world, mediated through Christian tradition and implemented by the agency of the churches. Initiated by God and appropriated by humans, this work of salvation through faith will be completed for each believer at death and for humanity as a whole at the end of history.

Salvation is spiritual and moral; there is some social spin-off into the life of the world but only secondarily and at a remove from the fundamental spiritual mission. The social manifestations of salvation will show up mainly in acts of charity and mercy and in the dutiful fulfilling of one's station in life. All this is slanted in a decidedly individualistic direction or, if cast more communally, primarily in terms of a traditional precapitalist "ideal" world that no longer jibes with actual societies today. Communal thinking is mainly reserved for the peace and prosperity of the churches necessary to further their work of spiritual salvation, and the criteria for the churches' effectiveness draw heavily on capitalist notions of success: that is, growth in membership and budget, consumer satisfaction, and so on.

As I noted in the first part of this chapter, the still-regnant orthodox theologies are those recast under feudal and aristocratic auspices (in their Catholic forms) and under early bourgeois and protocapitalist auspices (in their Protestant forms). They are stamped with the marks of hierarchic thinking that parallel the social hierarchies of the secular world and are manifest in those of the churches. They tend to split reality into material and spiritual sectors, to drive a wedge between the public and the private, and to regard people as individual atoms with secondary social connections.

Taken together, all these features of orthodox theologies, unless strongly countered by critical social thinking, support the mission of the bourgeoisie to promote and defend capitalist society. These theologies worked with considerable vision and coherence for their respective times, but they have become ever more outmoded and reactionary as the capitalist program has revealed its limits: its structural inability to include the great majority of the world's people within its "success story," and its tendency to make social and cultural life painful even for those whom capitalism rewards materially.

Postorthodox theologies have in various ways mitigated the church-world dualism of the older orthodox theologies. They have done so under the ideological and social tensions and pressures created by the one-sided and limited accomplishments of capitalist society. Liberal theology stressed the historical foundations of Christianity, the personal competence of believers to develop their powers in the world, and the necessity of social reforms to alleviate the most inhuman life conditions. Neo-orthodox theology provided a strong basis of resistance against fascism and authoritarian Communism but offered no grounds for a social ethic to confront capitalism per se. Existential theology conceded the erosion of clear moral and religious norms in capitalist society and sought to make an asset out of spiritual rootlessness in order to fashion authentic individual identities against the tide of social anomie. Process theology recognized the organismic interaction between nature and society and between individuals and social collectivities, and it sought to show how the divine is a given dimension of the human in order to alleviate many of the presumed conflicts between religion and science.

Among these postclassical theologies, only liberal theology produced a notable social thrust; in the Social Gospel movement of American Protestantism and more indirectly in Catholic Action programs preceding the rise of liberation theologies. The circumscribed limits of these social action efforts can be explained by the naive guilty conscience and excessive social optimism of progressive sectors of the bourgeoisie. They proceeded on the assumption that the leadership of capitalist society could be persuaded by reason and moral suasion to improve the conditions of social life. They were at the same time very limited in their sensitivity to racism, sexism, and imperialism.

The social aspirations of liberal theology were restricted by capitalist ideology at the outset and did not seriously aim to overturn the fundamental systemic conditions that produced the ills they addressed. As they exhausted their theoretical and strategic resources, some adherents of the Social Gospel and Catholic Action either turned back toward orthodox theologies or settled for "social holding actions" within neo-orthodox, existentialist, or process frameworks. Others were propelled onward toward the emerging liberation theologies, once they recognized that the confines of bourgeois social thought had to be transcended if the contradictions of society were to be relevantly and cogently dealt with.

LIBERATION THEOLOGIES AND SOCIAL CONFLICT

In this confused and frustrating theological climate, where none of the existing theologies could address the social plight of humanity adequately, liberation theologies emerged in the 1960s with a fundamentally new orientation. Retaining the familiar sources of Christian theology, the liberation schema added further sources and set them all, new and old, in a radically different context, precisely that of the fundamental involvement of all aspects of human life in the process of universal salvation. Liberation theologies rejected the schizoid notion of two planes of existence, the one spiritual and the other material, affirming in its place the irreducible and indivisible unity of spiritual and material welfare as a promise and a possibility for all people.

Furthermore, the "liberation" orientation located integral spiritual-material salvation itself directly in the lives of people in all their social connections. Church and world were no longer regarded as respectively prior and derivative arenas of religious reality. Rather, both were projected as different aspects of the one work of God on behalf of all people, which extends into the most mundane and openly "political" aspects of life. The "universal" note in Christianity, specified by orthodox theologies as belonging to the spiritual realm, was expanded to designate all people in all aspects of their material life.

The practical import of the new orientation was threefold. It signified that social analysis and social change were as much Christian obligations as any activity within the institutional church. It affirmed that every believer had an integral spiritual-material responsibility and calling that gave the involvement and initiative of laity equal weight with the role of clergy. And it drew dramatic attention to the grievous obstacles to spiritual and material empowerment within the churches themselves.

In one swoop, the theologies of liberation have presented both a comprehensive picture of the unity of the historic process of salvation as a project of comprehensive human redemption, and an equally encompassing ethic and practice mandating social analysis and action to redistribute power over resources and people in all realms, both "secular" and "sacred." The liberation perspective has unprecedented breadth and force. It has been able to address fully and cogently all the traditional topics of theology, to make "social sense" of them, and to claim biblical authority for its orientation. At the same time, it has redeployed this entire reconceptualized armory of theological topics to serve the goals of reconstituting church and society on entirely new foundations.

In doing so, liberation theologies broke free of the bourgeois containment of religious thought and practice, refusing at the same time to return to older feudal and aristocratic co-optations. Instead, it pointed onward toward a new socioeconomic era more or less consonant with socialism in broad terms, without, however, prescribing the detailed lineaments of the new society or offering any particular socialist society as a model.

In fact, liberation theologies differ in the degree of explicitness with which they identify their social and theological goals and presuppositions as socialist, emphasizing rather that each socially oppressed group must develop its own integral process of liberation suited to its context. What is truly fresh and decisive in liberation theology and what causes it to strike fear in the hearts of so many—especially among leaders in business, government, and the churches—is precisely this radical conceptual breakthrough. Shattered are the old premises in Christian practice and social theory about what theology is and what theology leads to. Liberation theologies have the audacity to envision new arrangements of power and wealth in society and church as not just a legitimate but an imperative Christian goal and at the same time a possibility attainable within the resources God has granted to human beings.

From our earlier analysis of the links between social class and religious identity, we saw that in all the social classes, without exception, people generally do not gain whatever social analysis they have from the churches themselves. They bring mostly unexamined social presuppositions to their churches, which church teaching and practice tend to fortify or adorn. On occasion those presuppositions may be indirectly challenged or brought under suspicion, but in a manner tangential to the main function and aim of the churches.

The will to undertake social analysis and the resources to do so must normally be sought by Christians outside the institutional church—at least this was the prevailing reality until the various theologies of liberation began to find lodgment in the churches. This "conscientizing" political and social intrusion of liberation outlooks into congregations and church agencies is fed by the power of religious symbols and ignites a combined religious and social impulse. It threatens the aloofness of a church as a supposedly social and political "neutral space." The hierarchy's fear that more and more believers will connect their faith with radical social criticism and action, converting churches into "committed space," reveals how integral and holistic the liberation perspective really is when counterposed to the socially fragmented and theologically abstract outlook of all previous theologies. It clearly transcends the effects of previous attempts to go beyond orthodox traditionalism, attempts that remained captive to an increasingly ossified bourgeois mentality.

The development of theology and ethics over the course of Jewish and Christian history indicates that the struggle over liberation theologies and practices is of critical importance to everyone desiring major social change, religious or not. Religious belief and practice constitute a significant inhibitor or facilitator of social change. This is true even though religion is seldom the primary initiator of social change. Inasmuch as religion lends an aura and stamp of legitimacy to social attitudes of one stripe or another, no calculus of social change achievable in a given context can afford to ignore religion as potential obstacle or aid.

If my analysis is correct, liberation theologies constitute the very first thoroughgoing, frontal religious-ideological challenge to capitalist society. They stand on a par in magnitude and import with the theologies of the Protestant Reformation. Protestant theologies, appearing more or less concurrently with the rise of the bourgeoisie, encouraged the development of a "youthful" capitalism. Liberation theologies, appearing at the point of chronic capitalist crisis in its "overripe maturity," toll the death knell of capitalism's long monopoly on moral and spiritual discourse within Western Christian circles.

As Michael Zweig shows in Chapter 1, liberation theologies reject the capitalist understanding of human nature that isolates people from one another and fragments them internally, leaving them ripe for manipulation as virtual commodities in an irrational and unjust economic order. Liberation theologies see the ground and goal of human life to be a just and people-affirming society in which wealth serves the basic human needs of everyone instead of indulging the inordinate cravings of a relative few.

Liberation theologies claim that this impulse to genuine social and economic democracy, beyond the narrow confines of bourgeois political democracy, is supported by the weight and thrust of biblical and theological traditions, once those traditions are read critically without capitalist blinders. Liberation theologies promise and, more important, deliver a sustained, broad-gauged critique that simply refuses to confine itself to the categories and proposed solutions of capitalist ideology and economic behavior.

The theoretical formulations of liberation theologies rise in large measure from the reflected social experience of oppressed and marginalized people in their diverse painful circumstances, and they resonate with the misgivings about capitalism that have taken hold of many within the middle classes. Liberation thought and liberation practice go hand in hand, evoking and criticizing each other in an ongoing, life-involving process, empowering and motivating socially active Christians on a worldwide scale. In the person of these Christians, many of whom are active in secular organizations, liberation theologies boldly expose and confront the inhuman and illogical costs of a capitalist ideology and world system that has not only outlived its contributions to humanity but reveals itself ever more clearly as the salient barrier to further progress for the great majority of humankind.

One final conclusion of great strategic importance emerges from a historical materialist study of the social correlates of theology and ethics: the urgency of Christian liberationists and Marxist liberationists to think and work together, at first drawing on one another's experiences and insights and then, step by step, pooling them. Religious liberationists need to develop their theological and ethical insights in the direction of social theory and strategy. Secular liberationists need to develop their social theory and strategy with regard to the reality of religious ideology and practice as critical factors for or against social change. Each without the other is poorer in theory and feebler in practice. The delivery of humankind from the throes of capitalist economics and social organization may very well depend upon a close and sustained collaboration between religious and secular liberationists. Religious activists and Marxists can be together among a far larger company of people of many religions and sociopolitical persuasions, whose combined efforts on many fronts can mend and transform the world.

3

AN ETHICAL CRITIQUE OF
CAPITALISM: CONTRIBUTIONS OF
MODERN CATHOLIC SOCIAL TEACHING

Gregory Baum

Critiques of capitalist economic structures have been elaborated at all levels within the Catholic hierarchy, including national and regional assemblies of bishops. In response to the appalling conditions of life that hundreds of millions of Catholics and others experience in the modern capitalist world, and in the presence of powerful mass movements to confront these conditions, church leaders have sought ways to bring Catholic teaching to bear on the daily needs of the common people.

Liberation theology is the most recent and vibrant development of Catholic social doctrine. It has emerged in Latin America, where mass suffering has been particularly acute, but its influence and vision have extended into North America as well. The link between liberation theology and the popular masses is well known. But it is no less important to understand that liberation theology finds sources of support in the teachings of Pope John Paul II as well.

It is surprising to many that John Paul II should be associated with liberation theology. As Pamela Brubaker so clearly shows in Chapter 4, John Paul's teachings concerning women are profoundly reactionary. His antipathy to Marxism has been abundantly expressed, and he has consistently opposed the leading proponents of liberation theology in Latin America and elsewhere.

Nonetheless, there is much in papal teaching that lends weight to liberation theology. Whatever one's evaluation of John Paul's other theological pronouncements or his record in the papacy, his critique of capitalism is a crucial tool for activists within and without the Church who are working for justice and equality. Catholics should study it to discover how it applies to their concerns for economic justice. Others, including Marxists, can use papal teaching to evaluate and enhance their own critiques of capitalism. Through such broad-based reflection and praxis, the genuine insights of papal teaching will be deepened. Furthermore, the process will broaden the common ground on which different religious and secular currents advocating economic and social justice can meet and link their efforts.

THE SOCIAL CONTEXT OF CHURCH TEACHING

Since Vatican Council II (1962–65), Catholic social teaching has turned toward a deeper and more pointed critique of modern capitalism, elaborating and extending earlier critical reflections. The process has been a contradictory one, reflecting the conflict of interests in the larger society to which the Church has been responding. In this regard, the historical development of church teaching, including the writings of John Paul II, has exemplified the dynamic interaction between social conditions and religious doctrine described by Norman Gottwald in Chapter 2.

The Catholic Church has never fully reconciled itself with modern, capitalist society. The revolution of the burgher class threatened the feudal-aristocratic society from which capitalism emerged, including the place occupied in it by the Catholic Church. To resist the spread of modern society, the Catholic Church identified itself with the conservative sectors of European society and defended the old order against the new.

As capitalism became the dominant order in the world, the Church struck a long peace with the system and its rulers. According to revised church teaching, the market was a useful economic and social institution, but since it did not protect the common good or the poor from exploitation by the rich, the market had to be limited by government regulation and humanized by an ethical culture of fraternity.

From the time of Leo XIII at the end of the nineteenth century, Catholic social teaching condemned the abuses and excesses of capitalism but not capitalism as such. The Church defended private property, even though it understood private property, contrary to liberal opinion, as an institution that included social responsibility. In its defense of private property, the Church strongly and unambiguously condemned socialism.

Leo XIII led the Church to criticize modernity, especially the individualism, utilitarianism, and secularism promoted by the philosophy and the institutions of liberalism. But unlike socialist doctrine, which criticized capitalism with an eye to the future possibilities of human development, the Church criticized modern liberal society by contrasting it with an idealized picture of the past. Against the contractual basis of the recently emerged capitalist society and its strong individualism, church teaching defended the older, organic concepts of feudal society, the traditional notion of the common good, and the ancient virtues of social solidarity and respect for hierarchy.

The surprising shift to the left that has taken place in the Church's teaching since the 1960s preserves a good deal of continuity with the past. There remain the resistance to liberal philosophy and liberal economics, the emphasis on the common good and social solidarity, and the call for an ethical culture of justice and compassion. What is new is "the preferential option for the poor," the reading of society from the perspective of the disadvantaged. But modern Catholic teaching is often contradictory, not least the pronouncements of John Paul II. The new injunction to identify and overcome structures of oppression often comes into conflict with continuing strands of more conservative thought.

The experience of the Latin American Church in the 1960s and 1970s was especially important in the evolution of Catholic social teaching. Thanks to the influence of liberation theology it became clear to the Latin American bishops that the organic, corporatist concept of society did not apply to their societies, divided as they were between a small sector of wealthy and middle-class people and the great majority, impoverished and excluded from all social participation.

In two important church documents, the "Conclusions" of the 1968 Medellín Conference and the "Final Document" of the 1979 Puebla Conference, the Latin American bishops chose a conflict model to describe their own society. They recognized the division of society between the rich and the poor and argued that human justice and God's justice demanded "the preferential option for the poor": that is, solidarity with the poor and their struggle for emancipation.[1]

But Catholic social teaching is not without its ambiguities. Because of the effort to preserve a certain continuity with past teaching, there are passages in the contemporary documents that continue to promote a corporatist approach to society. Conflict and struggle then appear as brief interruptions of an underlying harmony, to be repaired by concessions on the part of the powerful, compromises on both sides, and the creation of a new consensus.

Another ambiguity is the fact that in most situations the Catholic Church applies its own social teaching in neither its internal organization nor its social counsel. Many bishops nominated by John Paul II in Third World countries and in the developed countries have tended to be conservative personalities, defenders of the status quo, indifferent or hostile to the new social teaching. Despite his trenchant critique of capitalism, which in many ways parallels the insights of liberation theology, John Paul II has been unwilling to allow the critique to become the basis of truly revolutionary practice.

Still, it is important that these and other reactionary aspects of church teachings do not obscure the progressive aspects that are emerging. These can be seen even in two important encyclicals of Pope John Paul II, *Laborem Exercens* (On labor) of 1981 and *Sollicitudo Rei Socialis* (On social concern) of 1987, as well as in the pastoral letters of the Canadian and American bishops.[2] The shift to the left in these church documents is supported with religious enthusiasm by a significant minority in the Church, the Christian left, manifested in a faith-and-justice movement embodied in a network of groups, centers, and individuals committed to emancipation and sustained by frequent meetings and an appropriate literature. In some parts of the world, these Christians constitute the core of the political resistance against oppression. In fact, it is due to this movement, especially in the Third World, that a change has taken place in the Church's official teaching. The shift to the left has come from below.

The radical church documents offer an ethical critique of capitalism that has modified Catholic social teaching and drawn it closer to left-wing politics. Three ideas in John Paul II's encyclicals, for example, have a close affinity with ideas developed by Karl Marx in his early manuscripts, at a time when he too engaged in ethical reflection on liberal institutions.

In these early writings Marx introduced the concept of alienated labor.[3] Wage labor in the factory system robbed workers of the fruit of their labor and estranged them from their own humanity. Workers were meant to be the subjects of production. It was capitalism that made them into objects of production. We note in passing that Marx offered here an ethico-philosophical critique of capitalism, not a scientific one, for to speak of human alienation and the human destiny to be subject presupposes a normative concept of human nature.

81

In one of his first essays, Marx proposed an even more radical concept of alienation.[4] He argued that people became estranged from their human nature whenever they were prevented from assuming collective responsibility for society and the institutions to which they belonged. People were meant to be the subject of their society. This was democracy. Political democracy in capitalist countries, Marx argued with some vehemence, was not very democratic: it proudly proclaimed that all citizens were equal before the law, and in doing so disguised the crass economic inequality between workers and owners and the total absence of democracy in the economic institutions.

In his early manuscripts Marx also defined the human as a "species being" (*Gattungswesen*),[5] a term derived from German idealism. Humans differ from animals inasmuch as the human struggle for survival and well-being is oriented toward the entire species, the whole of humanity. Against John Locke and the liberal philosophers, who promoted individualism, Marx defined the human as a social animal.

These three ideas in Marx are developed from a Christian perspective in the papal encyclicals. First, John Paul II argues that the dignity of labor is such that workers are entitled to participate in the decisions affecting the work of their hands and the organization of the work process. Workers are meant to be subjects, not objects of production. The Pope calls this "the priority of labour over capital."[6]

Workers are alienated from their human nature when they are excluded from ownership and coresponsibility, as they are both in capitalism and in Communism as represented by the Soviet and East European collectivism of the post–World War II era. In capitalism the fate of the workers depends on decisions made by the owners and directors of the industries, and in Communism on the decisions of the appropriate agency of the state bureaucracy. In both systems, wages are the important reality for the workers, and the struggle for just wages must continue for the time being. But eventually wage labor must be replaced by worker coownership; eventually workers will be the owners of their giant workbench.

For John Paul II, worker ownership is no unfailing guarantee of social justice. What is required for justice is that the industries be run to serve the well-being of the whole society. Workers who make decisions regarding the industries must therefore be responsible to a government that protects and promotes the common good.

In this context, John Paul II has also elaborated the Catholic position on property. As has been done since Leo XIII, he defends the rights of property, but only conditionally. The title to property, whether it be private, cooperative, or public, is valid only if the industries or the land actually serve the common good of society.[7] But more than any pope before him, John Paul II recognizes that it may not be possible to hold privately controlled property to standards of public interest. In such a situation, he has extended Catholic teaching to countenance collective, public ownership of means of production as a way to bring the fruits of labor's effort to bear in workers' interest.

But public ownership offers no guarantee that production will serve the needs of society. As in capitalism, where private ownership tends to serve the accumulation of private profit, a government may run the economy to enhance its power at home or expand its power abroad without regard to the welfare or needs of the workers. As is his custom, John Paul II formulates his ideas as critiques of both capitalism and collectivism. Because of oppression and sociopolitical marginalization of workers and the poor in both systems, protest movements and organized efforts to change the economic structure have an ethical foundation in capitalist societies no less than in socialist ones.

In his encyclicals John Paul II also defends the theory, formulated by the young Marx, that humans are meant to be subjects of their society and decision-making participants in all the institutions to which they belong.[8] In the past, Catholic social teaching opposed egalitarianism. The Catholic conservative tradition distinguished between the *majores*, the responsible leaders, and *minores*, the simple people, and demanded that "the leaders" serve the common good of society and "the simple people" obey their laws and regulations. Perhaps it was his experience in Poland that made John Paul II put great emphasis on what he calls "the subjectivity" of peoples.[9] Societies are just only if they allow the responsible participation of their members.

Governments may serve or claim to serve the well-being of their societies, but from an ethical perspective they are just only if they recognize the "subjectivity" of the people, their right to share responsibility in defining their culture and shaping their society. John Paul II does not suggest, however, that this necessarily calls for parliamentary democracy. One can imagine other institutional forms that respect the subjectivity of a people.

It is unfortunately both characteristic and remarkably inconsistent that John Paul II does not introduce the principle of subjectivity into the one institution over which he has power: namely, the Catholic Church. In ecclesiastical matters the Pope has all the instincts of a conservative, frightened of democracy as the beginning of chaos. In 1988 he went so far as to silence Leonardo Boff, one of the leading voices of liberation theology in Latin America, when Boff insisted publicly that the Church open itself to the active and creative participation of the common people.

Yet in his encyclicals John Paul II advocates the concept of universal solidarity. With Hegel and the young Marx and Abraham Lincoln as well, he argues that freedom is indivisible: if some remain oppressed, all remain imprisoned in one way or another. The alienation inflicted on some has adverse effects on the whole of society. If the wealthy nations of the North promote their own economic development to the detriment of the poor nations of the South, then even the northern ·nations will suffer. Why? Because the economic mechanisms that widen the gap between rich and poor countries also widen the gap between rich and poor classes in the North. Human development, the Pope argues, is "a duty of all towards all." [10]

The ethical discourse of universal solidarity is not always free of ambiguity. Universal solidarity is sometimes used as an ethical argument against class struggle and thus in favor of a corporatist concept of society. Many ecclesiastical texts, however, clearly recognize that universal solidarity begins with the poor and oppressed. Solidarity is not extended to the oppressor. Solidarity is preferential; it embraces those who struggle for justice. We note that the social perspective is here conflictual, not organic. Preferential solidarity aims at the reconstruction of the social order so that then, with the establishment of justice, solidarity may be extended to all. Preferential solidarity is the means; universal solidarity is the end.

In the encyclical *Laborem Exercens,* John Paul II argues that the workers are the dynamic element in both capitalist and Communist societies. Their exclusion from ownership and responsibility makes them the agents of social transformation in both societies. What counts in these struggles is that the workers develop solidarity in their own ranks and that those who are not workers, including the leadership of the Church, extend their solidarity to the workers' movement. The ethical imperative formulated by John Paul II is "the solidarity of labour and solidarity with labour." [11] For less developed countries, the Pope speaks of solidarity of the poor and with the poor. Universal solidarity here clearly begins with the poor and oppressed. [12]

84

In the mind of John Paul II, these innovative social ideas have nothing to do with Marxism. The Pope looks upon Marxism as an economistic and deterministic set of ideas that falsely claims the status of demonstrable science, that is devoid of humanistic reflection and insensitive to the aspirations of working people, a conservative, unimaginative ideology protecting the interests of the holders of power in so-called Communist regimes.

Even Western "scientific" Marxism does not appear attractive to the Pope. Against positivistic science on the left and the right, the papal encyclicals strongly emphasize the element of freedom and responsible choice that continues to be present in economic institutions. There are no economic "laws," only strong economic "trends." Economic systems are never completely internally determined. They always operate through specific, concrete institutions—industries, banks, decision-making boards—which people establish and for which they are responsible. Through human action, these institutions might be set up differently, even in the given system. In his analyses John Paul II always brings out both the "structuration" and the "human agency" present in the historical situation, even if he does not use this terminology.

Of special interest in this context is the concept of "structural sin," which John Paul II has reiterated in Catholic social teaching.[13] In another striking parallel with liberation theology, he argues that it is impossible to understand the present economic and political crisis simply as the multiplication of personal sins, the malicious acts of individuals. In the past, the churches used to "moralize." They created the impression that the problems in society were caused by pride and selfishness, and that if people only became more generous and loving, these problems would straighten themselves out.

Against this former trend, John Paul II speaks of "structures of sin," of mechanisms and institutions—created by people—which, following a logic built into them, inflict heavy burdens on certain sectors of society. As examples he gives colonialism and imperialism. Sister Amata Miller has used this framework in Chapter 7 to describe and interpret the advanced capitalist international economic system.

Even though people are shaped by the socioeconomic institutions through which they produce and live their lives, John Paul II brings out the agency and hence the responsibility that remains with individuals. Structural sin is always linked to personal sin, and individuals cannot escape responsibility by hiding behind generalized institutional or historical forces. Since systems always operate through specific, concrete mechanisms, decision-makers do make some choices and so have some responsibility for increasing or lightening the burden on people's backs. Increasing the unjust burden is sinful.

More than that, systems that create oppression also generate opposition and provoke critical ideas. In this situation, the Pope argues, personal sin is present in people who refuse to listen to criticism, who defend social injustice, and who oppose social change or seek to slow it down in order to protect their own privileges.

Against any form of determinism, the Church defends human agency and responsibility. Christian theology is suspicious of totalizing systems and evolutionary theories that predict the direction of history. History remains open. In times of great anguish such as our own, this openness of history to human agency and the unexpected is a source of hope.

THE CHURCH AND GLOBAL CAPITALISM

Recent church documents also provide an ethical critique of present-day global capitalism. The social analysis of the present economic crisis as presented in the papal encyclicals has been endorsed and developed by the Canadian bishops and, less consistently perhaps, by the U.S. bishops as well. According to these documents, world capitalism is entering upon a new and brutal phase which, unless stopped, will dispossess and disenfranchise ever widening sectors of the world population.[14]

After World War II, at different speeds in different countries, capitalism became a somewhat more benign economic system in the advanced countries. The Great Depression convinced people that capitalism was an essentially unstable system subject to economic cycles and that for this reason governments should extend a helping hand to industries and the general population during periods of decline. And the war demonstrated that greater government control actually made the national economy thrive.

Capitalists became willing to enter into an unwritten contract with society: in return for government assistance and broad popular support for capitalism, they promised to favor high levels of employment, support welfare legislation, and respect labor organizations that did not threaten the capitalist domination of society. This more benign phase of capitalism was successful for a time. It produced great wealth in the industrialized countries and created the hope of upward mobility among ordinary people. People believed that if they themselves did not make it, at least their children would.

This phase has come to an end. The capitalists' unwritten contract with society is coming apart. Unemployment is steadily rising, welfare legislation is slowly being dismantled, and labor organizations find themselves attacked from all sides. The gap between the rich and the poor, and more especially between rich countries and poor countries, is ever widening.

What is taking place is a giant reorganization of the economy on an international basis around privately owned, giant transnational corporations. These macrocorporations are not concerned with the well-being of the society in which they were originally located. On the contrary, they have become so powerful that they are able to blackmail national governments to do their will: to introduce neoconservative economic policies at home and adopt foreign policies that will protect their overseas interests and allow them to compete more successfully with transnationals based in other parts of the world. The national economy thus becomes a slave of the international market.

The Canadian bishops have described this process in some detail.[15] They point to the changes taking place in the structure of Canadian capital as a symptom of the reorientation of the global economic system. They show that capitalism, following its own logic and no longer restrained by government policies, creates industrial and financial centers of power that become wealthy at the expense of the less developed hinterland. This process impoverishes the developing countries of the South, and in the North the same process creates unemployment and regional disparity and thus widens the gap between rich and poor.

John Paul II refers to this trend as "economic imperialism." During a visit to Canada he said, "Poor people and poor nations of the South— poor in different ways, not only lacking food, but also deprived of freedom and other human rights—will sit in judgement of those people of the North who take these goods away from them, amassing to themselves the imperialistic monopoly of economic and political supremacy."[16]

Without saying so explicitly, papal teaching seems to recognize that capitalism has become a global economic system, with centers of power in North America, Western Europe, and East Asia, each competing with the others. These centers are surrounded by the dependent regions of the rest of the world, including the countries of Eastern Europe, who suffer from the domination of the major capitalist powers.

In his encyclical *Sollicitudo Rei Socialis*, John Paul II deals specifically with the inequality between the developed North and the slowly developing South. Why is the South sinking into ever greater poverty and powerlessness? Why is the gap between rich and poor widening all over the world? John Paul offers two reasons for this. The first one is the organization of world capitalism in a manner that enhances the wealth of the industrial and financial centers in the North.[17] The economic mechanisms that regulate the flow of capital, resources, and goods have been set up by the powerful and wealthy to the detriment of the poor nations in the South. Sister Amata Miller gives a full account of these dynamics in Chapter 7.

Writing in the 1980s, before the fall of the Berlin Wall and the transformations of Eastern Europe and the Soviet Union, John Paul II identified a second major cause of increasing Third World misery. The Cold War had divided the North into two hostile and competing camps, a division detrimental to the nations of the South and harmful to the entire human family. The two blocs constituted empires that promoted antithetical ideologies—liberal capitalism and Marxist collectivism—each claiming to have universal validity.[18] The competing superpowers fostered regional wars by proxy and spent hundreds of billions of dollars in preparation for total war.

The division of the North into two hostile blocs, each pursuing an end it regarded as absolute, had a devastating impact on the South.[19] Countries in the South that wanted to free themselves from colonial bondage and start their own development were forced to choose between one and the other side. And in choosing, they tragically entered into the destructive East-West dynamics of the Cold War.

The two empires in the North understood the South not in terms of its own problems and aspirations but in geopolitical terms, in terms of the power struggles of the East-West conflict. Because countries of the South had to choose between the two blocs, their populations became divided over the choice. The countries were thus weakened by internal conflicts that sometimes even led to civil war. In some cases one country found itself adjacent to another that had opted for the opposite bloc, a situation often leading to hostility, armed struggle, and impoverishment.

More profoundly still, by opting for one of the two blocs, these countries were drawn into one or another ideology, liberal capitalism or Marxist collectivism, each one in its own way discontinuous with their own cultures, values, and mores. Such economic development produces human alienation and inevitably leads to failure. The difficult task of these regions is to create structures of economic development that respect their own cultural and religious heritage and thus strengthen the people in their sense of self-identity and self-respect.

John Paul II has raged against the ideological bipartition of the North as one of the principal causes of the world's ills.[20] Even with the end of the Cold War and the collapse of Soviet and East European collectivism, the prospect for humane progress for the world's peoples is far from assured. Widespread restoration of more or less full capitalist markets is bringing great misery to working people in formerly collectivist societies and intensifying capitalist rivalries among the major powers. Meanwhile, the ideological hold of capitalist individualism is tightening everywhere.

These are the very evils that have been the principal targets of Catholic social teaching since Vatican Council II, even as the evils of collectivism have also been criticized. With the collapse of the socialist alternative, if the Church maintains its critique of capitalism, it will become a more prominent global pole of opposition, no longer a mediating force between capitalism and socialism. In this period of capitalism triumphant, Catholic social teaching will be severely challenged as it continues to focus on the inhuman side of capitalist society.

Liberation theology has already begun to blaze this oppositional path, but it is under attack. Papal teachings, while in many ways supportive of radical social action, are ambiguous in their substance and hostile to liberation theology as such. It remains to be seen whether liberation theology will be able to continue within the framework of Catholic teaching as a doctrine of empowerment whereby poor and working people can effectively challenge and overcome the capitalist system.

The ethics of solidarity, as we have seen, holds a central position in the Church's social teaching. This is not an "idealistic" position, not the ethical approach scathingly designated by Marx and Engels as "utopian socialism." The ethics of solidarity does not imply that if all people become more loving, then social injustice will disappear and present structures will not have to be changed. On the contrary, the ethics of solidarity begins with the preferential option for the poor, feeds the social struggle for reconstruction, and aims at the creation of a more just society on the global level.

In my opinion it was the great weakness of Marxism to have so little to say on the motivation for social struggle, apart from the collective self-interest of economic classes. Making use of a distinction introduced by Max Weber,[21] we can say that movements for social reconstruction are successful if they are driven by a complex set of motivations: "purpose-rational," referring to the self-interest, personal and collective, of the people involved; "value-rational," referring to the alternative vision of society entertained by the people; and "emotional," referring to cultural factors such as national resistance or religious conviction.

The Catholic ethics of solidarity incorporates these three motivations. The ethics of solidarity has a purpose-rational dimension for all concerned, for masters and slaves alike, because without bold social change, world society is seriously threatened; it has a value-rational dimension because it is based on an alternative vision of society; and it has an emotional component because it is filled with religious yearning.

Toward Economic Justice

My analysis of Catholic social teaching makes it seem clearer and more precise than do the ecclesiastical documents themselves. The reason is that church documents are usually not perfectly consistent: they do not pursue the same perspective throughout; they often repeat phrases taken from an earlier perspective without acknowledging the difference. Even bold church documents want to preserve continuity with past teaching. Nor do the radical principles affirmed in one papal document necessarily appear in the appropriate place of the next papal pronouncement. These inconsistencies reflect also the conflicting social interests expressed in the process by which the documents are drafted.

Some readers wonder whether radical principles deserve to be taken seriously when they are uttered only once or twice and fail to reorient the entire approach to social theory. As I mentioned above, John Paul II does not apply his own social theory to the self-organization of the Catholic Church or to the political orientation of the Vatican administration. On the contrary, at this very time the Vatican makes every effort to tame the progressive bishops of Brazil whose "preferential option for the poor" has shaped their entire pastoral approach, while the same Vatican did not reproach the reactionary bishops of Argentina for their alliance with the political right and their silence during the years of terror in the 1970s and early 1980s. Nor has John Paul II ever recognized the ethical foundation of the women's movement. There are many reasons to be skeptical.

Still, in my opinion the evolution of Catholic social teaching encourages an important social movement within the Christian churches and makes a significant contribution to contemporary social theory. The recent shift in the official teaching has been brought about through a multiple dialogue: dialogue with the prophetic texts of the Bible, with the voices of oppressed groups and classes, and with critical political and social science, including Marx and Weber. Catholic social theory has come to entertain a conflictual understanding of society which challenges both the traditional organic concept found in conservative thought and the pluralistic concept embraced by liberalism. In this new strand of theological reflection, the struggle for justice is understood as calling for preferential solidarity. Church teaching provides strong arguments against the present "neoconservative" economic trend and the "neoconservative" culture associated with it.

From my point of view, however, the greatest merit of the more recent Catholic social theory is its contribution to the critical dialogue taking place among social thinkers of the left.

First, Catholic social theory, as mentioned above, consistently rejects institutional determinisms of any kind. Despite the logic and the pressure of institutions, a certain human freedom remains. Catholic social theory defends the agency and the creativity of consciousness, even though the collective self-understanding of people is largely shaped by the economic institutions in which they labor and live. Because of this dimension of freedom, social theory should not understand itself as an exact science. It cannot predict the future. History remains ever open. Catholic social theory has little sympathy for evolutionary or revolutionary theories of history that anticipate the final outcome. It rejects all this-worldly eschatologies, including the Marxist expectation of the classless, reconciled society.

Yet the openness of history is itself a source of hope. The contradictions of society always generate critical thought and countervailing movements. Sometimes unexpected historical events—wars, severe economic crises, or ecological disasters—create conditions that allow these countervailing movements to acquire political power.

Second, Catholic social theory emphasizes the abiding importance of ethics. Despite their passionate ethical convictions, Marxist theorists too often refrain from ethical reflection. They lack an ethical discourse and provide no norms for the interaction of comrades in the movement. Nor have they formulated adequate values to guide the new societies they have sought to build where they have had power. Catholic social theory can make a contribution to these movements by contributing its sense of the importance of ethics, in particular the abiding relevance of love and compassion.

Third, the preferential option for the poor, we note, is not the equivalent of the option for the proletariat. In Catholic social theory, preferential solidarity embraces the workers and the poor: that is, the popular sector of low-income people, casual workers, the unemployed, people on welfare. The marginalized sector includes the native peoples, major sectors of the other despised races, and poor women.

The social struggle against the unjust order calls for the building of a solidarity network, possibly around a political party, that brings together labor unions and representative organizations of other disadvantaged groups. Such a network could receive the active support of all citizens who love justice, including church and synagogue groups.

What emerges here is a more pluralistic concept of the left. Each of these concerned groups will have a slightly different perspective, and only as the solidarity among them is strengthened through joint action and the give-and-take of negotiations will a single political orientation emerge. Unity of social analysis is not the starting point but the end result. Each group will have to compromise a little in relation to its own collective self-interest in order to support a more universal political movement, one representing all the poor and oppressed and aimed at transforming the unjust social order.

Finally, Catholic social theory recognizes the importance of social passion in the struggle for economic justice. While the great religious traditions of humanity have been compromised by their entanglement with ruling classes and ruling-class culture, they are nonetheless heirs of an original religious yearning for love, justice, and peace.

Religion has an ideological and a utopian dimension. At present we observe both right-wing and left-wing movements in the world religions. In the Christian churches, Catholic and Protestant, the left-wing movement has affected official teaching. Even the political left is beginning to recognize that it must allow its supporters to retain their cultural and religious traditions, to find in them spiritual resources for the social struggle. Secular people have a great humanist tradition to draw upon, and religious people have their own inheritance, which, though marked by ambiguity, is able to nourish the yearning for justice and strengthen political commitment.

Such Christians believe that the infinite and incomprehensible source of all life, love, and justice, which they call God (and see revealed in Jesus Christ), is operative in human history, especially in people's struggles against injustice and oppression. To stand against the established powers in solidarity with workers and the poor is for Christians a place of new religious experience.

NOTES

1. The preferential option for the poor was endorsed and explained by the Latin American bishops in the "Final Document" (nn. 1134–40) of the 1979 Puebla Conference, reprinted in *Puebla and Beyond: Documentary and Commentary*, ed. John Eagleson and Philip Scharper (Maryknoll, N.Y.: Orbis Books, 1979).

2. John Paul II, *Laborem Exercens*, in Gregory Baum, *The Priority of Labor: A Commentary on Laborem Exercens* (New York: Paulist Press, 1982); John Paul II, *Sollicitudo Rei Socialis* in *The Logic of Solidarity: Commentaries on Sollicitudo Rei Socialis*, ed. Gregory Baum and Robert Ellsberg (Maryknoll, N.Y.: Orbis Books, 1989); Canadian Conference of Catholic Bishops, "Ethical Reflections on the Economic Crisis," in *Ethics and Economics*, ed. Gregory Baum and Duncan Cameron (Toronto: Lorimer, 1984); National Conference of Catholic Bishops, "Economic Justice for All: Catholic Social Teaching and the U.S. Economy," *Origins* 16, no. 24 (1986). See also Gregory Baum, *Theology and Society* (New York: Paulist Press, 1987).

3. Karl Marx, "Alienated Labor," in *Karl Marx: Early Writings*, ed. T. B. Bottomore (New York: McGraw-Hill, 1964), pp. 120–34.

4. Karl Marx, "On the Jewish Question," in *Early Writings*, pp. 3–31. See also Bertell Ollman, *Alienation: Marx's Conception of Man in Capitalist Society* (Cambridge: Cambridge University Press, 1970).

5. Marx, "Alienated Labor," pp. 126–28.

6. John Paul II, "The Priority of Labour," in *Laborem Excercens*, n. 12. See also "Work and Ownership," n. 14.

7. "The means of production cannot be possessed against labour, they cannot even be possessed for possession's sake, because the only legitimate title to their possession—whether in the form of private or collective ownership—is that they should serve labour" (ibid., n. 14).

8. John Paul II, "Man as Subject of Work," in ibid., n. 6. "We can speak of socializing the means of production only when the subjectivity of society is ensured, that is to say, when on the basis of his work each person is fully entitled to consider himself a part owner of the great workbench at which he is working with everyone else" (n. 14).

9. John Paul II, *Sollicitudo Rei Socialis*, n. 15: "No social group, for example a political party, has the right to usurp the role of sole leader, since this brings about the destruction of the true subjectivity of society and of the individual citizens."

10. Ibid., nn. 38–40, 32.

11. John Paul II, *Laborem Exercens*, n. 8.

12. John Paul II, *Sollicitudo Rei Socialis*, n. 39.

13. Ibid., nn. 36–37.

14. Baum and Cameron, *Ethics and Economics*, pp. 52–54.

15. See Canadian Conference of Catholic Bishops, "Ethical Reflections on the Economic Crisis," pp. 5–18. This document created a nationwide debate in Canada. Many critics accused the bishops of being Marxists. Of course they were not, but their analysis was undoubtedly influenced by the positions adopted by the Latin American bishops and liberation theology, which had been formulated in dialogue with the neo-Marxist dependency theory elaborated by such scholars as André Gunder Frank and Samir Amin.

16. Quoted in Baum, *Theology and Society*, p. 96. The theory of imperialism, first developed by the liberal J. A. Hobson and modified by V. I. Lenin, has been reformulated by more recent neo-Marxist scholars. See, e.g., Harry Magdoff, *Imperialism: From the Colonial Age to the Present* (New York: Monthly Review Press, 1978); and I. M. Zeitlin, *Capitalism and Imperialism* (Chicago: Markham, 1972). In some form, the theory appealed already to Pope Pius XI, who made use of it in his 1931 encyclical, *Quadragesimo Anno*, nn. 105–9, in *Seven Great Encyclicals*, ed. William Gibbons (New York: Paulist Press, 1963), pp. 153–54.

17. John Paul II, *Sollicitudo Rei Socialis*, nn. 16–17.

18. Ibid., nn. 20–21.

19. Ibid., nn. 22–23.

20. See Gregory Baum, "The Anti-Cold War Encyclical," *The Ecumenist* 26 (July–August 1988): 65–74.

21. Max Weber, *Basic Concepts in Sociology* (New York: Citadel Press, 1969), p. 59.

4

ECONOMIC JUSTICE FOR WHOM?
WOMEN ENTER THE DIALOGUE

Pamela K. Brubaker

Any dialogue between religion and economics must include women and take account of women's needs and experiences if it is to develop an inclusive and equitable emancipatory practice. Feminist liberation theology has a contribution to make to such a dialogue.[1] First of all, it is committed to the social, spiritual, and material well-being of women specifically and humanity more generally. Second, like other liberation theologies it is experiential, but feminist liberation theology pays particular attention to women's experiences of oppression—experiences that are often overlooked in other liberation theologies. Furthermore, feminist liberation theology insists that an emancipatory practice begin with the experience and needs of poor Third World women.[2] It is in their lives that sexism, racism, and economic exploitation are most vividly intertwined.

This chapter attempts to bring women's experiences of economic vulnerability and struggle to the dialogue between liberation theology and economics, arenas in which women's experience is too often hidden. After presenting a global sketch of women's experiences of economic reality, I discuss some of the ways this reality is rendered invisible or marginal in both liberation theology and economics. I conclude with some guidelines for illuminating and addressing women's economic vulnerability and creating an empowering social practice for women and men.

My own understanding of women's economic vulnerability reached a turningpoint at the 1985 United Nations End of the Decade for Women Conference and Forum in Nairobi, Kenya.[3] It was among the fifteen thousand women at this nongovernmental gathering that I grasped more fully the global character of our political economy and the need to integrate a global perspective into our socioeconomic analysis.

A young African woman told how the debt crisis increased the work load of her mother and other women who remained in her village. I thought of my own mother, who still lives on our family farm, and of the impact the farm crisis was having on rural women and their families in the United States. A Latin American woman described the devastating impact of budget cuts in social service programs on the lives and health of women and children in South and North American countries. An Asian woman linked the shutdown of unionized factories and loss of jobs in industrialized countries to the growth of sweatshops filled with women workers of color, both in Western cities and in free trade zones in Third World countries. These narratives concretely linked women around the world in the material terms of their everyday lives and called for a common struggle for global economic justice.

COMMON THREADS BIND: A SKETCH OF WOMEN'S ECONOMIC REALITY

"Women hold up half the sky," an old Chinese proverb, has become a popular slogan that seems to affirm women's social worth, yet it understates women's social contribution. Statistics gathered during the United Nations Decade for Women (1975–85) indicate that although women make up half the world's population and one-third of the official work force, women do two-thirds of the world's work because they are responsible nearly everywhere for unpaid domestic work in addition to their participation in paid labor. Women's work is a significant contribution to family and societal well-being: most studies indicate that women's unpaid household and subsistence work alone, if given economic value, would add one-third to the world's gross national product. Yet women receive only one-tenth of the world's income and own less than one-hundredth of its property.[4]

In three of the key indexes of economic reality—work, income, property—the inequities between women and men as groups are striking. Further, women are disproportionately represented among the poor, the illiterate, the unemployed, and the underemployed. In the United States, two out of three poor adults are women. The United Nations Development Program discovered that in developing countries women are "the poorest of the poor." Globally, women outnumber men among the illiterate by three to two. A woman's chance of getting an education in the developing world is about two-thirds that of a man's. Women's unemployment rates in developed countries—with the exception of Great

Britain, Canada, and the United States—range from 10 to 100 percent higher than those of men; in developing countries they average 50 percent higher. A growing number of women cannot find full-time jobs and are forced to work part-time instead; women make up around three-quarters of the part-time work force in developed countries.[5] Despite their striking cultural, racial, and socioeconomic diversity, women are bound to a subordinate social position by "common threads of powerlessness, of marginality and of dispossession."[6]

What does all this mean in terms of women's everyday lives? It means that women are concentrated in the lowest-paying jobs, receive only about three-quarters of the wage of men doing similar work, and are more vulnerable to unemployment. It means that although women grow nearly half the Third World's food, they find it difficult to get the land, credit, or agricultural support services that men do. It means that most women work a double day or second shift, since very few men share equitably in the work of caring for children or a home. It means that women who head households because of divorce or migration—nearly one-third of all households—often find it difficult to meet their families' basic needs.[7] In short, many of the world's women are *overworked and underpaid*.[8]

Although common threads bind women to a subordinate position, there is no universal woman. Women's experience is shaped not only by gender but also by race, ethnicity, class, and nationality. The differences in the everyday lives of Black and white women in apartheid South Africa may be more glaring than that of Black and white women in the United States, but racist institutions and practices in the United States contribute to African American, Hispanic, Asian, and Native American women's being more economically vulnerable than European American women.

Black female full-time wage and salary workers have been paid about 90 percent of the wages received by similarly employed white workers for the past decade. Black women's unemployment rate during that period has been some two and a half times that of white women; Hispanic women's rate is half again as high as white women's.[9] Half of Black female householders live in poverty, while only about one-quarter of white female-headed households do.

Although working-class white women are obviously more vulnerable to impoverishment and socioeconomic marginalization than middle-strata and wealthy women, even middle-class women face barriers to self-fulfillment. Their full participation at the higher levels of the economic pyramid, which one would expect by virtue of their class, is severely hampered by what has come to be known as the "glass ceiling," which upwardly mobile professional women cannot yet penetrate because of gender discrimination. Still, women in most developed countries are usually more able to meet their basic needs than those in underdeveloped countries, although there are significant racial/ethnic and class differences among women within each of these countries.

According to the Society for International Development, the seriousness of the plight of the majority of the world's women is "largely unrecognized and underestimated."[10] This is also true of the plight of women in the United States, whether it be the second shift of employed women or the difficulty of poor and low-income women in meeting their basic needs and those of their families.[11] I believe that several factors contribute to the invisibility of economic vulnerability as women experience it: women's relative political and economic powerlessness; their exclusion from or marginalization within policy-making bodies; and the benefits that all economies, whether capitalist or socialist, overdeveloped or underdeveloped—as well as individual men—receive from women's unpaid and underpaid labor.

These facts of life are mirrored in the theoretical concepts and principles of religion and social science, which also subordinate and obscure women's reality. Norman Gottwald explores this general dynamic in his discussion of the relation between values and social structures in Chapter 2. I focus in this chapter on conceptualizations concerning women in both religious ethics and economic theory, and the challenges that feminist liberation theology directs at them. This is vital because the way we see a problem, even whether or not we perceive in a given situation any problem at all, does much to determine our response to it.

Feminist theology arises out of the oppressed condition of women as women use theological reflection to support their own liberation. Third World women theologians, gathered in their first intercontinental dialogue, claimed theologizing as a way in which women struggle for their right to life, to liberation from oppression. They also insisted that theology include an analysis of the root cause of "women's multiple oppression."[12]

LIBERATION FOR WHOM? A FEMINIST CRITIQUE
OF LIBERATION THEOLOGIES

As Michael Zweig points out in Chapter 1, liberation movements have emerged during the past three decades in most of the world's religions. Social and economic justice, participation, and human rights for all people are common goals for these movements. Some feminists, however, charge that women's needs and experience are not fully included in these movements' emancipatory practice. This section documents this charge by analyzing recent progressive social pronouncements by the Roman Catholic Church and by the World Council of Churches, which is composed primarily of Protestant and Orthodox Christian groups.

My special attention to Christian religious doctrine is not meant to obscure the fact that Jewish and Muslim women have made similarly important, often parallel, critiques of their religious communities. Buddhist women too have begun an upsurge of critical, liberatory activity.[13] The neglect of women's reality characteristic of all these religions and spiritual movements grows out of a common social setting. Even though the oppression of women in society is filtered through each religion in a way particular to its own beliefs, the lessons learned by a close examination of Christian doctrines apply in broad terms to the treatment of women in other religions as well.

Neither Roman Catholic nor World Council liberation theology and ethics adequately address the economic vulnerability of women. While the movement within these organizations to recognize the radical obligations for social and economic justice as conditions for human liberation, and their embrace of the preferential option for the poor and oppressed has been constructive, the depth of women's oppression has not been touched. Women's economic vulnerability, a specific manifestation of women's oppression, is at best marginal and often invisible in the pronouncements of these organizations.[14] Furthermore, their understandings of human nature and social organization distort women's moral agency in ways that deny full human liberation to women. Because there are distinct reasons for this distortion, I discuss the two groups separately.

World Council of Churches Social Teaching

Early in the twentieth century, Protestant and Orthodox Christian churches around the world began to express concern about contemporary social problems. Through the efforts of various American and European church leaders, the Universal Christian Conference on Life and Work met in Stockholm, Sweden, in 1925. About five hundred representatives from various Christian communions (Episcopal, Lutheran, Methodist, Orthodox, and Reformed, among others) came together in the hope of uniting in practical work and "to insist that the principles of the Gospel be applied to the solution of contemporary social and international problems."[15]

This conference was a turningpoint in Christian history in that participating denominations accepted "the urgent duty of applying the Gospel of Christ in all realms of human life," after a long period in which many had distinguished between spiritual and worldly realms.[16] The work of the conference was continued through the Life and Work movement, which in 1948 joined with the Faith and Order movement to become the World Council of Churches (WCC).[17] The World Council has continued to address contemporary social and international problems through education, advocacy, and the funding of projects and programs.

Since the 1960s there has been a shift in the World Council's social pronouncements, due in part to the growing number of Third World churches in its membership. Until that time the World Council had advocated "the responsible society" as a standard of judgment of existing societies and a guide in specific choices. This notion required "that power be made responsible to law and tradition, and be distributed as widely as possible through the whole community" and that "economic justice and the provision of equality of opportunity be established for all the members of society." The Council rejected the ideologies of both laissez-faire capitalism and Communism.[18]

At the fifth assembly of the World Council (Nairobi, 1975) the notion of the "just, participatory, sustainable society" replaced "the responsible society" as the Council's central social ethical criterion. With the articulation of this criterion, the WCC began to move away from many of the liberal presuppositions that had informed its notion of the responsible society. Doing so has involved a change in stance from seeking balance and a presumed harmony of goals and interests among different classes and nations to embracing the option for the poor and oppressed. Understandings of justice within Council pronouncements have shifted from a liberal focus on distributive justice to a more radical understanding of social justice, which stresses participation.

Finally, the Council has moved from advocacy of mainstream economic models, which stress the centrality of market activity, to an insistence instead on the participation and social control of productive sectors. The fifth assembly questioned the logic of the market and charged that " 'growth' in an economic order based on the so-called 'free market' system has a built-in exploitative tendency where resources are unevenly distributed." The assembly rejected economic and social goals, patterns of resource ownership, and decision-making processes that are oppressive to the poor, so that "the creative powers of people to satisfy their needs and decide their destiny" might be released.[19]

Although the World Council has addressed and criticized the operation of markets in society, however, it has not adequately addressed another central tenet of classical liberal doctrine: the dichotomy between public and private spheres of life. This conceptual split is partially responsible for obscuring women's oppression in society because such a dichotomy within liberalism separates the domestic sphere of family life from the public realm. The Council's failure to consider this issue weakens its ability to address women's oppression in its pronouncements.[20]

Political theorist Carole Pateman has described the impact of the public-private split on socioethical discourse:

> The family is based on natural ties of sentiment and blood and on the sexually ascribed status of wife and husband (mother and father). Participation in the public sphere is governed by universal, impersonal and conventional criteria of achievement, interests, rights, equality and property—liberal criteria, applicable only to men. An important consequence of this conception of private and public is that the public world, or civil society, is conceptualized and discussed in liberal theory in abstraction from, or as separate from, the private domestic sphere.[21]

The relationship of the family and household to the economy and how this relationship shapes women's participation in the economy are not addressed to any significant extent in World Council ethics, even recent liberation ethics. Rather, the assumption too often is that insofar as women participate in the economy, their participation is no different from that of men. This is what Beverly Thiele calls the "vanishing act" of universalism, in which language that purports to be inclusive obscures the male bias of a theory.[22] Consequently, women's double day, low wages relative to those of men, occupational segregation, and other specific aspects of economic vulnerability are usually invisible or marginal to the Council and seldom addressed specifically in its pronouncements.

In 1968 the fourth assembly of the Council condemned the denial of full human rights to women by established patterns in family, church, and society.[23] But because it did not identify or analyze such patterns or propose policies for change, the Council left the impression that serious problems in this area do not exist. Its social justice agencies were slow to accept the reality of women's economic vulnerability. Reinhild Traitler was told by her colleagues in the Commission on the Churches' Participation in Development that

> in view of the really demonic nature of the powers we were dealing with, it [women's liberation] was an emotional "belly-ache." Only later (and very gradually) did we all come to realize that the women among the poorest of the poor are still the poorest of all. The extent of suffering is always in inverse proportion to the measure of power and rights that one has. We gradually realized that in many third-world countries women have little power and fewer rights.[24]

More recent WCC assemblies (Nairobi 1975, Vancouver 1983) have addressed sexism as a structure of injustice, as women have insisted that their oppression be taken seriously, yet the Council is still hesitant to criticize patterns of family organization. The sacralization of the family has prevented it from taking family relations seriously as an arena of justice. In 1968 the World Council's Department on the Cooperation of Men and Women asserted that "the family is the privileged community to which is given the grace of conjugal love, the mystery of a unity wherein the physical bonds and the spiritual bonds reinforce each other in order perfectly to fulfill the command of the Saviour: 'Love one another.' "[25]

The law in nearly all countries also treats the family as a privileged community. Women's movements around the globe are having great difficulty penetrating this privilege as they advocate legal protection against domestic abuse and marital rape—a difficulty reflected also in the World Council of Churches. For instance, the 1981 Community of Women and Men consultation sponsored by the Council was not able to speak directly to issues of family violence and sexual assault. Constance Parvey, staff for the consultation, reported "issues of sexuality are part of the socialized conspiracy of silence in the churches."[26] Women and children are the ones who suffer from this conspiracy of silence, as it is primarily women and children who are the victims of battering and sexual abuse within the family.

Feminist theologian Beverly Harrison has criticized Reinhold Niebuhr, an influential theologian in the earlier years of the Council, for not questioning the public-private dichotomy. Her critique can be extended to the Council itself. Niebuhr's contrast of the "interpersonal, humane relations of the family" with the "impersonal relations of the public arena" tended to sacralize family relations. Both Niebuhr and the Council failed to see that the "broader social injustices toward women . . . at the collective level were only extensions of the dynamic operating in the supposedly blissful arena of the family." [27]

The conspiracy of silence that Parvey challenged still continues in official pronouncements. Recently the Council launched the Ecumenical Decade of the Churches in Solidarity with Women (1988–98); one of its stated goals is to empower women "to challenge oppressive structures in the global community, their country and their church." [28] The family is not included in this listing or elsewhere in the official goals of the Decade. Nevertheless, some groups of women mobilized by the Council are challenging oppressive family structures. For instance, the first Decade program organized by Korean women is called "Education and Cultural Movement to Develop a Democratic Family Life." [29]

Unless the Council includes family relations within its socioethical analysis, it maintains its silence in the face of domestic abuse of women and children. It also fails fully to address the links between violence against women and their socioeconomic vulnerability. Furthermore, without a socioethical critique of the family, it cannot adequately speak to women's claim on the social wage nominally paid to the husband on behalf of the entire family. Until the public-private split is healed, the family demystified, and patriarchal family relations critiqued in its pronouncements, the Council cannot begin to create an effective emancipatory practice in solidarity with women.

Roman Catholic Social Teaching

The primary conceptual reason for the marginality of women's needs and experiences within Roman Catholic papal teaching and liberation theology is the perpetuation of a static, natural-law view of women's nature.

Even recent pronouncements, such as those of the Latin American bishops at Puebla, the encyclicals of John Paul II, and the United States bishops' pastoral letter on the U.S. economy, which show increasing concern for women's marginality, have not moved beyond these conceptions. For instance, the Puebla documents speak of woman's fundamental role as that of mother and charge that this role must shape women's social participation. Such understandings are not brought to bear on fathering or men's social participation.[30]

Earlier papal teaching, which Pope John Paul II has recalled, legitimates and perpetuates women's economic vulnerability and dependency by insisting that nature destines women to be mothers and that this role is incompatible with participation in the labor force.[31] Women's economic dependency is perpetuated by this stand, as is women's exclusive responsibility for unpaid household labor. For instance, John Paul II contends that it is "wrong from the point of view of the good of society and of the family" to abandon the care and education of children for "paid work outside the home" if doing so contradicts or hinders the primary goals of the mission of a mother.[32] John Paul II is echoing Pope Pius XII, who taught that "every woman is destined to be a mother. . . . The Creator has disposed to this end the entire being of woman, her organism, and even more her spirit, and above all her exquisite sensibility."[33]

In this view of womanhood the ability to give birth totally defines a woman's personhood. "Motherhood" becomes a woman's entire identity and purpose in life. In actuality, such a view obscures the social construction of this role. Mothering is presented as a natural function, given women's biological capacity for childbearing. Responsibilities such as full-time child care and the physical and emotional care of home and family, which are not necessarily connected to childbirth at all, are linked "naturally" to this capacity. As Giglia Tedesco, an Italian Catholic legislator, points out, this teaching transforms maternity "from a human relationship into a social role which then becomes a social handicap for women."[34]

Furthermore, neither the economic value nor the physical character of household labor and child care is generally recognized. In part this is due to conceptualizations of work in economic theory which are discussed later in this chapter. But it is also related to the tendency of most religions to sacralize the family, which we have already seen in World Council of Churches teaching. In Catholic teaching, domestic work is also spiritualized or idealized as "nurturing" or "creating the family hearth," as in this statement from Pope John XXIII: "At all times and in all circumstances they [employed women] are the ones who have to be wise enough to find the resources to face their duties as wives and mothers calmly and with their eyes wide open; to make their homes warm and peaceful after the tiring labors of daily work; and not to shrink from the responsibilities involved in raising children."[35]

It is significant that the responsibilities of raising children and making a home "warm and peaceful" are not seen as part of the "tiring labors of daily work." But how else can one describe food preparation, cleaning, laundry, and the many other tasks involved in domestic labor? This sacralization of family life also obscures the fact that Pope John was legitimating women's double day. Even recent teaching that highlights women's marginality and economic vulnerability has not seriously challenged the double day and thus justifies social relations that contribute to women's socioeconomic marginality and exploitation.

The contribution—usually unpaid—of women to agricultural work, particularly in Third World countries, is described by Ann Seidman in Chapter 6. But these contributions are not acknowledged in church pronouncements on international development or the food crisis in Africa, where women produce 80–90 percent of food for domestic consumption. Nor are women's specific needs and concerns—such as their access to land, credit, and support services—taken into account by the suggested strategies.

The mystification of women's work is particularly ironic in light of the consistent advocacy of "the just wage" as a central norm of Catholic social teaching. For example, John Paul II insists that the just wage is "the concrete means of verifying the justice of the whole socioeconomic system," because wages are the practical means through which most people have access to goods intended for common use.[36] Catholic social teaching has gotten around this omission by defining the just wage as a family wage. But it has never specified that women are to have a say in the allocation of the family wage received by the male, so there is no guarantee that women will have access to the goods that the just wage is to ensure.

Such views prevent Roman Catholic social teaching from recognizing women's economic inequality, because women's economic dependency is seen as "natural." Presuppositions about "woman's nature" are more clearly illuminated in other papal pronouncements. An examination of some of these documents shows that natural-law assumptions about woman's nature not only obscure women's economic vulnerability but also distort women's capacity for moral agency.

Samuel Bowles and Herbert Gintis consider moral agency in Chapter 9, where they characterize social action as "the individual constituting him- or herself by developing personal powers through acting in the world." Moral agency is the ability to act in the world and thereby to become fully responsible. Feminist liberation theology believes that our ability as women to constitute ourselves fully as self-determining members of human communities is critical to our liberation. Feminist ethicist Ruth Smith explains why this is so: "Becoming the subject of one's own action is a social and historical process key to liberation politically, socially, and psychologically so that we no longer collude in our own oppression and so that we can attempt to change conditions of life negation and alienation into conditions of affirmation and fulfillment."[37] If Catholic social teaching is committed to human liberation, it must also liberate women. This requires, among other things, supporting rather than distorting women's capacity to act as moral agents.

Roman Catholic social teaching has affirmed the equal dignity and worth of women and men since Pius XII, but never without qualification. In his encyclical *Casti Connubii* (On Christian marriage), Pius XII affirmed "a true equality" in the dignity of women and men, in contrast to a "false equality": any change in the civil rights of a married woman must always give regard to "the natural disposition and temperament of the female sex, good morality, and the welfare of the family."[38] Women's equality and participation is consistently limited—in later papal teaching, Vatican Council II documents, and statements of regional bishops—by "her nature" and "her proper role." This approach denies women's full moral personhood through what Canadian philosopher Kathryn Morgan calls a "difference in kind": theories are generated "about the nature of woman which claim that women differ from men either in degree or kind such that women are not entitled to full moral agency."[39]

A brief review of some of the main points of John Paul II's letter *Mulieris Dignitatem* (On the dignity and vocation of women) clearly indicates how traditional notions of femininity limit women's ability to act as adult human beings. The Pope affirms the mutuality and equality of male and female, but he also maintains the notion of "that dignity and vocation that result from the specific diversity and personal originality of man and woman." Consequently, "even the rightful opposition of women to what is expressed in the biblical words 'he shall rule over you' (Gen. 3 :16) must not under any condition lead to the 'masculinization' of women. In the name of liberation from male 'domination,' women must not appropriate to themselves male characteristics contrary to their own feminine originality." Precisely what John Paul II means by this becomes apparent in his definition of femininity: "receiving so as to give of self, *always in response to the love of God or of husband.*"[40] The implication is that a woman is not to take initiative. Thus her ability to act as a full moral agent is denied because of her assumed "difference in kind" from the male, and one is left to wonder how women may rightfully oppose being ruled over by men.

The conceptualization of femininity as "receiving" also informs Catholic teaching against artificial contraception and against women's ordination to the priesthood, positions that some see as oppressive to women. In his encyclical *Humanae Vitae* (On human life), Paul VI discusses "the generative process" without ever mentioning women as the bearers of life,[41] thus rendering women's reproductive labor as invisible here as their actual domestic labor is in most other social teaching. John Paul II also uses this understanding of femininity as the basis for the denial of ordination to women, as they cannot represent Christ who *first* gave of *himself.*[42]

Catholic women are challenging the denial of their full moral agency and personhood. In the United States, the group called Catholics for a Free Choice demands that women be recognized as morally capable human beings with the capacity to make decisions about their reproductive powers. Other groups have organized to press for women's ordination to the priesthood and a more democratic church structure.

Some people dismiss these as concerns of privileged First World women, since they appear to focus on "quality of life" issues rather than direct economic improvement. Women are also challenging these views in Latin America, however, where liberation theology first emerged. Some Peruvian women, for example, contend that "a woman's dignity resides in the fact that she is a human being, graced by God with the potential for realizing herself fully as a person. This self-realization must not be limited to her maternal role." They admonish:

In fidelity to its commitment to embrace a preferential option for the poor, the church cannot remain silent in the face of the intense suffering and exploitation of women. If it is to be faithful to its commitment to human liberation, the church must not ignore the sin of sexism so manifest both in the structures of society and in daily interpersonal relationships. Neither must it support patriarchy within society as a whole or in the structures of its own institution.[43]

The World Council of Churches and the Roman Catholic Church cannot adequately engage women's economic vulnerability without an appropriate socioeconomic analysis. Such an analysis requires a critical exploration of existing approaches to economics in relation to their ability to illuminate women's economic vulnerability. The ability of a socioeconomic theory to account for the sources of suffering and oppression of poor Third World women is a fundamental criterion of feminist liberation theology.

Economics: A Dismal Science for Women

Part of the reason that women's economic vulnerability is hidden in theological ethics is that it is hidden in the economic theories used in doing these ethics. In both mainstream and Marxist economics, basic categories of analysis are gender-blind. Yet as we have seen, women and men generally do not participate in the economy in the same ways. Feminist critics charge that the "economic *man*" of economic theory is just that. Thus, women's economic reality is hidden, and neither approach to economic analysis adequately accounts for or addresses women's economic vulnerability.

A full assessment of the usefulness of each approach is beyond the scope of this chapter; I generally concur with Michael Zweig's assessment of mainstream and Marxist economics in Chapter 1. My concern here is to consider the ability of each to illuminate women's economic reality.

Mainstream Economics

Mainstream economics is not particularly useful to feminist liberation theology for the same reasons that it is not useful to other liberation theologies. As Zweig points out, it is static, ahistoric, based on extreme individualism, and narrowly focused on market activities. These characteristics contribute to its failure to deal adequately with women's economic situation.

Mainstream economics, in its treatment of people as individuals, obscures gender, race, and class differences among them. This is clearly inappropriate: women suffer *as women*, and their suffering needs to be recognized and accounted for, as does the suffering of people of color and of poor and working-class people. The interstructuring of gender, race, and class oppression in people's lives needs to be illuminated if we are to overcome this oppression.

The failure of most mainstream economics to account for wage differentials between men and women, whites and Blacks, illustrates this point.[44] Mainstream economics focuses on market exchange—the buying and selling of commodities and labor—as the central human economic activity. According to its logic, relative wages are determined by the interaction of supply and demand in the labor market. In principle, neither gender nor race would make a difference in the wages a worker receives. When sex and race wage differences do exist, they are usually attributed to differences in human capital, such as education or work experience, or to preferences for certain types of jobs, rather than to discrimination. Yet research has established that women of all racial groups and men of color often receive lower wages than white male workers with similar education and skills.[45] The individual, ahistoric approach of mainstream economics cannot account for this difference. Its narrow focus on market activity obscures sexist and racist social dynamics.

Some critics of mainstream economics question whether relative wages are in fact determined by the market. The institutional approach looks at the impact of social institutions and practices, such as the family or sex-role stereotyping, on market activity. Perhaps the best-known example of this approach is "the feminization of poverty" analysis. Diana Pearce coined this term in 1978 to describe what she saw as the key factors in the increasing proportion of women among poor people in the United States.[46]

Pearce and most liberal feminist theorists point to the wage discrimination that women face in the labor market as perhaps the main cause of women's poverty, discrimination usually attributed to the practice of sex-role stereotyping. Pearce identifies the increase in the number of female-headed households as another significant factor, thus highlighting the significance of institutions such as the family in the distribution of income within a society. Proponents of this approach argue that virtually all women are vulnerable, as divorce or widowhood may throw even middle-strata women into poverty.

Critics charge that the feminization-of-poverty analysis overstates the vulnerability of white women to impoverishment. A smaller proportion of white women than of Black and Hispanic women are poor—only about one-quarter of white, single, female heads of household; slightly over half of Black and Hispanic ones—and those who do fall into poverty tend to stay there for shorter periods of time than do women of color. Furthermore, this approach ignores or underestimates the impoverishment of working-class men, particularly Black men. For example, Black male unemployment rates are two and a half times those of white women. Economist Pamela Sparr points out that a Black woman would have a better statistical chance of escaping poverty by changing her race than by changing her gender.[47]

Pearce's primary solution to the feminization of poverty is government intervention in the labor market to overcome sex segregation and wage discrimination. Pearce still holds to the belief that the market would "work" if sexist institutions could be successfully challenged; she still analyzes this problem from within mainstream economics. She is so focused on why the market does not work on behalf of women that she does not see how it does not work on behalf of others.

The institutional approach has moved somewhat beyond the individualism of mainstream economics, but it has not addressed the multidimensional sources of women's economic vulnerability. It has not sufficiently challenged the way mainstream economics assigns economic value only to those goods and services exchanged in the market, thus denying economic value to domestic work. It is also unable to recognize or account for the way capitalist development itself creates and maintains broad socioeconomic inequality throughout society. One consequence of these failings is that institutional approaches obscure the links women might forge with others who are marginalized and exploited in capitalism.

Marxist Economics

I believe that a more useful approach to women's economic vulnerability will emerge from a critical appropriation of Marxist economics. Four characteristics commend it to feminist liberation theology. First, radical political economics attends to poverty and oppression, forms of suffering that are often obscured in mainstream economics. Second, the political economy is understood as a sociohistorical reality, in contrast to mainstream understandings of the economy as subject to natural laws and thus limited in possibilities of transformation. Third, its historical materialist methodology attempts to illuminate everyday life experiences, whereas mainstream economics tends to look at individuals abstracted from concrete life experience. Finally, radical political economics sees the political economy as a whole and understands that economic activity is inseparably related to the sociocultural matrix of human social life. I concur with Beverly Harrison's assessment of radical political economics as "demonstrably superior" to mainstream economics in its capacity "to critically break open our experience."[48]

Yet Marxist economics cannot fully account for women's economic vulnerability without a structural analysis of sexism and racism. Let us return to the question of wage differentials between men and women, whites and Blacks, to illustrate this point. Marxist economics focuses on the processes and relations of production. Class—people's relationship to production—is a privileged category of analysis. Class relations within capitalist societies are seen to be conflictual social relations. Simply put, owners, not workers, determine the aims of production and gain advantage from—exploit—workers. Michael Zweig elaborates the Marxist view of class relations in Chapter 8.

This approach can account for wage hierarchies as a capitalist strategy to increase profits and manage the labor force, but a strict class analysis cannot explain why it is that women of all races and men of color are the ones to receive lower wages. Its privileged category, like that of mainstream economics, is gender-blind and race-blind.[49]

Feminist critics such as Heidi Hartmann have charged that most Marxist analysis of what it has called "the woman question" has focused too exclusively on women's relation to capital rather than women's relation to men. Although Marx was concerned about the oppression of women, the usual Marxist solution to women's oppression has been women's participation in the work force and the socialization of domestic work. Women's social equality was to follow automatically from the economic independence presumed to arise from participation in the labor market outside the home.

In countries where this solution has been attempted, however, it has been inadequate to overcome women's subordination. Since very few socialist countries have adequately socialized domestic work or child care, socialist women also work a double day. Where domestic work or child care has been socialized, it is usually performed by women at low wages, thus perpetuating their subordination and marginalization.[50]

Some theorists contend that one reason for this failure is men's resistance to such changes. Marxist economics has not adequately accounted for the ways individual men or economies benefit from women's unpaid or underpaid domestic labor and child care. As Hartmann points out, "Men have a higher standard of living than women in terms of luxury consumption, leisure time, and personalized services."[51]

In Marx's analysis, the wage paid to the worker should be the amount needed to support the reproduction of the entire family. But like Catholic teaching, which also regards the wage as a family wage, Marx paid very little attention to domestic labor or child care. He too saw human reproduction and the sexual division of labor as "natural." In his analysis of capital, he noted that the reproduction and maintenance of the working class are necessary conditions of capital reproduction, but he concluded that "the capitalist could safely leave [their] fulfillment to the labourer's instincts of self preservation and propagation."[52] The sexual and generational division of labor, he said, springs up "naturally" and is thus "based on a purely physiological foundation." Lise Vogel suggests that a series of nineteenth-century ideological notions that have not been sufficiently challenged is behind these formulations.[53]

Marx shares these naturalistic assumptions with Catholic social teaching, but whereas the popes have sacralized such a division of labor, Marx saw it as a form of slavery for women and urged as its remedy the full participation of women in the labor force. Actual family relations are more complex: although some women have experienced marriage as institutionalized slavery, others, including many Black and working-class women, find in family life a source of support and resistance to oppression.[54]

An adequate analysis will break with these naturalistic notions and undertake a historical materialist analysis of family relations. Marxists have generated at least three different accounts of the oppression of women which do make this break. First, some Marxists see the oppression of women as a cultural leftover or atavism from a previous mode of production that will wither away on its own. This explanation was used in the Puebla documents of the Latin American bishops to account for sexist attitudes and practices. But such an interpretation, although historical, is not sufficiently materialist. As Brazilian economist Heleieth Saffioti notes, hierarchical gender and race relations are not just "fossilized vestiges of the former class relations in which they were rooted originally"; they are also "a discrete aspect of the concrete totality within which they stand."[55] In other words, capital uses these hierarchical relations to assign women and people of color to marginal positions in the labor force or to exclude them altogether. Thus, there is a material basis specific to capitalism for the continuation of race and gender hierarchies.

A second Marxist explanation points to women's differential position in capitalist social reproduction, a position rooted in women's childbearing capacity. Proponents of this perspective note the importance of women's domestic labor and child care to the maintenance and reproduction of the working class, although they disagree about the value of domestic labor. Some think domestic labor indirectly produces surplus value for capitalist exploitation; some think it directly produces surplus value; and others argue that it creates only use value.[56] This is a critical point, given that traditional Marxist economics sees the material base of oppression in capital's appropriation of the surplus labor created by the working class.

This explanation provides a nuanced historical materialist account of women's oppression which builds on many of Marx's insights about capital accumulation. It provides a material basis for woman's oppression through her role in social reproduction or by seeing housewives as direct producers of surplus value. Nevertheless, I think that it still tends to reduce women's oppression to class oppression. It does not analyze in depth women's relations with men or the ways individual men, including working-class men, benefit from women's domestic labor. The capitalist class is seen as the primary oppressor of women and beneficiary of their oppression. Thus, whatever its merits, this analysis presents only a partial explanation of women's oppression. It is particularly weak in accounting for their sexual exploitation and abuse. Class relations can exacerbate such violence, as Dalla Costa notes in describing working-class men's physical abuse of their wives as a safety valve for their frustration over their own oppression. But this manifestation of women's oppression is not reducible to a form of class oppression; it cuts across and is perpetuated within class lines, as is the case with women's socioeconomic marginalization and the exploitation of women's reproductive and productive labor.[57]

A third account of women's oppression attempts to overcome a narrow focus on social relations generated by capitalism by positing capitalism and patriarchy as dual systems that shape contemporary society. Heidi Hartmann is a pioneer of this approach, which identifies itself as socialist feminist. Hartmann sees capitalism and patriarchy as semiautonomous systems that join together in the oppression of women. For instance, she points to the family wage as serving the interests of both men and capital: "The family and women's work in the family serve capital by providing a labor force and serve men as the space in which they exercise their privilege."[58] Socialist feminists tend to draw together Marxist analysis and radical feminism (also called cultural feminism by some) to analyze patriarchy and the sexual division of labor. According to Hartmann, patriarchal gender relations govern "the production and reproduction of people and their gender identities."[59] Men are the primary beneficiaries of this division of labor, of which the material base is men's control over women's labor power and sexuality.

The strength of this position is that it provides a material basis for women's oppression which does not reduce it to class exploitation, while also recognizing the oppressive character of capital accumulation. Socialist feminism recognizes the economic value of women's domestic labor and its benefits to both men and capitalism. This perspective begins to illuminate the multiple sources of women's oppression historically and materially.[60]

Although a multidimensional historical analysis is not easy to carry out, there is some agreement among socialist feminists as to the elements of such an approach. Lourdes Beneria and Martha Roldan characterize it as a "paradigm to include all factors having an influence on the complexity" of the lives of women on the periphery. It needs to "capture the dynamics" of the totality of real life without losing sight of its different elements: "multiple relations of domination/subordination—based on race, age, ethnicity, nationality, sexual preference [that] interact dialectically with class and gender relations."[61] I find this the most promising approach, as it most fully accounts for the multidimensional character of women's economic vulnerability and is thus the most useful for feminist liberation theology.

TOWARD AN EMPOWERING SOCIAL PRACTICE

Feminist liberation theology begins with the needs and experience of poor Third World women and develops its practice in solidarity with them. This is a dialogical theology that moves from particularity and attempts to account for specificity. Each of our truth claims is perspectival, but as we come together in dialogue we can hope for enhanced truthfulness.[62]

I have participated in this dialogue as a white, middle-class woman from the overdeveloped United States. I have listened and continue to listen to Third World women in order to learn from them. In this dialogue the elements of an integrated, multidimensional perspective have begun to emerge. An adequate analysis that fully illuminates conflict and suffering must account concretely for the structures and practices which create that conflict and suffering, globally and historically. Drawing on what I have learned, I suggest five criteria for an adequate illumination of women's economic vulnerability in any socioeconomic analysis.

First, all socioeconomic analysis must be set within a global perspective, because our social and economic reality is shaped by a global economic system. This means analyzing the international division of labor and processes of capital accumulation, taking into account how they are conditioned by other social and historical processes.

Second, gender must be addressed intentionally and systematically throughout an analysis. This means accounting for the differential participation of women in the economy and the differential impact of the economy on them.

Third, both the material and the ideological bases of women's subordination and their interrelation must be accounted for. It is inadequate to treat women's oppression simply as cultural. Yet ideological and cultural dynamics must be recognized and proposals for cultural change addressed.

Fourth, an effective integration of race, sex, and class as simultaneous social dynamics is necessary, because racism and class exploitation are not reducible to gender, nor is sexism or racism reducible to class oppression.

Finally, all analyses of social or economic trends must be placed in concrete historical perspective. This means taking into account the actual history of slavery, of colonialism, of racial and ethnic oppression, of the subordination of women, and of working-class exploitation.

From what I have heard and learned, I have also formulated criteria to evaluate public policy. They consider whether actions for economic justice include women, a necessary next step in the struggle for global economic justice.

First, every policy for economic development, whether in developed or developing countries, must be scrutinized for the impact it will have on people and the environment. Only policies that enhance people's participation and ease women's work load should be accepted. Environmental protection, certainly important to all people, has a special significance for women and children pushed onto the most marginal land in Third World countries, as described by Ann Seidman in Chapter 6. Economic justice for women requires particular attention to the environment.

Second, all areas of work must be open to women, and more equitable value (comparable worth) assigned to sectors that have been devalued, such as the service work traditionally assigned to women. Occupational segregation, whether based on race or gender, needs to be overcome.

Third, basic needs—food, clothing, shelter, health care, education—must become inviolable priorities, with explicit budgetary provisions, in both developed and underdeveloped countries.

Fourth, child care and domestic work need to be shared by women and men in families and by the larger society. Alternative patterns of family relations must have the same legal status as more traditional ones.

Fifth, in the formulation and adoption of specific socioeconomic goals and policies, their capacity to influence the self-determination of both women and men must be assessed. Processes for ensuring people's role in setting their own goals and priorities must be developed.

Sixth, empowerment of marginalized groups, particularly women, must be a key part of any proposal for socioeconomic development.

If economic justice for all is to become a reality, we must engage in a project of structural transformation. We need to move toward equitable access and control of the resources of production and reproduction in our socioeconomic organization. Hierarchical relations of domination and subordination based on class, race, gender, ethnicity, age, or sexual preference must be replaced by reciprocal egalitarian relations.

This is an outline of a project around which diverse groups can come together. Within this project the specific agendas of particular groups, such as peoples from different cultural and ethnic heritages, need to be recognized and supported.[63]

THE CONTRIBUTION OF FEMINIST LIBERATION THEOLOGY

Such a project of structural transformation requires many changes; we are only beginning to realize their depth. Other chapters address aspects of this project; here I want to attend to what feminist liberation theology can contribute.

Our contribution grows out of our critique of economic and theological discourse. I have identified common problems that need to be overcome if women's oppression is to be illuminated and addressed: naturalistic notions of women and human reproduction which obscure the extent of women's oppression and rob women of their right to self-definition; and the public-private dichotomy in which universalism and individualism characterize the "public sphere," while the family is privatized and sacralized.

Feminist liberation theology is just beginning to envision what it would mean to overcome static conceptions of women and to heal the public-private split. Our work is provisional and perspectival. A deep and sustained dialogue among women of different classes, racial/ethnic groups, and nationalities is necessary for a fuller vision to emerge. I offer what follows as my understanding of some necessary elements of an empowering social practice that enables human liberation for both women and men.

Traditional notions of femininity such as those advocated by Pope John Paul II deny women the possibility of being moral actors, as women are always to receive—to react to—the initiative of men. Such a conception also places a burden on men, who are expected always to be initiators. Both results discourage relations based on mutuality and reciprocity. I think the limits on liberation for either women or men that such a conception sets are apparent. The constraints that the public-private dichotomy places on human liberation may not be so clear, however. I want to explore the impact of this split on moral agency and suggest some ways of healing it.

The privatization of the family during capitalist development and the resulting public-private dichotomy in liberalism have deeply shaped our understandings of what it means to be a man or a woman. Too many accept the resulting "masculine" and "feminine" characteristics as natural, if not ordained by God. The social construction of masculinity and femininity is obscured by the dichotomy, which presumes the separation of these two spheres.

Sociologist Talcott Parsons, for instance, insists that women are naturally expressive rather than instrumental. Conservatives such as George Gilder use this supposedly natural difference to assert the necessity of the traditional sexual division of labor, which assigns women to home and family, and men to politics and production. And radical cultural feminists such as Mary Daly and Susan Griffin cite these different traits in proclaiming the "natural" moral superiority of women.[64] All miss the ways in which specific characteristics are developed by particular forms of socioeconomic organization, a process Samuel Bowles and Herbert Gintis analyze in Chapter 9.[65]

For instance, bourgeois society stresses sentimentality in the family but rationality in the public arena. Because bourgeois women are assigned responsibility for family relations, they are encouraged to develop nurturing and relational characteristics. Men, assigned to the public arena, are expected to be rational—that is, not emotional. Such a dichotomy robs both women and men of the opportunity to become full human beings. This split must be healed if we are to develop an empowering social practice of human liberation.

The distortion of moral character created by the public-private dichotomy is exacerbated by the liberal conception of the moral agent as autonomous and rational. Healing the split requires a shift from an understanding of the self as "an autonomous, detached rational subject" idealized in the public arena to an understanding of "an integrated, other-connected self" who incorporates "a sense of imagination, moral empathy and moral feeling."[66]

Moral principles such as justice, participation, and equality will be transformed when they are grounded in a communitarian conception of human beings rather than an individualistic one. Beverly Harrison has described a transformed understanding of justice as "a radically relational understanding of justice as rightly ordered relationships of mutuality within the total web of social relations. The givenness of reciprocal, interdependent social relations must be presumed in liberation moral theory. All of our moral norms must be reciprocal, stressing mutuality both of responsibility and control."[67] A transformed understanding of participation will attend to those factors that constrain the participation of women and other marginalized people, whether they be long hours of paid and unpaid labor or sociocultural prohibitions. And equality requires not just equal education and opportunity but equal access to power and resources. Empowerment of women and other oppressed peoples is a condition for both participation and equality, as is a woman's right to control over her reproductive powers.[68]

Another task necessary for healing the moral rift created by the public-private dichotomy is bringing moral norms such as equity and social justice, usually confined to the public arena, into the family and household.

Doing so is critical to desacralizing and demystifying the family. As part of this process we need to develop an ethic of rights and obligations for interpersonal relations which deals with sexual relations and which takes seriously the actual domestic labor that supports personal and family life, rather than idealizing or spiritualizing it.

Conversely, virtues such as nurturance and openness, which have been confined in the "private sphere," need to be reclaimed as morally valuable characteristics for all people and for public life. Women need to empower themselves and each other to reflect on what they have learned from childbearing, mothering, and domestic labor in regard to their own identities, interpersonal relations, and the social conditions that support child rearing and family life.[69] These activities and practices are not natural activities grounded in instinct; they must be recognized as involving moral agency and human initiative.

Bell Hooks insists that women and men must learn to value the work they do, whether paid or unpaid, "as a significant and meaningful gesture of power and resistance" to the reigning market values in our current political economy.[70] Working-class and poor women in particular have much to offer to such a change in practice, because their work has been especially critical to their families' survival.

Our utopian vision will be transformed as we heal the public-private dichotomy. As Peruvian Catholic feminists claim in challenging static organic conceptions of "woman's nature," motherhood is a relation open to the whole world. Opening this relation to all goes beyond bringing virtues such as nurturance and openness into all of life. It means a change in how work is understood, organized, and rewarded. Marx's utopian man who produces, reads, and goes fishing becomes the woman or man who also cooks, cleans, and cares for infants, children, and people of all ages.

A critical evaluation of our current social practice is necessary to the development of an inclusive emancipatory social practice. Religious communities in particular need to take account of their own role in legitimizing the oppression of women. Scripture, theology, ethics, religious history, ministry, ritual, and other areas of religious teaching and practice need to be examined in this light. Such a project would play a significant role in challenging and transforming beliefs and practices that perpetuate sex-based stereotyping and oppressive gender identities as part of the larger project of transforming the structures of domination and exploitation. Together, religious and secular people can create an empowering social practice that includes both women and men in its liberating vision and activity.

Notes

1. My use of the singular is not meant to imply that there is only one feminist liberation theology. The literature indicates a range of views as well as some common ground. I am speaking from what I see as common ground, knowing that no one woman can fully represent feminist liberation theologies. For a sampling of the literature in addition to the texts cited by Michael Zweig in Chapter 1, see Judith Plaskow, *Standing Again at Sinai: Judaism from a Feminist Perspective* (San Francisco: Harper & Row, 1990); Rosemary Radford Ruether, *Sexism and God-talk: Toward a Feminist Theology* (San Francisco: Harper & Row, 1983); Katie Geneva Cannon, Ada Maria Isasi-Diaz, Kwok Pui-lan, and Letty Russell, *Inheriting Our Mothers' Gardens: Feminist Theology in Third World Perspective* (Philadelphia: Westminster Press, 1988); Riffat Hassan, "Women in the Context of Change and Confrontation within Muslim Communities," in *Women of Faith in Dialogue*, ed. Virginia Mollenkott (New York: Crossroad, 1987, pp. 96–109); Virginia Fabella and Mercy Oduyoye, eds., *With Passion and Compassion: Third World Women Doing Theology* (Maryknoll, N.Y.: Orbis Books, 1988). For a specific focus on feminist ethics, see Barbara Andolsen, Christine Gudorf, and Mary Pellauer, eds., *Women's Consciousness, Women's Conscience: A Reader in Feminist Ethics* (Minneapolis, Minn.: Winston Press, 1985).

2. I use the term "Third World" to include those Third World people who live in the First World, whether they are recent immigrants or second-generation (or more) residents. I follow common usage of the terms "of color" and "racial/ethnic" in designating non-white and European peoples.

3. For an insightful but brief account of this conference, see Nilufer Cagatay, Caren Grown, and Aida Santiago, "The Nairobi Women's Conference: Toward a Global Feminism?" *Feminist Studies* 12, no. 2 (1986): 401–12.

4. *The State of the World's Women, 1985* (London: New Internationalist Publications, 1985), p. 3. This report summarizes the volumes of research collected by the United Nations and its various agencies. There has been no indication of a significant change in this situation since 1985. For a useful account of how economic value is determined, see Marilyn Waring, *Counting for Nothing: What Men Value and What Women Are Worth* (Wellington, N.Z.: Allen & Unwin, 1988).

5. Ruth Sivard, *Women . . . A World Survey* (Washington, D.C.: World Priorities, 1985). In using the terms "developed" and "developing" countries, I am following the usage of the United Nations documents. I am convinced that more accurately descriptive terms might be "overdeveloped" and "underdeveloped," which more clearly indicate the exploitative character of the relationship between these countries. See, e.g., Maria Mies, *Patriarchy and Accumulation on a World Scale: Women in the International Division of Labour* (London: Zed Books, 1986), pp. 39–40.

6. Society for International Development, "World Crisis and Women: Risk of Dispossession or an Opportunity for Empowerment," *Compass* 27 (April 1986): 1. The universality of women's subordination, this report concludes, is "best exemplified in the usage of women's labour as a 'shock-absorber' for tensions resulting from unemployment and instability due to the ongoing transformation of work." The Society for International Development is an international, nongovernmental organization committed to creating alternatives to capitalist growth models of development.

7. Research has shown that a woman's class position is generally tied to that of her husband. When he leaves or dies, a woman often loses class status and experiences a sharp decline in financial resources, no matter what her previous class position. For a discussion of this phenomenon in the United States, see Mary Corcoran, Greg J. Duncan, and Martha S. Hill, "The Economic Fortunes of Women and Children: Lessons from the Panel Study of Income Dynamics," *Signs* 10, no. 2 (1984): 232–48.

8. The statistics in this paragraph are taken from Sivard, *Women . . . : A World Survey*, and *The State of the World's Women, 1985*. Another useful text is Robin Morgan, ed., *Sisterhood Is Global: The International Women's Movement Anthology* (Garden City, N.Y.: Anchor Books, 1984), which includes for each country a breakdown of relevant statistics, a brief history, and an article by a local woman.

9. These statistics are extracted from *Labor Force Statistics Derived from Current Population Survey 1948–87* (Washington, D.C.: U.S. Department of Labor, 1988), and *Handbook of Labor Statistics* (Washington, D.C.: U.S. Department of Labor, 1989).

10. Society for International Development, "World Crisis and Women," p. 2.

11. Some basic texts on U.S. women include Rochelle Lefkowitz and Ann Withorn, eds., *For Crying Out Loud: Women and Poverty in the United States* (New York: Pilgrim Press, 1986); Ruth Sidel, *Women and Children Last: The Plight of Poor Women in Affluent America* (New York: Penguin Books, 1986); Ann Statham, Eleanor M. Miller, and Hans O. Mauksch, eds., *The Worth of Women's Work: A Qualitative Synthesis* (Albany: State University of New York Press, 1988); and Arlie Hochschild with Anne Machung, *The Second Shift: Working Parents and the Revolution at Home* (New York: Viking Press, 1989).

12. "Final Document: Intercontinental Women's Conference," in Fabella and Oduyoye, *With Passion and Compassion*, p. 186.

13. In addition to the sources cited in note 1, see, e.g., Beverly W. Harrison, *Making the Connections: Essays in Feminist Social Ethics*, ed. Carol Robb (Boston: Beacon Press, 1985), for a critique of Christianity; Blu Greenberg, "Confrontation and Change: Women and Jewish Tradition," in Mollenkott, *Women of Faith in Dialogue*; Fatima Mernissi, "Femininity as Subversion: Reflections on the Muslim Concept of Nushuz," in *Speaking of Faith: Global Perspectives on Women, Religion, and Social Change*, ed. Diana Eck and Devaki Jain (Philadelphia: New Society, 1987); and Lenore Friedman, *Meetings with Remarkable Women: Buddhist Teachers in America* (Boston: Shambala, 1987).

14. For an analysis of the movement in Roman Catholicism, see Mary Hobgood, *Catholic Social Teaching and Economic Theory: Paradigms in Conflict* (Philadelphia: Temple University Press, 1991). For a comparative analysis of Roman Catholic

and World Council pronouncements, see Marvin Ellison, *The Center Cannot Hold: The Search for a Global Economy of Justice* (Washington, D.C.: University Press of America, 1983); and Pamela K. Brubaker, *Rendering the Invisible Visible: Methodological Constraints on Economic Ethics in Relation to Women's Impoverishment* (Ann Arbor, Mich.: University Microfilms, 1990).

15. G.K.A. Bell, ed., *The Stockholm Conference 1925* (London: Oxford University Press, 1926), p. 1.

16. W. A. Visser't Hooft, "The Historical Significance of Stockholm 1925," in *The Gospel for All Realms of Life: Reflections on the Universal Christian Conference on Life and Work* (Geneva: World Council of Churches, 1975), p. 15.

17. I can only sketch here the history and development of the World Council. For a thorough account, see W. A. Visser't Hooft, *The Genesis and Formation of the World Council of Churches* (Geneva: WCC, 1982). Paul Abrecht, ed., "Fifty Years of Ecumenical Social Thought," *Ecumenical Review* 40 (April 1988), a special issue of the World Council's journal, includes a history of the development of the Council's social teaching. Ans J. Van Der Bent, *Vital Ecumenical Concerns* (Geneva: WCC, 1986), is a useful compendium of WCC pronouncements on ecclesiological and social issues.

18. W. A. Visser't Hooft, ed., *The First Assembly of the World Council of Churches: Official Report* (London: SCM Press, 1949), pp. 79–80. Another useful review of World Council social thought is Richard D. N. Dickinson, *Poor, Yet Making Many Rich* (Geneva: WCC, 1982).

19. David Paton, ed., *Breaking Barriers: Official Report of the Fifth Assembly* (Grand Rapids, Mich.: Eerdmans, 1976), pp. 128, 122–23. For further development of these perspectives, see the report of the 1983 Vancouver Assembly in David Gill, ed., *Gathered for Life* (Geneva: WCC, 1983); and the documents from the March 1990 Convocation Covenanting for Justice, Peace, and the Integrity of Creation (JPIC) in Seoul, Korea (available from the JPIC office of the WCC in Geneva), in which the Roman Catholic Church also participated and through which the Council initiated an attempt to develop a new political and economic paradigm. A useful summary of the work of the Council's Advisory Group on Economic Matters has been compiled by Catherine Mulholland in *Ecumenical Reflections on Political Economy* (Geneva: WCC, 1988). For an updated report, see "The World Economy and the Debt Crisis," in *Justice, Peace, and Integrity of Creation: Appendices to 2nd Draft Document* (Geneva: WCC, 1990).

20. Another significant factor is the unity agenda of the Council: as a part of its attempt to overcome the ecclesiological divisions within Christianity, the Council strives for consensus. The role of women tends to be seen as a church-dividing rather than church-uniting issue, because some members of the Council oppose the ordination of women and support traditional forms of family life. For an insightful discussion of this topic, see Melanie A. May, *Bonds of Unity* (Atlanta, Ga.: Scholars Press, 1989). Although great strides have been made in recent years as the number of women on the Central Committee and among the representatives at assemblies continues to grow, women are still struggling to become full participants in the life and work of the Council.

21. Carole Pateman, "Feminist Critiques of the Public/Private Dichotomy," in

Feminism and Equality, ed. Anne Phillips (New York: New York University Press, 1987), p. 106. Note that what is presumed to be natural in this citation is in fact also socially constructed: what counts as a blood tie varies from culture to culture.

22. Beverly Thiele, "Vanishing Acts in Social and Political Thought," in *Feminist Challenges: Social and Political Theory,* ed. Carole Pateman and Elizabeth Gross (Boston: Northeastern University Press, 1986), pp. 30–43.

23. See Norman Goodall, ed., *The Uppsala Report 1968* (Geneva: WCC, 1968), p. 92.

24. Reinhild Traitler, "An Oikoumene of Women?" *Ecumenical Review* 40 (April 1988): 179.

25. Madeleine Barot, *Cooperation of Men and Women in Church, Family, and Society* (Geneva: WCC, 1964), p. 8.

26. Constance Parvey, "The Community Study: Its Mixed Messages for the Churches," in *Beyond Unity-in-Tension: Unity, Renewal, and the Community of Women and Men,* ed. Thomas F. Best (Geneva: WCC, 1988), p. 39. The consultation did condemn prostitution and the traffic in women, but these are seen as occurring in the so-called public sphere.

27. Beverly Harrison, "Sexism and the Language of Christian Ethics," in Robb, *Making the Connections,* pp. 27–28. For an illuminating analysis of the contradiction between equality, property rights, and patriarchal rights in liberalism, see Herbert Gintis, "Social Contradictions and the Liberal Theory of Justice," in *New Directions in Economic Justice,* ed. Roger Skurski (Notre Dame, Ind.: Notre Dame University Press, 1983), pp. 91–112.

28. *Ecumenical Decade 1988–1998: Churches in Solidarity with Women* (Geneva: WCC, 1988), p. 1.

29. Shin Sun, "A Vision of the Women's Committee," *In God's Image,* June 1988, p. 5.

30. See "Evangelization in Latin America," nn. 841, 846, in *Puebla and Beyond: Documentary and Commentary,* ed. John Eagleson and Philip Scharper (Maryknoll, N.Y.: Orbis Books, 1979).

31. See Michael Zweig (Chapter 1) and Gregory Baum (Chapter 3) for discussion of this earlier teaching.

32. See John Paul II, *Laborem Exercens,* n. 19, in Gregory Baum, *The Priority of Labor: A Commentary on Laborem Exercens* (New York: Paulist Press, 1982).

33. *The Pope Speaks: The Teachings of Pius XII,* ed. Michael Chinigo (New York: Pantheon Books, 1957), p. 58.

34. Giglia Tedesco, "Laborem Exercens: A Handicap for Women," *NTC News* (Rome) 8, nos. 11–12 (1981): 1.

35. John XXIII, "The Woman of Today," in *The Pope Speaks* 7 (1961): 172–73.

36. John Paul II, *Laborem Exercens,* nn. 16–19. I am not arguing here that "wages for housework" is a necessary or adequate norm for economic justice for women. Rather, I am using the just wage in relation to domestic work as an example of the invisibility of women's economic contribution in Catholic social teaching. This is also true of World Council social teaching, and in both such invisibility is due in part to the economic theory they are using.

37. Ruth L. Smith, "Feminism and the Moral Subject," in Andolsen, Gudorf, and

Pellawer, *Women's Consciousness, Women's Conscience*, p. 250.

38. Pope Pius XII, *Casti Connubii*, n. 77, in *Seven Great Encyclicals* (New York: Paulist Press, 1939).

39. Kathryn Pauly Morgan, "Women and Moral Madness," *Canadian Journal of Philosophy*, supp. vol. 13 (n.d.): 204; reprinted in *Feminist Perspectives: Philosophical Essays on Method and Morals*, ed. Lorraine Cole, Sheila Mullett, and Christine Overall (Toronto: University of Toronto Press, 1988), pp. 146–67.

40. John Paul II, *Mulieris Dignitatem*, August 15, 1988, *Origins* 18 (1988): 261–83, nn. 10–11 (emphasis added).

41. Paul VI, *Humanae Vitae*, n. 14, in *The Gospel of Peace and Justice: Catholic Social Teaching since Pope John*, ed. Joseph Gremillion (Maryknoll, N.Y.: Orbis Books, 1976).

42. John Paul II, *Mulieris Dignitatem*, nn. 26–27.

43. "Reflections of Peruvian Women on the Occasion of the Visit of Pope John Paul II" (approved English translation), in *Women in the Church*, New LADOC Keyhole Series 2 (Lima, Peru: Latin American Documentation, 1986), pp. 2–3.

44. My discussion of mainstream economics is informed in particular by Nancy S. Barrett, "How the Study of Women Has Restructured the Discipline of Economics," in *A Feminist Perspective in the Academy: The Difference It Makes*, ed. Elizabeth Langland and Walter Gove (Chicago: University of Chicago Press, 1981), pp. 101–9; and Elaine Donovan and Mary Huff Stevenson, "Shortchanged: The Political Economy of Women's Poverty," in Lefkowitz and Withorn, *For Crying Out Loud*, pp. 47–60.

45. See, e.g., Corcoran, Duncan, and Hill, "The Economic Fortunes of Women and Children."

46. Diana Pearce, "The Feminization of Poverty: Women, Work and Welfare," *Urban and Social Change Review* 11, no. 1 (1978): 28–36; reprinted in Lefkowitz and Withorn, *For Crying Out Loud*, pp. 29–46.

47. Pamela Sparr, "Reevaluating Feminist Economics," in Lefkowitz and Withorn, *For Crying Out Loud*, p. 64. Another insightful critique of this approach is Linda Burnham, "Has Poverty Been Feminized in Black America?" *Black Scholar* 16, no. 2 (1985): 14–24; abridged version in *For Crying Out Loud*, pp. 69–83. Sparr and Burnham also criticize Karin Stallard, Barbara Ehrenreich, and Holly Sklar, *Poverty in the American Dream: Women and Children First* (Boston: South End Press, 1983); although these authors claim to be using a socialist feminist analysis, gender takes precedence over class and race in their work. A more useful socialist feminist approach is that of Wendy Sarvasy and Judith Van Allen, "Fighting the Feminization of Poverty: Socialist-Feminist Analysis and Strategy," *Review of Radical Political Economics* 16, no. 4 (1984): 89–110.

48. In addition to my own analysis, my assessment of the usefulness of radical political economics for feminist liberation theology is deeply indebted to Beverly Harrison, "The Role of Social Theory in Religious Social Ethics," in Robb, *Making the Connections*, pp. 54–82. Because full discussion of this topic is beyond the scope of this chapter, I strongly encourage a reading of Harrison's essay.

49. Heidi Hartmann, "The Unhappy Marriage of Marxism and Feminism: Towards a More Progressive Union," in *Women and Revolution: A Discussion of the Unhappy Marriage of Marxism and Feminism*, ed. Lydia Sargent (Boston: South End

Press, 1981), pp. 10–11.

50. A classic text on this topic is Hilda Scott, *Does Socialism Liberate Women?* (Boston: Beacon Press, 1974).

51. Hartmann, "Unhappy Marriage," p. 9. Also see Heidi Hartmann, "The Family as the Locus of Gender, Class, and Political Struggle: The Example of Housework," *Signs* 6, no. 3 (1981); reprinted in *Feminism and Methodology: Social Science Issues,* ed. Sandra Harding (Bloomington: Indiana University Press, 1987), pp. 109–34. More recent research indicates that a higher standard of living is still the case for men in countries around the globe.

52. Karl Marx, *Capital* (New York: International Publishers, 1967), 1:572.

53. Ibid., 1:351. Lise Vogel discusses this passage in her book *Marxism and the Oppression of Women: Toward a Unitary Theory* (New Brunswick, N.J.: Rutgers University Press, 1983), pp. 60–62. Some Marxists continue to account for the sexual division of labor in this functionalist way. See, e.g., Linda Burnham and Miriam Louie, "The Impossible Marriage: A Marxist Critique of Socialist Feminism," *Line of March* 17 (Spring 1985). For accounts of the social construction of this division, see among others Peggy Sanday, *Female Power and Male Dominance: On the Origins of Sexual Inequality* (Cambridge: Cambridge University Press, 1981); and Mary O'Brien, *The Politics of Reproduction* (Boston: Routledge & Kegan Paul, 1981).

54. Womanist theologian Delores Williams offers an insightful discussion of these differences in "The Color of Feminism; or, Speaking the Black Woman's Tongue," *Journal of Religious Thought* 43, no. 1 (1986): 42–58.

55. Heleieth I. B. Saffioti, *Women in Class Society* (1967), trans. Michael Vale (New York: Monthly Review Press, 1978), p. 297.

56. This debate becomes very technical, and the literature on the subject has become immense. For a summary of the debate, see Vogel, *Marxism and the Oppression of Women,* pp. 17–24. Vogel defends the position that domestic labor produces only use value (pp. 156–58). Saffioti is a primary proponent of the view that domestic labor indirectly produces use value; see *Women in Class Society,* p. 96, and her "Women, Mode of Production, and Social Formations," *Latin American Perspectives* 4, nos. 1–2 (1977): 27–37. Mariarosa Dalla Costa, "Women and the Subversion of the Community," in *The Power of Women and the Subversion of the Community* (Bristol: Falling Wall Press, 1973), pp. 19–54, argues that domestic labor directly produces surplus value, and she has organized an international Wages for Housework campaign around this view. For a useful discussion of the implications of this debate for the analysis of the impoverishment of women and for public policy, see Hilda Scott, *Working Your Way to the Bottom: The Feminization of Poverty* (London: Pandora Press, 1984), pp. 129–46.

57. Dalla Costa, "Women and the Subversion of the Community," p. 42.

58. Hartmann, "Unhappy Marriage," p. 22.

59. Heidi Hartmann and Ann Markusen, "Contemporary Marxist Theory and Practice: A Feminist Critique," *Review of Radical Political Economics* 12 (1980): 87–94. For an alternative socialist feminist view that stresses the conflict between patriarchy and capitalism, see Ann Ferguson and Nancy Folbre, "The Unhappy Marriage of Patriarchy and Capitalism," in Sargent, *Women and Revolution,* pp. 314–38, which defines patriarchal relations (p. 317) as "the social context for specific forms of human

(typically, female) labor: labor devoted to bearing and rearing children and nurturing adult men. In order to emphasize the importance of the labor process itself, we utilize the concept of sex-affective production." I believe this is a promising approach to an analysis of women's unpaid work.

60. Sarvasy and Van Allen, "Fighting the Feminization of Poverty," presents an integrated rather than dualist analysis of women's oppression through the heuristic category of women's dual role. Some useful texts that include a multidimensional analysis are Gita Sen with Caren Grown, *Development, Crises, and Alternative Visions: Third World Women's Perspectives* (New York: Monthly Review Press, 1986); Arthur Brittan and Mary Maynard, *Sexism, Racism, and Oppression* (Oxford: Basil Blackwell, 1984); Eleanor Leacock and Helen I. Safa, eds., *Women's Work: Development and the Division of Labor by Gender* (South Hadley, Mass.: Bergin & Garvey, 1986); Mies, *Patriarchy and Capital Accumulation;* Maria Mies, *Women: The Last Colony* (London: Zed Press, 1988); and Swatsi Mitter, *Common Fate, Common Bond: Women in the Global Economy* (London: Pluto Press, 1986).

61. Lourdes Beneria and Martha Roldan, "Industrial Homework, Subcontracting, and Household Dynamics in Mexico City," in *The Crossroads of Class and Gender* (Chicago: University of Chicago Press, 1987), pp. 1–16.

62. Sources that discuss this theological approach include Introduction and "Final Statement of the Latin American Conference on Theology from the Perspective of Women," in Fabella and Oduyoye, *With Passion and Compassion,* pp. ix–xv, 181–83; Letty Russell, "From Garden to Table," in Russell, *Inheriting Our Mothers' Gardens,* pp. 150–55; and Sarah Cunningham, "A Meeting of the Minds," in Mollenkott, *Women of Faith in Dialogue,* pp. 9–16. The character of truth claims is also a crucial issue in feminist theory. For a recent review of the debate, see Mary E. Hawkesworth, "Knowers, Knowing, Known: Feminist Theory and Claims of Truth," *Signs* 14, no. 3 (1989): 533–57. See also Harding, *Feminism and Methodology;* Teresa de Lauretis, *Feminist Studies, Critical Studies* (Bloomington: Indiana University Press, 1986); Donna Haraway, "Situated Knowledges," *Feminist Studies* 14, no. 3 (1988): 575–99; and Allison M. Jagger and Susan R. Bordo, eds., *Gender/Body/Knowledge: Feminist Reconstructions of Being and Knowing* (New Brunswick, N.J.: Rutgers University Press, 1989).

63. These criteria for adequate analysis and public policies are significantly informed by Sen and Grown, *Development, Crises and Alternative Visions;* and "The Dakar Declaration on Another Development with Women," *Development Dialogue* 1–2 (1982): 11–16.

64. Some feminists support claims of women's moral superiority with the findings of psychologist Carol Gilligan, whose *In a Different Voice: Psychological Theory and Women's Development* (Cambridge, Mass.: Harvard University Press, 1982) argues that women are more concerned with relationship than with the rules that concern men. It should be noted that Gilligan is primarily interested in challenging the claim of moral developmentalists that women are morally inferior to men because they do not attain to universal standards of justice, rather than in asserting the moral superiority of women. I agree with those critics who charge that Gilligan does not sufficiently attend to the social construction of the differences she notes. See Martha J. Reineke, "The Politics of Difference: A Critique of Carol Gilligan,"

Canadian Journal of Feminist Ethics 2, no. 1 (1987): 3–19.

65. Anthropologist Nancy Scheper-Hughes presents compelling evidence of the connection between such characteristics as maternal nurturance and forms of socioeconomic organization in her description of the maternal withdrawal of care from sickly infants and children in regions with high infant mortality rates ("Death without Weeping," *Natural History*, October 1989, pp. 8–14). Other theorists have pointed out that the form of family relations idealized in liberal theory and bourgeois society is race- and class-specific. The conditions for its attainment were available only to the white middle strata and the wealthy. See, e.g., Leith Mullings, "Uneven Development," in Leacock and Safa, *Women's Work*, pp. 41–57.

66. Morgan, "Women and Moral Madness," pp. 224–25. Morgan's discussion focuses on the individual person; I am attending to communities as well. In speaking of the healing of the public-private split, I am drawing on the Jewish notion of *tikkun* discussed by Michael Lerner in Chapter 5 and by Plaskow, "The Repair of the World," in *Standing Again at Sinai*, pp. 211–38.

67. Beverly Harrison, "The Role of Theological Reflection in the Struggle for Liberation," in Robb, *Making the Connections*, p. 253.

68. In an egalitarian male-female relationship, reproductive decisions would be mutual, but this is not the reality of most women's lives. Since women suffer nearly all the risks and costs of unwanted pregnancy, they must ultimately be the ones to decide how their reproductive powers will be used. This includes the right to have children as well as not to have children. See Beverly W. Harrison, *Our Right to Choose: Toward a New Ethic of Abortion* (Boston: Beacon Press, 1983); Betsy Hartmann, *Reproductive Rights and Wrongs: The Global Politics of Population Control and Contraceptive Choice* (New York: Harper & Row, 1987); and Committee for Abortion Rights and Sterilization Abuse, *Women under Attack: Victories, Backlash, and the Fight for Reproductive Freedom*, ed. Susan E. Davis (Boston: South End Press, 1988).

69. See Martha A. Ackelsberg, "Communities, Resistance, and Women's Activism," in *Women and the Politics of Empowerment*, ed. Ann Bookman and Sandra Morgen (Philadelphia: Temple University Press, 1988), pp. 297–313, for a useful discussion of the limits of liberal and Marxist political conceptions and an examination of the implications of women's activism for an adequate conception of democratic politics that focuses on the politics of relationship generated by the concerns of everyday life.

70. Bell Hooks, *Feminist Theory: From Margin to Center* (Boston: South End Press, 1984), p. 103. See also Bonnie Thornton Dill, " 'Making Your Job Good Yourself': Domestic Service and the Construction of Personal Dignity," in Bookman and Morgen, *Women and the Politics of Empowerment*, pp. 33–52.

5

JEWISH LIBERATION THEOLOGY AND EMANCIPATORY POLITICS

Michael Lerner

As we enter the 1990s, many people, tired of political struggle that seems to be going nowhere, are making their way back into religious communities, searching for a meaning and purpose in their lives that they did not find in political movements. Other activists feel betrayed by that move—and see the return to religion as nothing more than the final cop-out of a conservative period, the much-to-be-regretted consequence of the Reagan and Bush years.

In fact, the recent return to religion has often been a return to a kind of religious consciousness that is a willed forgetting of the social and political world. But emphasis on this point obscures a more important insight: the psychological and spiritual needs that lead people back into a religious world view are *legitimate and fundamental human needs that have not been addressed by the progressive movements for social change, whether Marxist or more conventionally liberal.* It is my contention that until those needs *are* addressed, progressive movements will remain deeply limited, their victories always extremely partial, their defeats inevitable.

Yet this is not a plea that liberals and progressives should now include a new *constituency,* "religious people," or convert to a particular religious community. Nor should the traditional concerns of progressive movements be abandoned in favor of a strictly spiritual agenda. Rather, the set of truths and the way of looking at the world embedded in Jewish liberation theology, which in important ways are also echoed in Christian liberation theology, could be appropriated and integrated into the self-understanding and strategic focus of a secular liberatory movement for social change.

Skepticism about Jewish theology as a progressive force may now be particularly acute among Jews and non-Jews alike as we watch right-wing

fanatics in Israel using the language of Judaism to justify the brutalization of the Palestinian people. It is a tragedy for the entire Jewish people
to find its history and religious beliefs—for thousands of years among
the most powerful challenges to the world's various systems of oppressions—appropriated by moral cretins who represent them to the world
as merely another special interest, quite comfortable in joining other
oppressive systems.

Jewish theology, like all religious belief, has been used to justify a
wide range of behaviors and attitudes; often these religiously based conclusions are diametrically opposed to one another, even though they are
nominally drawn from the same tradition. In this regard, the assertion
of a Jewish liberation theology must confront other readings of Jewish
tradition which are profoundly conservative and reactionary, much as
Christian liberation theology must address a long history of reactionary
Christian doctrine and practice.

Human history, and our own personal experiences, have too often
been filled with rabbis, priests, or ministers who offer readings of the
religious texts to turn them into the handmaiden of any and every political or philosophical world view, no matter how oppressive and contrary
to the needs of human dignity. Such sectarian and reactionary religious
practice has contributed to the distrust many progressive people display
toward *all* religion.

The conflict between the tradition of Jewish liberation theology and
more conservative Jewish religious traditions is an important subject that
lies beyond the bounds of this chapter. Nevertheless, I want to argue
here that a Jewish theology of liberation has insights of universal significance—not only for Jews and people in alternative religious traditions
but also for the millions of secular Americans who tend to believe that
religion itself is part of the problem, not part of the solution.

A word of preparation for those who think of theology as a set of
abstract theories about the nature of God. In Jewish theology, God reveals Him- or Herself in a series of events in Jewish history, and it is in
making sense of these events that we understand our relationship to God.
God is revealed to the Jews through a historic process that is ongoing.
Thus, Jewish theology is about the experience and self-understanding of
a people as it struggles to understand itself and its relationship to God.
One reaches an understanding of the divine through an understanding
of the people and its teachings.

For this reason, Jewish history is especially rich in lessons of interest to those drawn to contemporary liberation theology and ethically based social movements. The Jewish people has conceptualized itself as a vanguard people that has a task of changing the world in some way. Its actual experience has been one of struggling and failing, struggling and failing. Yet in the course of time, Jews have built up approaches to the world that have made it possible to survive 3,500 years of this process.

For those who may be temporarily overwhelmed by the depression engendered by the political victories of the forces of oppression and domination, the experience and accumulated wisdom of the Jewish people may be an important basis for learning how to survive in the meantime. Yet it is my contention that there is much more here: a way not only to survive but ultimately really to transform society.

There are two fundamental elements in Jewish liberation theology: the balance between celebration and transformation, and the dual injunctions to fight idolatry and to maximize compassion. Let me explain.

Judaism was not the first religion to recognize that there was something in the universe that transcended human reality—a force or power or presence that radiated through the world and yet transcended it. Human beings have long recognized something remarkable, special, unique, taboo, holy—and have tried to relate to it through prayer, ritual, dance, song, and awe.

What was unique about Judaism was that it identified this force in the universe as a *moral* force that rejected the inevitability of oppression and that demanded and made possible world transformation. The claim that there exists a God, then, a one unique God who rules over the universe, became a claim about the possibility of a moral order. God was no longer simply an embodiment of arbitrary or capricious power. God became power joined with the injunction to improve the world.

The very power or force that shaped and governed the universe is the force that makes for the possibility of human salvation. The way things are in the world is not the way they ought to be or should be—and the power of God is on the side of transformation toward a moral order. This transformation is possible (though not inevitable) because the governing force in the universe is *not* the principle of order and necessity but the principle of freedom and transcendence.

When asked by Moses to name His or Her name so that Moses will have some way of identifying this deity to the Israelite slaves, God says, "I shall be who I shall be. Tell them 'I shall be' sent you." Here we see that the religious world view of Jewish tradition has insisted that the universe is governed by a principle of possibility for transformation, of becoming. It is an outlook that readily provides a basis for a transformative social practice.

The beginnings of the Jewish story emerge as the story of opposition to the two great Middle Eastern empires of the time. First, Abraham is commanded to leave the Babylonian world. Rather than attempt to reform the existing order, he is to found a new order and a new people. A new religion emerges not in a simple act of faith, not in a new conception of God, not simply in a new set of ritual acts—but rather in the political act of rejecting an entire social order.

Second, Moses leads the Jewish people in the first recorded slave rebellion—a revolutionary act that became the cornerstone of Jewish identity and history, and a cornerstone of contemporary Christian liberation theology as well. One of the most powerful empires the world had ever known finds itself defeated and even humiliated by a group of ordinary human beings, slaves, people who had been debased and defeated, people who are the paradigm case of powerlessness and despair.

It would have been conceivable for the Jewish people to emerge from slavery, forget that part of their past, and then go on to build a religion appropriate to their new status as a people of power and eventually of land. Instead, Judaism became centered on this paramount act of liberation and transformation: the overthrow of the power of a mighty empire. It was this aspect of Judaism that made it most subversive and most offensive to ruling classes throughout history: its insistence on making not just a religion that was about how wonderful the physical world is but a religion that insisted there was nothing inevitable about the hierarchies of the social world. Judaism taught that the most fixed and seemingly immovable powers of the world could be struggled against, that the power of ordinary people could triumph over the claims of the entrenched ruling elites.

Nor was this just a claim that it had happened once to one group of people. Rather, Judaism proclaimed a message of potentially universal significance: the power that created the universe *is the same power* that champions the powerless and creates the demand for a moral universe infused with justice and compassion. Celebration of the grandeur of creation goes hand in hand with transformation of the social world.

The revolutionary message was enshrined in a religious practice. Judaism reshaped the nature of holidays, which had been built around the harvest, to reflect moments in the historical legacy of the Jewish liberation in the exodus from Egypt and travel to the promised land. And it also created a new holiday, the Sabbath, which became the living embodiment of the revolutionary message.

One day a week, proclaimed Judaism, it is forbidden to work: the Sabbath is both a day to celebrate the grandeur of creation and the day to remember and celebrate the liberation from slavery. To be sure, taking one day out of seven from the masters of the world is only a reform—it does not in itself overthrow the existing systems of oppression. Yet the notion that a people could establish this kind of reform, proclaim to the world that no ruler could have control over it on this one day, introduced to the world the notion of putting permanent constraints on ruling classes that previously had known no constraints to their absolute power.

The revolutionary message in Judaism made us the enemies of every ruling class—even when we did not intend to be. Many a Jewish community throughout our history has attempted to vitiate this dynamic, to assure the rulers that we could and would serve them well if only they tolerated and protected us. At times this strategy has worked, and we have secured for ourselves the space to live and flourish.

Yet to the extent that we stayed true to Judaism, we were propagating a message that was fundamentally and irredeemably subversive. No ruling class could long tolerate us without simultaneously protecting itself by trying to generate among its own population a set of anti-Jewish feelings that could be exacerbated when circumstances warranted. Particularly at moments when popular discontent at their rulers' oppression might lead the masses to rebellion, anti-Jewish sentiment has been used as a substitute target for anger and aggression.

Judaism, then, was a religion which in its essence called for social transformation. It did not sanctify existing hierarchy as God-given, or ignore worldly oppression while attending to some higher consciousness or transcendent reality. Judaism placed at its center the notion that the social world was real, that it should and could be different, and that the greatest power in the world was a power that sided with those who wished to build a just and ethical social world.

Yet there was a balance in this religion as well, a recognition that the anger and frustration of fighting against oppression was not enough to sustain a community. Yes, one must struggle for transformation, for *tikkun*. But simultaneously one must rejoice, must stand in awe, wonder, and radical amazement at the grandeur of creation. One must join with others in celebration of that which is already available to us in the myriad of miracles that daily confront us in the natural world.

The Jewish tradition contains this balance between celebration of creation and the call to transform reality still further toward justice. The "is" and the "ought" do not negate each other: the very force that makes what is, is also the force that commands us to fight for that which ought to be. There is no need to separate one's politics from one's spiritual life: the community of joy and celebration can also be the community of struggle and transformation.

So committed was Judaism to the fundamental unity of the ethical and the spiritual that its chief obsession was to fight against idolatry: the worship of gods who embodied the partial truths of the realm of the spirit without embracing the moral and transformative imperative to create a just and humane world. The idolaters might seem to be worshiping the spirit that pervades the universe, but in fact they were killing that spirit—making it into mere objects, artifacts of wood and stone—to the extent that they were unable to recognize the moral content to that force.

Idolatry is to take the part for the whole, to take that which is and accept it as that which ought to be, to accept reality and flow with it rather than to challenge reality and transform it. No religion has an automatic safety valve against idolatry; every religion might transform itself into a service of forces that have no relationship to the fundamental ethical imperative to remake the world according to the criteria of justice and compassion.

Idolatry could and did pervade Judaism itself. The prophets were not talking about some other guy who was bad—it was to chastise the Jews themselves that they came forward, challenging every accommodation with injustice. They ridiculed religious practices that had lost touch with the God of liberation, the God who had demanded that Jews struggle for a new world.

And yet there was within Judaism a recognition that human beings who were challenged to remake this world were fundamentally fallible and conflicted. People have the potential to move toward a world of justice and compassion, but also the possibility of recreating a world of cruelty and evil. For Judaism, every human being becomes the locus of this struggle, the inheritor of both possibilities.

Thus the story of Abraham. According to the midrash, he is traumatized as a child. One legend tells of his being thrown into a pit with wild animals by the king, who has discovered that Abraham will not worship the idols of the land. Another describes a conflict with his own father, himself a chief idolmaker. When Abraham hears the voice of God, it is to tell him to clear out of this land, to go to another place, a place that God will show him.

Yet inevitably, Abraham brings not only his awareness of God but also his traumatized self. Much of the Abraham story that follows is a story of a man deeply conflicted, a man who is struggling with two voices, the voice of God and the voice that masquerades as divine but is actually the reflection of the legacy of cruelty. At times we can recognize Abraham's transcendence—as when he challenges God to live up to the highest moral possibilities in dealing with Sodom by not allowing the good to be destroyed with the bad. At other times Abraham is simply acting like a scoundrel—particularly in his treatment of Sarah.

The conflict is made most explicit when Abraham thinks that he is hearing the voice of God tell him to sacrifice his only son. We can recognize here the repetition compulsion that so dominates human history: Abraham came from a society in which child sacrifice was commonplace; it is not unusual for cruelty done to children to reemerge in their own adult lives—for Abraham, in the form of a divine command.

In this story we have an ancient treatment of a central problem of our contemporary world: that most people have been shaped by psychological stresses that incorporate the oppressions of the past, the pains and traumas visited upon our parents, and their parents, in a great chain of negativity reaching endlessly into the past and brought forward to us; and that we then pass this negativity on to the next generation, feeling that our patterns of behavior are "common sense" and our cruelty the call of some higher truth.

So we march off to wars or turn our backs on the suffering of others or inflict pain on those whom we love—and do so in the name of some higher cause (nationalism, religion, family loyalty, "the revolution," art, intellectual accomplishment, political correctness, self-fulfillment) that actually just masks for us the degree to which we are trapped by repetition compulsion to pass on to others the cruelty and pains that were visited upon us. The greatness of Abraham appears at the moment in which he demonstrates the possibility of compassion overcoming cruelty: it is the God of compassion who calls out to him to stop him from this child sacrifice. Abraham's story symbolizes the great promise of Judaism: that the repetition compulsion can be transcended.

If Judaism is a message of optimism, its optimism is embodied in this claim: that the way things have been is not the way things must be, that the world can be radically altered, that the chain of negativity need not be passed on from generation to generation. Abraham's greatness is not, as some existentialists would have it, that he was willing to sacrifice his son though it violated the very ethical norms of the God of justice and compassion. Rather, the great lesson of Abraham is that he was able to overcome the very human conflict within him and refuse to sacrifice his son, thereby breaking the chain of negativity and becoming a beacon of hope that compassion can triumph over cruelty.

The message of optimism is repeated over and over again in Torah: compassion can triumph over cruelty. The importance of Sinai as the event following the exodus from Egypt is this: that the Jews have not been freed so that they can recreate the evil of Egypt. And there is no more frequently repeated injunction than this: when you go into your own land, *do not oppress the stranger, remember that you were strangers in the land of Egypt.* The point of your political liberation is not that you can trade places with the oppressor, acting unto others as some people acted toward you. The goal of your liberation is that you break the chain of negativity.

And yet . . . and yet there is also recognition in the Torah itself that at any moment there are real limits to such personal transcendence. We have been deeply scarred by our past, and to some extent we will unconsciously recreate the patterns of previous life. So, when God is faced with a people that has gone through the experience of political liberation and almost immediately reverts to some form of idolatry at the Golden Calf, the instant anger and outrage are replaced with compassion and the building of a religious system that takes into account human limitations and human needs at that historical moment.

A long set of detailed rituals is established, from animal sacrifice to the building of a physical sanctuary, all of which provide the external forms for a people who need the externals, who are not capable of total and permanent transcendence, who waffle between moments of "getting it" and most moments, in which they cannot stay fully in touch with the important truths they have momentarily grasped.

God does not abandon the demand for transcendence: the divine injunction is also the source of human hope—that it really is possible to break through the chains of seeming necessity. But Torah seems to be saying something else as well: that there is a need for compassion for our weakness, an understanding that at any given moment there will be limits to transcendence, and that it is necessary to make compromises with human weakness.

The problem, of course, is that the compromises can become the substance of a religion and the demand for transcendence be lost. Cruelty and the acting out of pain on others can become the social content of religion. Hence, every generation must call forth its own prophets, who demand transcendence and testify to the possibility of possibility that is God.

The history of the Jewish people is a history suffused with this tension—as is the Torah and all its interpretations. We see it played out today in the treatment of Palestinians by Israel's Jews, and in the opposition to that oppression from other Jews, in Israel and around the world. It is a tension also found in every other religious tradition and in the world of secular politics as well. There is no liberation tradition that has not been appropriated also by the forces of oppression, or has not at least been used in an oppressive manner. Consider, for example, the crimes of Stalin, done in the name of a system that was to transcend human degradation.

So I do not need to be reminded of the moments in which Moses begins to hear a very different kind of God from the God who calls for loving treatment of the stranger. And whether we adopt the traditional interpretation that says Moses himself wrote every part of the Torah, or whether we imagine a group of scribes, working under Ezra in the fifth century B.C.E., who gathered together and wove fragments of stories and written documents from the past to create the Torah scroll we have now, the conflicts in authorial voice reflect the human conflicts in those who received the divine inspiration that made Torah possible. The conflicts within these people that made it possible for them to hear voices of cruelty as voices of God are conflicts that still tear at our human souls today.

We cannot hide from ourselves that the Jewish people is like all other peoples and that we have never completely overcome the legacy of cruelty. As surely as the dominant voice in Judaism became a voice of compassion, there were other voices, always there, pointing to the passages of Torah that reflected the legacy of cruelty. There were always the commentators who kept alive the vision of a Jewish people who would take revenge on the *goyim*, always aspects of the popular culture that defended against feelings of self-degradation by ridiculing and degrading the *goyim*, always the voices that prayed for revenge and for a return to power. These we hear too often today from positions of power in Israel, as they were present in older ghetto and *shtetl* life, where there was also brutality, mutual exploitation, and cruelty alongside the very many acts and traditions and institutions that manifested compassion, mutual care, and spiritual sensitivity.

To reverse Lord Acton's familiar comment, it is also true that power-lessness tends to corrupt. The more one is abused, the more one can develop a tendency to abuse in turn. The voice of compassion within Jewish tradition acted as a counterforce to this tendency, but in and of itself, it could not always be sufficient to counter the psychological power of endless external abuse. To the extent that Jewish life in the past several thousand years has been subjected to oppression, violation, beatings, expulsions, and finally mass murder, its inner life would ineluctably reflect the impact of this brutalization.

Thus, no matter how spiritually deep and ethically alive Jewish life in the diaspora became, it was also in some respects distorted and oppressive, if not in comparison with the even more deeply distorted lives of the majority populations in whose oppressive societies Jews were forced to seek haven, then at least in comparison with the highest ideals of Jewish ethical teachings. This was not simply a picture of the morally pure being oppressed by the evil others. Jewish life itself incorporated and reflected some of the ugliness and pain that had been imposed upon it by an oppressive reality.

Given this history of Jewish oppression in feudal Europe and the limitations of *shtetl* life, it is no surprise that Jews welcomed the rise of capitalism with its challenge to the authority of the Church and rejoiced at the emancipation from the ghettos made possible in the aftermath of the French Revolution. At least from the time of Spinoza, Jews have contributed to the intellectual and material foundations of modern capitalist society wherever they have been allowed to participate.

Precisely because it offered a path out of social oppression, Jews adopted, and to some extent helped shape, the spirit of liberalism that was the philosophy of the emerging bourgeoisie. That liberalism placed at the center of its agenda the emancipation of individuals from the constraints of the social-economic-religious order of feudalism, in which the major aspects of one's life were dictated by the norms of the external community. Although a private sphere would remain in which people should be free to choose their own religious and ethical values, the public world must be rid of all systems that had previously operated in a coercive manner.

For Jews, this promised an escape from the repressive norms of their own ghetto life, but much more important, it meant an end to a larger world defined around religious categories that would always make us the "other"—and thereby subject to physical as well as legal assault. The secularization of the world would, we hoped, provide us with physical security and freedom from persecution. If, in the process, one might have to abandon deep spiritual truths and a rich cultural and intellectual legacy, that was a price many Jews were willing to pay, if they could thereby achieve freedom from physical oppression and liberation from those confining and repressive aspects of ghetto life that were sometimes incorporated into Jewish religious law and practice.

Jews became champions of civil liberties, the spokespeople for individual rights, the liberal force par excellence. In liberalism we found a political philosophy that both advanced our own interests and simultaneously allowed us to concretize into real politics the liberatory spirit of Judaism as the vanguard of the oppressed.

And yet liberalism had its limits as a liberatory philosophy. The most easily recognized limit became clear in the early decades of the nineteenth century: the fact that legal constraints had been eliminated did not create a social world in which each individual could fully actualize his or her own potential as a human being. Socialists of every stripe began to argue that freedom *from* constraint had not produced freedom *to* be fully human.

Instead of a world of human potential fulfilled, liberal capitalist society had become one in which some people, with massive amounts of economic power, were free to pursue their own interests to the detriment of the vast majority. Freedom of opportunity quickly boiled down to the freedom of the majority to sell their labor power to the owners of means of production—or starve to death. Great inequality of resources led to great inequalities in realized liberty.

Many Jews understood this reality and became leaders in the struggles to repair the deficit. Some were revolutionaries who sought to replace capitalism with an economic system based on substantive, not just formal, equality. Some were reformers who sought legal constraints on corporations, coupled with such economic benefits as social security, unemployment insurance, and medical care to offset the worst consequences of corporate greed and the self-seeking ethos of the capitalist marketplace. Even when undertaken in the secular language of Marx or modern liberal politics, Jewish participation in social justice movements has reflected the ancient Jewish religious tradition that challenges injustice and commands us to act to transform the world.

But the material inequalities of capitalism and the resulting differences in power and substantive exercise of rights have not been the only limits to the liberatory potential of capitalism's earliest promise. The very individualism that provided impetus to the creation of capitalist wealth contradicted the collective and co-operative essence of human society.

By denying mutual dependence and mutual responsibility in favor of self-assertion and self-gain, the liberal capitalist ethic set us adrift to find meaning in our lives only in our material possessions. And by banishing moral issues to the private realm, the very secularization of society that freed people from feudal state oppression has become a limit to the further advance of justice. For the entire power of the capitalist state and public discourse is committed to ignoring ethical matters, including of course the moral issues that arise in the creation of capitalist wealth. The result is that these moral issues are relegated to the "private" arena, considered merely a matter of individual taste. Many liberals have embraced this exclusion of moral discourse from the public arena because, when moral discourse *was* a matter of public concern (in the feudal era), it was also used as an instrument of oppression.

Perhaps as a result, public efforts to confront the limitations of capitalism as a vehicle of justice and human liberation have tended historically to focus on its failure to deliver economic or political equality. The system was criticized for not providing enough material satisfaction or for repressing the rights of women and minorities. Pressured by these often rather limited critiques, the system to some extent responded.

But capitalism simultaneously created a crisis in "meaning." Human beings need to be part of loving relationships, to do meaningful work, and to feel embedded in communities that share a higher spiritual and ethical purpose. Capitalism tore down existing frameworks of meaning and made friendships and loving relationships more problematic.

Friendships and long-term commitments in relationships and families are in crisis because the competitive marketplace rewards us to the extent that we develop personality styles adept at manipulating and controlling others—precisely the kinds of personalities least likely to promote love, intimacy, and commitment. And the breakdown of communities of meaning is powerfully connected to the triumph of individualism and the worship of individual choices as the highest meaning of life—itself a reflection of the capitalist marketplace, which thrives by its ability to generate endless new needs for consumption in people who have come to believe that these needs are simply a manifestation of their own personal choices, a reflection of their ability to define their own lives and find self-fulfillment through consumption of the latest product, therapy, exercise, spiritual discipline, or life-style.

Ironically, those who have confronted capitalism over issues of economic justice have usually restricted their agenda to the failure of the system to deliver material goods and political rights. Quality-of-life issues, the psychological traumas imposed on people by capitalism, questions of deeper human meaning—these are often dismissed as "soft" or "flaky" concerns. One of the weaknesses of Marxism, contributing to its marginalization, has been the reluctance of its adherents to acknowledge and analyze the spiritual dimension of human experience.

Just as surely as capitalism tends to impoverish people materially, so it tends to drain us spiritually. In one of the great ironies of political life in the United States today, it is right-wing champions of the market and classical liberal thought who have most clearly taken up the family crisis, the decline in public values, and the breakup of our communities. Unfairly, they have blamed these crises on the struggle for individual rights, claiming that these struggles (embodied in the civil rights movement and the movements of women and gays) have provided the pernicious individualism that undermines family and community. But as long as critics of capitalism fail to address the crisis in families and communities in a coherent way, fail to help people find a way to cope with the pain they feel in their daily lives, that pain will be manipulated by the right to justify its programs. The prospects for transforming society into a place of justice and human dignity will be all the more remote if the liberal and progressive forces fail to address the psychological and spiritual needs that are just as central to most people as their needs for economic security and political rights.

One step forward would be to reframe the progressive program as one committed to making the world safe for love and intimacy. The centerpiece of progressive pro-family politics could be reflection on the kinds of changes it would take in our workplaces and in our social and economic structures to make the world more likely to produce loving and committed relationships and strong families.

Any progressive pro-family program must reject traditional patriarchal hierarchies of power as fundamentally undermining of loving relationships. We therefore question the conservative fantasy that past societies based on hierarchies of power had stronger, more loving families. It is precisely the ethos of selfishness enthroned in the competitive marketplace that is the greatest and most significant source of the undermining of loving commitments in modern society. This leads us directly into questioning the fundamentals of the capitalist system itself, calling for social change in the name of our demand for a world that is safe for love and intimacy.

One hears sometimes that it is *wrong* to be asking these kinds of questions concerning values and spirituality while so many people are still in the throes of poverty and homelessness domestically, or being economically and politically exploited throughout the world. There is a fear that in talking about the crisis in meaning and the problems of building loving relationships we will find a convenient way to turn our backs on the suffering of others.

This is a legitimate fear, but misguided. The key question to ask is this: how will critics of capitalism ever be in a position where they *could* have the power to solve the issues of poverty and oppression? The answer is this: when they have a mandate to do so from the majority in an advanced capitalist society. But if that majority *experiences* its own life as in pain and responds significantly to those whom they believe can help them deal with that pain, then anyone who wishes to end poverty and oppression *must* address the crisis in meaning. This is both a fundamental political necessity and completely consistent with the programmatic agenda that progressive people have asserted against capital in the quest for better material existence.

The fact that the left has been reluctant to deal with these matters has contributed both to its social isolation and to the internal weaknesses so painfully felt within progressive movements. Lacking any sophisticated understanding of the psychological dynamics that limit our transcendence, the left in the 1960s adopted an existentialist view that we could be whatever we wanted to be by a simple act of will. All protests against "the system" notwithstanding, this neatly mirrors the dominant meritocratic ideology of contemporary capitalism—you can make it if you really try, you can become whoever you want to be if you have the smarts, courage, and energy.

Therefore, when we discovered that we ourselves, and our comrades in the movement, were unable immediately to transcend the sexism, the racism, the self-centeredness and egotism with which we had been raised in this society, we were ruthless toward each other and toward ourselves. We had no principle of compassion, no principle of *rachmones*, through which to understand our own failings. The movement quickly dissolved in a frenzy of self- and other-blaming. Movement activists frequently explained their retreat from politics by quoting a Pogo comic: "We has met the enemy and it is us."

Instead of understanding that we will inevitably be scarred by the inheritance of generations of oppression, we turned on ourselves with a ferocity that soon made most people regard the movement of the late 1960s and early 1970s as not adequately embodying any of the humanity we sought in the larger society. We had no compassion for our own inevitable limitations.

That same lack of compassion was communicated to everyone else. At the moment when mass attention in the United States was focused on the left—in the late 1960s and early 1970s—we projected a disdain for the majority of Americans so strong that the real elite of the society, represented by Nixon and Agnew, could campaign against the left by calling *us* elitists. Their charge stuck and remains central to the way Americans think of the left in the 1980s and 1990s, because the left projected a deep disdain for the American majority. The Weathermen's charge that the Vietnam War, racism, and sexism were the products of the "white skin privilege" of ordinary Americans reflected an attitude that continues to alienate most Americans from liberals and the left. They may not always have the intellectual sophistication or categories to understand every liberal or left-wing ideology, but the American people are acutely sensitive to those who disrespect them and their lives. They correctly sense this disrespect from many liberals and people on the left—and it is this, more than anything else, that guarantees our permanent isolation.

To respect the American public would mean to take seriously the spiritual as well as material pains in their lives as they experience them. A new respect would require us not to pathologize everyone's pain but instead to ask what are the social roots of what is experienced as an individual problem.

The fundamental psychological block to social change in America is rooted in this: the self-blaming that an individualistic and meritocratic society generates. Our dominant ideology teaches us to believe that we are individually responsible for whatever has happened to us—we create our own realities, in the language of mass psychology. It is this belief that paralyzes most of us. Because as we interpret our own pains as reflections of our deepest personal failings, we come to feel so inadequate that we cannot imagine ourselves engaged in struggle to change anything larger.

The right offers a solution to self-blaming: religious and nationalistic communities that offer well-defined enemies who are said to be the source of our problems. The cost: suspension of one's own intellect, adoption of a right-wing program, and commitment to the very economic and political institutions that are *really* the source of the problem. People are eager to adopt these ideologies because it feels good to decrease self-blaming.

A movement with a sympathetic understanding of Jewish liberation theology could offer a much more powerful alternative: a mass psychology of compassion, upon which could be based real programs to deal with both the spiritual and the material degradations imposed on people in capitalist society. How powerful it would be to have occupational stress groups at the workplace or in our unions, or family support groups in our communities, incorporating some of the strengths of the consciousness-raising groups of the women's movement but directing them toward helping people work through some of the aspects of their own personal lives which have been massively shaped and distorted by the dynamics of the larger social and economic structures.

Imagine how much more persuasive our movement would be if we found a way to talk meaningfully and sympathetically about the frustrations that people experience at work and encouraged people to begin to explore what their work world would look like if it were organized to promote their well-being (quickly adding that humanly satisfying work environments are also typically more productive). Imagine a movement that talked about the way people unfairly blame themselves for "not getting ahead"—and talked about the real constraints people face in the competitive marketplace.

How much more integral to people's lives we would be if we fully addressed the ways in which tensions from work get brought home into personal life—sometimes leading people to do everything they can to bury the frustrations, whether with drugs, alcohol, numbing television, or child and spouse abuse. In short, we must help people re-understand their personal lives, replacing inappropriate self-blaming with compassion for oneself and others. A mass psychology of compassion, practical *rachmones*, must become a central part of any progressive movement.

Here the lessons of Jewish teachings and history become important.

The fight to transform ourselves and our society becomes tempered with the compassion of understanding for human frailty. As I argued earlier in this chapter, Judaism is a religion whose commitment to reverence for the universe goes hand in hand with a commitment to the struggle for justice. Judaism makes central to its ontological commitment an awareness that the world is governed by a principle of freedom, not a principle of necessity. God is the force that makes possible the triumph of good by creating a world in which human beings have the ability to recognize an objective moral truth and the capacity to remake the world so that it is in harmony with that moral truth. But Judaism simultaneously stresses the need for compassion for the ways we will fail to achieve all the transcendence toward the good that we correctly strive for.

I do not argue that others should become Jewish—but I do argue that any liberatory social movement has much to learn from studying the development, rituals, and inner life of Judaism and attempting to appropriate creatively from these some of the wisdom that has made Judaism survive, particularly its delicate balancing of the demand for transcendence and the need for compassion.

We should, of course, never give up the hard-earned gains won in the struggles for individual liberty, human rights, and material advancement in capitalist society. But we will be able to advance still further if we recognize that what we have won is within a framework that revalidates the importance of some larger "we." We must project the notion that human beings are to be valued not only for what makes them distinct from others but for what makes us like one another in a human family. A healthy human being is not one who has learned to stand alone but one who can couple personal independence with the simultaneous need for others, who can allow him- or herself to be linked to and dependent upon a family and a community and, ultimately, a people.

It is here, in learning that we are each of us part of a larger "we" that transcends this historical moment and links the generations one to another in an everlasting quest for *tikkun olam,* for the healing and repairing of this world, that we can find some deep source of strength even as we accept and have compassion for our own and everyone else's human limitations.

III

STRUCTURES OF
MODERN CAPITALISM

6

MAN-MADE STARVATION IN AFRICA

Ann Seidman

In 1984, and again in 1988, films of emaciated women and children starving in Ethiopia invaded comfortable United States living rooms. Many compassionate U.S. citizens sent dollars, checks, even food parcels to relief agencies, hoping to help save some of the lives they had seen literally fading into oblivion on their television screens.

But religious and development-oriented groups working in Africa have long argued that starvation reaches far beyond the borders of Ethiopia to the disparate regions of a vast continent—a land mass three times the size of the United States, with a population exceeding 500 million. There, starvation, or diseases that malnourished bodies cannot fight, kill as many as a third to half of all children under five years of age. The average African born in the 1980s could expect to live only half as long as the average U.S. citizen.[1]

Yet in the 1980s Africa produced and shipped millions of tons of food and agricultural raw materials to the peoples and factories of Europe and the United States (see Table 6.1).

The conventional wisdom conveyed by the U.S. media—that drought, combined with a general decline in African food production, causes widespread hunger—misses the point. It fails to expose the roots of starvation planted deep in a man-made institutional system imposed on the newly independent countries of Africa by a century or more of colonial rule. Dominated by wealthy minorities, these inherited political economic structures direct Africa's best lands and more modern productive sectors to the export of low-cost crude agricultural crops and minerals to uncertain world markets.

Meanwhile, the vast majority of Africans, struggling with outmoded technologies to wrest food crops from infertile, poorly watered soils, barely subsist; they are chronically on the verge of starvation. In the

1980s the international recession and mounting world debt, coupled with drought and regional wars, pushed millions of peasants in all corners of the continent over that edge.

This chapter attempts to explain, first, how historically shaped institutions in Africa have marginalized the cultivation of food and those who produce it; second, why the international recession, drought, debt, and wars combined in the 1980s to cause widespread starvation; and finally, why religious and development-oriented groups have organized to urge a U.S. policy for Africa in support of liberation, peace, and development.

INSTITUTIONAL STRUCTURES

The pattern of imposed colonial rule in Africa varied from region to region and country to country, but everywhere it had essentially the same consequences. For a hundred years or more, English, French, Portuguese, and other colonial regimes shaped their institutional structures to coerce their African colonies to produce low-cost mineral or agricultural raw materials for export to their home-based factories. Everywhere, the colonialists devised land policies, taxes, marketing structures, credit, subsidies, agricultural research, and education to support relatively modern production only in enclaves dominated by colonial firms and, in some cases, settler farmers.

An analysis of Africa's colonial past helps us to understand why, as Table 6.1 shows, most African economies in the 1980s were still primarily engaged in the production of one or a few mineral or agricultural exports.

The Colonial Heritage

In West Africa, relatively few Europeans settled as farmers; they relied primarily on Africans themselves to grow export crops. Some West Africans have jokingly urged erection of a monument to the malarial mosquito, which scared away many Europeans. Others noted that their forebears fought for decades to keep out would-be settlers; in the Gold Coast (now Ghana), for example, it wasn't until just before World War I that the Ashanti lost their last battle against better-armed British troops.

Whatever the reason, instead of settling European farmers in West Africa, and in present Uganda and parts of Tanzania as well, the colo-

TABLE 6.1

Country (date) Exports	$ mil	% of Total Exports	Country (date) Exports	$ mil	% of Total Exports
Angola ('81)	1,874	100	Niger ('81)	454	100
Petroleum	1,539	82	Uranium	275	60
Burkino Faso ('83)	56	100	Cotton	22	5
Cotton	31	55	Rwanda ('80)	73	100
Burundi ('85)	109	100	Coffee	40	54
Coffee	98	90	Tea	12	16
Cameroon ('83)	1,082	100	Cotton	75	7
Petroleum	427	39	Asbestos	67	6
Coffee	195	18	Iron and steel	176	17
Cocoa	153	14	Ferro-alloys	114	11
Central African			Senegal ('84)	534	100
Republic ('80)	115	100	Groundnuts	82	15
Coffee	31	27	Phosphates	58	9
Cork and wood	33	29	Mineral fuels	98	18
Diamonds	28	24	Cotton fabrics	16	3
Congo ('80)	955	100	Sierra Leone ('85)	147	100
Petrol	855	89	Coffee	13	9
Ethiopia ('85)	337	100	Cocoa	23	16
Coffee	209	62	Vanadium	23	16
Ghana ('82)	717	100	Diamonds	45	31
Cocoa	418	58	Somalia ('81)	151	100
Aluminum[a]	168	23	Live animals	136	90
Ivory Coast ('85)	2,669	100	Sudan ('82)	499	100
Coffee	1,516	57	Unmilled cereals	116	23
Cocoa	848	32	Groundnuts	34	7
Liberia ('84)	449	100	Oil seeds	53	11
Iron ore	279	62	Cotton	125	25
Rubber	91	20	Togo ('84)	191	100
Madagascar ('85)	286	100	Cocoa	48	25
Coffee	103	36	Cotton	16	8
Spices	85	29	Phosphates	93	49
Mali ('82)	233	100	United Republic		
Live animals	84	36	of Tanzania ('81)	563	100
Cotton	130	49	Coffee	151	27
Mauritania ('84)	297	100	Tea	19	3
Iron ore	145	49	Spices[b]	52	9
Fish	136	46	Cotton	77	14

Continued on next page.

TABLE 6.1
CONTINUED

Country (date) Exports	$ mil	% of Total Exports	Country (date) Exports	$ mil	% of Total Exports
United Republic			Copper	313	35
of Tanzania (cont.)			Base metals	127	14
Sisal	32	6	*Zambia ('82)*	1,021	100
Diamonds	30	5	Copper	919	90
Zaire ('78)	899	100	*Zimbabwe ('83)*	1,026	100
Coffee	186	21	Tobacco	228	22

SOURCE: United Nations, *1986 International Trade Statistics Yearbook*, vol. 1 (New York: United Nations, 1988).

[a] The U.S. transnational corporation, Kaiser, imported alumina (instead of using Ghana's), processed it using Volta Dam electric power (for which it paid two-thirds less than did Ghanaian consumers), and exported it as aluminum; i.e., it profited from cheap hydroelectric power.

[b] Produced on the island of Zanzibar, which after independence joined Tanganyika to constitute the United Republic of Tanzania.

nial authorities found ways to force African peasants to devote more and more fertile land to the cultivation of export crops: coffee, cocoa beans, vegetable oil seeds, and cotton. The French and Portuguese used outright forced labor. The British imposed taxes, the payment of which required Africans to earn cash by cultivating export crops. In all cases, colonial buying firms, working closely with colonial banks, purchased crops from the peasants at low prices and shipped them overseas for processing in their own factories and then for sale—at a handsome profit—to the final consumers.[2]

Over the years, West African peasants cultivated more and more land near the ports and railroads to grow export crops, tying their national economies ever more tightly into uncertain world markets dominated by a handful of oligopolistic colonial firms. In more remote savanna areas, forced labor and taxes compelled hundreds of thousands of males to migrate to work as sharecroppers in the expanding export crop regions. The luckier Africans who owned land in those regions typically kept two-thirds of the income they obtained from the sale of the crops, paying the sharecroppers only one-third—not enough to support their families back home.

Meanwhile, using hoes and cutlasses in remote hinterlands, the women, children, and old folks could not clear and irrigate new lands to expand staple crops to feed the growing numbers of people engaged in producing and exporting minerals and export crops. Even in good years, they could barely grow enough to feed themselves. In Chapter 4, Pamela Brubaker discusses the special implications for women resulting from this pattern of colonial development.

In southern, central, and most of eastern Africa the colonial states, backed by superior military might, turned over to European settlers vast estates spreading over the most fertile, best-watered lands, pushing the African populations into overcrowded, infertile "reserves." Discriminatory marketing, extension, and credit facilities, combined with hut and poll taxes to force peasants to earn cash, left African males with little choice but to migrate to work at foreign-owned estates or mines. Their wives, children, and elders remained at home on neglected reserves, supposedly supporting themselves. The colonial settlers and mining companies then used the fact that the men were separated from "self-supporting" families to justify paying their workers extremely low wages.[3]

Consider Zimbabwe: At independence in 1980, fewer than six thousand settler and corporate farms stretched across the fertile, well-watered half of the nation's land area. The average estate spread over thousands of acres, although typically at least half lay un- or underutilized. Meanwhile, past government policies had crowded more than 900,000 African peasant families onto so-called Tribal Trust Lands—after independence euphemistically renamed "Communal Areas." Even the pre-independence regime admitted that these areas could support only half the number of Africans forced to live there. In 1980, per capita incomes averaged less than fifty U.S. dollars a year. Most of the men and some women had no option but to leave their families to migrate in search of paid jobs. Some 300,000 workers lived and worked on white-owned commercial farms, earning wages that averaged about twenty U.S. dollars a month. Studies showed that 80 percent of their children suffered severe malnutrition.[4]

Apartheid South Africa represented the culmination of the distorted pattern of institutions imposed by the colonial settlers. There, Europeans—a fifth of the population—exercised state power to push all Africans (except those who worked in white-owned factories, farms, mines, or kitchens) onto scattered fragments of land, so-called *bantustans* ("homelands"), which constituted barely 13 percent of the nation's total land area. In the 1980s the *bantustan* population reached twelve to fourteen million people, roughly half the nation's black majority, many of them with neither land to farm nor jobs. Those who could migrated to work for whites at wages far below the poverty line. Without land, paid jobs, or social services, the millions of women, children, and old men left behind suffered chronic hunger. Thousands of malnourished children and older folk died annually from curable diseases such as pneumonia and tuberculosis.[5]

High in the mountainous northeastern part of Africa, the armies of Ethiopia's emperors had managed to fight off outright European colonial rule. Nevertheless, especially after World War II, the imperial government accepted the orthodoxy proposed by its then U.S. advisers.[6] Landlords pushed peasants, who had formerly grown food crops, off their lands and planted coffee to sell on the world market, about a third of it to the United States. Like the former colonies elsewhere on the continent, Ethiopia depended primarily on coffee exports to earn the foreign exchange it needed to import manufacturing equipment and foodstuffs for its growing urban population. The 1974 drought and resulting famine aggravated the unrest that culminated in a military coup, followed by a major land reform. The new military government still encouraged the peasants to grow coffee, however; its leaders needed foreign exchange to buy not only machinery and equipment but also military hardware in order to pursue their destructive efforts to perpetuate their rule over neighboring peoples.

Marginal Postcolonial Changes

As the winds of change blew south across the African continent after World War II, more than fifty new African states attained political independence from their former colonial rulers. Nevertheless, often advised by World Bank and International Monetary Fund (IMF) experts, their governments typically sought to encourage peasants to grow even more export crops. Government officials viewed exports as a primary source of revenue to finance new schools, hospitals, roads, and ports as well as to support their swelling bureaucracies.

Meanwhile, in their efforts to expand export crops, most of the new African governments tended to neglect the production and storage of foodstuffs to meet their populations' needs. Women, children, and old folks, still struggling with hand hoes to till worn-out soils without fertilizers or irrigation, often chopped down trees for "free" fuel. These activities fostered the spread of desertification. At the same time, increasing numbers of young people migrated to the cities to escape rural poverty, and more and more countries became dependent on imported foodstuffs to feed their growing urban populations.[7]

By the 1980s, regardless of the differing historical circumstances and patterns of land settlement across the continent, the farmers of most African states had intensified their competition to sell more export crops to the transnational firms that straddled the world markets. A handful of such corporations, including Nestlé, bought most of the cocoa beans sold by Ghana, Nigeria, Togo, and the Ivory Coast and the coffee beans grown in the Ivory Coast, Kenya, Tanzania, and Ethiopia. They still shipped the beans for processing to their own factories, located in Europe and the United States or, in the case of southern African exports, increasingly in South Africa. A few giant tobacco firms, led by the British American Tobacco Company and the South African firm Rothmans, purchased African leaf from Zimbabwe, Malawi, and Tanzania. Every year, freighters carried peasant-grown peanuts and cotton, harvested from acreages stretching from Sudan through Senegal and Chad down to Tanzania and Zimbabwe, to provide cheap raw materials for European and North American factories.[8]

Like their colonial predecessors, these transnational agribusinesses maximized their global profits by holding down the prices they paid to the exporting countries. For example, Nestlé alone reported that its 1980–86 profits before taxes totaled about $8.5 billion, after taxes about $4.5 billion.[9] The fact that even after taxes Nestlé's global profits totaled about three times all the U.S. aid to southern Africa from 1946 to 1985 suggests, from an African perspective, the significance of this sum.[10]

Investing primarily to stimulate the independent African countries' expansion of crude mineral and crop exports, foreign firms drained away significant shares of the locally generated investable surplus. For example, in every year except two since Ghana became the first sub-Saharan African country to attain independence, U.S. investors sent back to the United States—as profits, interest, dividends, high salaries, and fees—more income than they brought into the continent.[11] Estimates indicate that transnational investors remitted to their home nations some 25 percent of the gross domestic product of Zambia and as much as 40 percent of GDP in still-to-be-liberated Namibia.[12]

In addition to this direct extraction of investable surplus, transnational firms indirectly drained potential investment funds by paying low prices for the crops they purchased from competing African countries. After processing the crops, the firms reaped high profits by charging much higher prices for the finished manufactures they sold to the final consumers—including buyers in African countries themselves. This practice constituted the underlying cause of the worsening terms of trade that forced many if not most African countries, especially in the late 1970s and 1980s, to borrow heavily abroad.[13] Amata Miller further analyzes and reflects on the problem of terms of trade in Chapter 7.

The example of tobacco purchased and processed in the United States illustrates the extent of the African countries' loss of potential surplus. Although they produced the essential raw material, and the manufacture of cigarettes and other final products constitutes a relatively simple process, tobacco-exporting countries retained only about 10 percent of the final value of the finished products. Tobacco-buying and -manufacturing oligopolies such as the British American Tobacco Company received about half the remaining value, out of which they paid the manufacturing and distribution costs, keeping the rest as profit. The other half was paid in taxes to the U.S. federal and state governments.[14]

In other words, the tobacco-growing countries lose to foreign firms and those firms' home governments nine of every ten dollars of the value of the cigarettes finally sold. Even though the leaf-purchasing companies must pay for transport, further processing, and marketing of the cigarettes, their profits have remained high. In the four years from 1983 to 1986, alone, for example, the British American Tobacco Company reported total profits of $6.9 billion before taxes, and $4 billion after taxes.[15]

It should be noted that to the extent that tax revenues in developed countries go up because Third World tobacco growers receive such low prices for their leaf, the growers subsidize First World governments. If the developed countries such as the United States simply returned the revenues obtained by taxing finished tobacco products, the leaf-growing countries would receive more than double the income their tobacco currently generates.[16]

Abortive Attempts to Industrialize

In the nearly three decades during which most African states attained political independence, their so-called "modern" export enclaves became increasingly dependent on expanding crude agricultural exports to finance the import not only of food but also of other manufactured goods: luxuries and semi-luxuries for high-income groups, and machinery and equipment for their modern agricultural and mining sectors. In an effort to reduce this growing external dependence, many African governments sought, by creating a hospitable investment climate, to attract foreign investments in new local industries.

The few manufacturing firms that came to the politically independent African countries, however, invested primarily in last-stage processing and assembly factories. They seldom processed locally grown food or fibers to boost local employment, incomes, and consumption. They usually imported their machinery, equipment, parts, and materials, thus requiring increased expenditure of the scarce foreign exchange earnings generated by the host countries' crude mineral and agricultural exports. They manufactured mainly luxuries for the more well-to-do, and a few semi-luxuries such as beer and cigarettes for urban wage earners. Located in urban centers, they tended to be relatively capital-intensive, providing few jobs for the growing numbers of unemployed.[17]

Transnational Corporate Investments in South Africa

Instead of investing in integrated industries to help the independent African states become more self-reliant, most transnational corporate managers apparently preferred to finance factories in South Africa. There, in the land of apartheid, they helped to build almost half the industrial capacity of the entire African continent. Even transnational agribusinesses, such as Nestlé and the British American Tobacco Company, located most of their African manufacturing operations not in the independent countries from which they bought crude agricultural produce but in South Africa. U.S. manufacturing firms alone poured over three-quarters of their post–World War II investment in Africa into South Africa's industrial sector.[18]

Providing the sophisticated technologies that enabled the minority regime to perpetuate its repressive rule at home and to dominate the independent countries of the region, foreign investors helped transform South Africa into a regional industrial subcenter.[19] From their South African regional headquarters, transnational manufacturing firms penetrated the neighboring countries' economies, siphoning out locally generated investable surpluses by buying their cheap raw materials and selling them high-priced manufactures—leaving their economies still primarily dependent on the export of crude or semi-processed materials to South Africa, Europe, the United States, or Japan.[20]

In short, by the 1980s the political economies of Africa had, if anything, become more rather than less dependent on the export of minerals and agricultural produce to transnational trading and manufacturing firms, which had set up their regional headquarters in apartheid South Africa and intensified their domination of African export markets. The spreading cultivation of export crops had increasingly marginalized the cultivation of food and those who grew it. Women, using outmoded tools to grow 70–80 percent of Africa's food crops in neglected hinterlands, could barely feed their own families, let alone produce enough surplus to sell to the mushrooming urban–export enclave populations. Malnutrition and hunger-related diseases remained rife throughout much of the African countryside, from the Ethiopian highlands to South Africa's overcrowded *bantustans*.

THE CRISIS OF THE 1980S

In the 1980s a combination of international recessions and growing debt, repeated and prolonged droughts, and military conflicts pushed the rural populations of many of the fragile, externally dependent economies of sub-Saharan Africa over the line from chronic malnourishment to outright starvation.

The International Economic Crisis

So-called recessions in the developed countries curtailed demand for the exports on which sub-Saharan countries relied to earn the foreign exchange they needed to buy machinery, equipment, and the increasing amounts of foodstuffs needed to support their expanding export sectors. As a result, their export prices fell dramatically, slashing their foreign exchange earnings. In the fourth quarter of 1977, for example, Ethiopia, the Ivory Coast, Uganda, and Tanzania were selling coffee for $2.68 per pound, but by 1983 the highest world coffee price—despite considerable fluctuation—was only a little more than half that.[21] This meant that the peasants in those countries had to cultivate almost twice as much coffee per year to earn the same amount of foreign exchange for their country as they had six years earlier.

In terms of real purchasing power, the value of other exports also slumped, while international inflationary pressures pushed up the cost of imports, including oil and manufactured goods.[22] In country after country, lack of foreign exchange to buy petroleum, spare parts, materials, and equipment led to layoffs and growing unemployment in the import-dependent modern sectors. By the mid-1980s, for example, lack of essential inputs forced most factories of Zambia and Tanzania to operate at less than half their capacity.[23] In 1985, as rains threatened to rot maize stacked under canvas in eastern Zambian depots, shortages of gas, tires, and spare parts hindered truckers from carrying the food to people in southern Zambia, southwest Zimbabwe, and northeast Botswana, where drought had destroyed their crops.[24]

The Impact of Drought

Throughout the continent, repeated and prolonged droughts aggravated the impact of the crisis. The use of the best, most well-watered lands for export crops meant that drought hit hardest the marginal, neglected food-producing hinterlands. In Ethiopia, years of drought forced people living in the fragmented overcrowded lands of Wollo and Tigrai to sell their cattle, eat their seed, and leave their lands—to crowd into the food distribution centers starkly pictured on U.S. television screens. As the blistering sun withered crops in the less-publicized savanna lands of Sudan, Mali, and Niger and parched the peasant farm areas of Zambia, Zimbabwe, Botswana, and Mozambique, hundreds of thousands of peasants in those countries, too, ate the last of their seed, sold their livestock, and migrated to the towns in a desperate search for help.

IMF "Conditions"

Drought, coupled with an inability to earn enough foreign exchange to buy essential imports, forced more and more African governments to borrow heavily abroad. Many turned for help to the International Monetary Fund. Pursuing monetarist policies, the IMF imposed austerity measures as a condition of its aid. Regardless of the objective factors causing each individual country's difficulties, the IMF has insisted on reduced government spending and the layoff of government workers. It has increased taxes on lower-income groups. And it has demanded devaluation of the national currency, which raises the prices paid for all the imports—including the increasing amounts of foodstuffs—on which the typical economy depends.[25]

Further, although African governments have the potential capacity to reduce their countries' external dependence, IMF experts have insisted on decreased state participation in their economies. It has pressed instead for government measures that would further "open up" African economies to "international market forces," assuming (while ignoring evidence of transnational corporate domination) that competition will stimulate increased efficiency.

In sum, from Sudan in the north to Zimbabwe in the south, far from ameliorating the impact of international recession and drought, IMF policies have tended to impose the burden of the resulting crisis on both the rural and the urban poor.[26]

Intensified Militarization and War

In several parts of the African continent, militarization and localized warfare aggravated the negative impact of adverse weather and economic conditions on peasant populations. Wars not only diverted funds from development programs but also killed or maimed tens of thousands of African peasants.

Unfortunately, instead of fostering peaceful solutions, U.S. policies especially in southern Africa aggravated the factors leading to military conflict. Despite repeated droughts and growing hunger in the 1980s, the United States increased food aid to Africa by only 40 percent—but U.S. military sales in the region soared by 150 percent. The number of states receiving U.S. military "aid" jumped from nineteen to thirty-six.[27]

The basic disregard for the lives of the African people underlying U.S. policy in the area was clearly expressed by Assistant Secretary of State Chester Crocker—the architect of President Ronald Reagan's so-called "Constructive Engagement" policy—when he declared in 1981, "First, southern Africa is a region of unquestioned importance to U.S. and Western economic and strategic interests."[28] Behind this assertion lay the reality of the U.S. transnational corporate investments in South Africa's mines and manufacturing, and the desire to project the domination of capital throughout southern Africa.

The result has been enormously destructive warfare in Mozambique, Angola, and elsewhere. In Angola alone, by 1987 nearly thirty thousand people, mostly peasants, had lost arms, legs, or eyes to U.S.-supplied Claymore (antipersonnel) land mines. Hundreds of thousands of peasants deserted the countryside, and over two million Angolans faced starvation.[29]

TOWARD LIBERATION, PEACE, AND DEVELOPMENT

Many development-oriented organizations and religious groups working in Africa rejected long ago the common explanation that drought and the low productivity of the peasants are the sole causes of starvation in Africa. Instead, as the analysis outlined above becomes more widely understood, there is growing recognition of the consequences of inherited institutional structures, aggravated by mounting foreign debt and the world economic crisis. Drought certainly contributes to famine. But the historical and social context of African countries, made all the more precarious for the mass of peasant food producers by war, explains why drought pushes millions of the most vulnerable among the African populations into conditions of outright starvation.

Over a thirty- to forty-year period the southern African independent states, working together with a liberated South Africa, could achieve self-reliant, balanced agricultural and industrial development capable of providing increasingly productive employment opportunities and rising living standards for all the region's inhabitants. Plentiful natural and human resources are available, but African economic structures and the purposes of U.S. intervention in the area prevent progress.

Ironically, if southern Africa could emerge as a vibrant economic region, it would provide a growing market for machinery and equipment produced by U.S. workers. Thus, support for the full liberation of South Africa is not only an essential first step in a program designed to end hunger throughout the African continent; it would also help to lay a sound foundation for peace, jobs, and social justice on both sides of the Atlantic.[30]

Notes

1. *World Population Data Sheet 1983* (Washington, D.C.: Population Reference Bureau, 1983).

2. For detailed discussion and further information, see Ann Seidman, *Planning for Development in Sub-Saharan Africa* (New York: Praeger; and Dar es Salaam: Tanzania Publishing House, 1974).

3. The income that colonial government statisticians estimated as sufficient for the average African family of six to survive was typically based on the assumption that the family spent over 50 percent of its income on food and most of the rest for a one- or two-room shack and a few clothes, leaving almost nothing for education or recreation; see, e.g., the cost-of-living indexes in the typical statistical digest published by almost all former British colonial governments.

4. For detailed analysis of the land question and the consequences for the Zimbabwean peasant, see Zimbabwe, *Report of the Commission of Inquiry into Incomes, Prices, and Conditions of Service* (Salisbury: Government Printer, 1981). The commission was chaired by Roger Riddell.

5. For details, see Ann Seidman, *The Roots of Crisis in Southern Africa* (Trenton, N.J.: Africa World Press, 1985).

6. In the post–World War II era, until 1974, the U.S. government was Ethiopia's main source of extensive military and economic aid. After the 1974 coup, when the U.S. refused to support their efforts to carry out land and other reforms, Ethiopia's new military leaders, many of them trained in the United States, turned to the Soviet Union for economic and military aid.

7. The growing literature describing the consequences of these policies includes Paul Harrison, *The Greening of Africa: Breaking Through in the Battle for Land and Food* (London: IIED/Earthscan, 1987); Jane Hayes, "Not Enough Wood for Women: How Modernization Limits Access to Resources in the Domestic Economy of Rural Kenya" (Ph.D. diss., Clark University, Worcester, Mass., 1986); and Erik Eckholm et al., *Fuelwood: The Energy Crisis That Won't Go Away* (London: IIED/Earthscan, 1984).

8. Carl Widstrand, ed., *Multinational Firms in Africa* (Dakar, Senegal: African Institute for Economic Development and Planning; Uppsala: Scandinavian Institute for African Studies, 1975). For southern Africa, see Ann Seidman and Neva Makgetla, *Outposts of Monopoly Capitalism: Southern Africa in the Changing Global Economy* (Westport, Conn.: Lawrence Hill, 1980).

9. *Moody's Industrial Manual* (New York: Moody's Investors Service, 1987).

10. U.S. Agency for International Development (AID), *Annex I, Africa: Fiscal Years 1975 and 1986* (Washington, D.C.: AID, 1984, 1985).

11. *Survey of Current Business*, published by the U.S. Department of Commerce, provides annual reports on foreign investments in its August, September, and October issues.

12. See Republic of Zambia, "Analytical Balance of Payments," in *Monthly Digest of Statistics* (published monthly in Lusaka by the Central Statistical Office); and R. H.

Green, report to workshop, "Towards Economic Development Strategy Options for Independent Namibia," held by the UN Institute for Namibia in Lusaka, April 1982.

13. See *International Financial Statistics: Country Reports*, published monthly by the International Monetary Fund, for current consequences of the imports, exports, and balance of payments of African states.

14. See Ann Seidman, "A Comparative Analysis of the Tobacco Industries of Kenya, Thailand, and Zimbabwe" (paper presented to workshop sponsored by the UN Center on Transnational Corporations in New York, 1983).

15. *Moody's Industrial Manual* (1987).

16. Furthermore, if they could reinvest those additional sums to create more balanced, integrated national economies, they might reduce their dependence on the export of tobacco, which has negative health effects on consumers.

17. See Ann Seidman, "An Explanation of the Distorted Growth of Import Substitution Industry: The Zambian Case," *Journal of Modern African Studies* 12, no. 4 (1974); and Ann Seidman, "The Need for an Appropriate Industrial Strategy to Support Peasant Agriculture," *Journal of Modern African Studies* 24, no. 4 (1986).

18. See *Survey of Current Business*.

19. Seidman and Makgetla, *Outposts of Monopoly Capitalism*.

20. Tied into the South African Customs Union, Botswana, Lesotho, and Swaziland buy as much as four-fifths of their manufactures from South Africa, while their unemployed males—like those from South Africa's own *bantustans*—migrate to South Africa's urban centers in search of (low-paid) jobs. Road and railway links, as well as South African institutional ties, destabilization, and IMF pressures (see below), force Malawi, Zimbabwe, Zambia, and even Mozambique to buy almost half of South Africa's manufactured exports. See Seidman, *The Roots of Crisis*.

21. See the International Monetary Fund's *International Financial Statistics*, supp. vol. 12 (1987).

22. Ibid. E.g., the world price for cocoa beans, which reached $1.84 per lb. in U.S. dollars in 1977, hovered at best between $1.00 and $1.59 in the 1980s. The tea price, which rose to $1.62 per lb. in 1977, fluctuated between $0.86 and $1.07 in the 1980s with the exception of a brief spurt to $1.55 in 1984. On the other hand, prices soared on the manufactured goods that Africans had to buy. Given 1980 = 100, the indexes of the prices of manufactured exports from the United States rose to 124; from the United Kingdom, to 143; from West Germany, to 118; and from France, to 194.

23. Seidman, "The Need for an Appropriate Industrial Strategy."

24. During a research trip to southeastern Zambia, I saw for myself the maize piled high under scanty canvas coverings, waiting for transport.

25. IMF experts assumed that higher taxes on companies would hinder private investment, ignoring evidence that instead of reinvesting, those companies tended to remit home a major share of their locally generated profits, as the *Survey of Current Business* reveals.

26. Numerous critiques have exposed the counterproductive consequences of the IMF's typical package of "conditions." For discussion and an annotated bibliography, see Ann Seidman, *Money, Banking, and Public Finance in Africa* (London: Zed Press, 1986).

27. Beth Perry, talk presented to a meeting of religious and private voluntary organizations concerned with aid to Africa, at Maryknoll Fathers and Brothers, Maryknoll, New York, May 14, 1985.

28. Chester Crocker, prepared statement before the U.S. House of Representatives Subcommittee on Africa, Committee on Foreign Affairs, hearing of September 16, 1981: *United States Policy towards Southern Africa: Focus on Namibia, Angola, and South Africa* (Washington, D.C.: U.S. Government Printing Office, 1983).

29. Cf. V. Mallet, "Fighting Brings Hunger to a Land of Plenty," *Financial Times* (London), June 29, 1988.

30. For a more detailed development of this thesis, see Ann Seidman, *Apartheid, Militarism, and the U.S. Southeast* (Princeton, N.J.: Africa World Press, 1990).

7

GLOBAL ECONOMIC STRUCTURES:
THEIR HUMAN IMPLICATIONS

Amata Miller, IHM

We live in a world in which one in four persons suffers from hunger on a daily basis, in which the economic gap between rich and poor nations continues to widen, and in which poor nations labor under crushing debt burdens. In this world, living standards decline inexorably year by year in many nations of Africa and Latin America. At the same time, people in the rich nations of the Northern Hemisphere, with less than one-quarter of the world's population, consume over three-quarters of the world's production of goods and services each year. These few chilling facts lay out in human terms some of the effects of the operations of the global economy.

Economists and religious leaders are among those who have sought to understand why these realities exist. Grappling with the questions from their different perspectives, some among them have come to similar conclusions. This chapter brings together the insights of economists and of contemporary leaders of the Roman Catholic Church about the functioning of the global economy. Because the subject is such a complex one, it is especially important to clarify at the outset my own perspective.

First, my focus is on the impact of the international economy on the people of the poorest countries of Africa, Asia, and Latin America for whom the "magic of the market" has belied the promises of its proponents. My discussion probes the working of what Pope John Paul II has called "structures of sin" in the modern world.[1] The failure in practice of conventional neoclassical economics to meet the needs of the poor of the world has attracted the attention of political economists as well as theologians.[2] Economists have had three decades to analyze the effects of applying the conventional wisdom about economic growth in newly independent nations. Church leaders and thinkers have reflected on these same effects—on the lives of the people of these nations. Their reflections have led religious leaders to call for a "preferential option for the poor."

Second, this chapter draws on the economic analysis of those who find neoclassical economic theories inadequate for understanding current global economic realities. These critics of the conventional wisdom, who include but are not limited to economists working in the Keynesian and Marxist traditions, are looking for better tools with which to address the question "Why are the poor being left behind?"[3]

Third, my method employs the schema called the "Pastoral Circle," originally set forth by the Center of Concern in Washington, D.C., to embody the method of theologizing of which "liberation theology" is one expression.[4] This method begins with reflection on the experience of injustice from the perspective of the affected group. Next, the insights of the social and behavioral sciences are explicitly brought to bear on the reality in a process of social analysis. Then, in a process of theological reflection, the realities newly understood are confronted with the principles drawn from the biblical and ethical tradition. This in turn leads to action planning by the affected community and further reflection on the new experiences.

Fourth, one clearly asks different questions about the functioning of the global economy from the vantage point of those marginalized by it than one would from the perspectives of its beneficiaries. I present my analysis in the spirit of the late Michael Harrington's 1977 book, *The Vast Majority: Journey to the World's Poor*. Harrington observed that the people of the United States are among the most generous the world has ever seen, responding with compassion to every kind of disaster afflicting both friend and foe. But, he challenged, most Americans in their "cruel innocence" do not have the slightest understanding that at the root of the human suffering they deplore is a global system dominated by the U.S. economy. He concluded that if Americans could understand this, it could be the beginning of change.[5]

This chapter is grounded in the belief that combining the insights of the social sciences with the motivational power of religious faith will help generate the new political will required for action for social transformation toward a more just and humane world.

DEVELOPMENT OF CATHOLIC
SOCIAL TEACHING SINCE JOHN XXIII

My reflections on the realities of global poverty are based on the modern social teachings of the Roman Catholic Church contained in the encyclicals of the popes, in the documents of Vatican Council II and the 1971 Synod of Bishops, and in the pastoral letters of various national conferences of bishops. Of these last, the documents of the Latin American bishops' meetings at Medellín in 1968 and Puebla in 1979 have most profoundly influenced the Church's teaching with regard to the global economic order. In addition, the 1986 letter of the U.S. bishops, *Economic Justice for All* (cited below), is valuable as a specific application of the tradition of Catholic social teaching to the U.S. economy and its role in the world, particularly as that role affects the poor nations.

The recognition that the structures of *both* capitalist and socialist systems are proving inadequate to respond to the needs of the poor of the world has developed progressively over thirty years in Catholic social teaching. Each of the papal documents reflects the times in which it was written and, in particular, the conclusions of economists and other social scientists of the various periods in which they were issued. John XXIII shared the optimism about development on the Western model characteristic of the First Development Decade in the 1960s. Paul VI reflected the learnings of the late 1960s that the previous twenty years of development strategy had benefited some in the poor nations but left the poorest behind and even worse off than before. John Paul II, writing in the 1980s, called the existing structures "incapable" of dealing with the scandal of world poverty and named them "sinful structures." Thus, the popes have come to share the verdict of radical political economists that minimal reform is not enough to meet basic human needs.

Modern Catholic social teaching began with Pope Leo XIII's 1891 encyclical, *Rerum Novarum* (On the condition of workers), which identified the "social question" as that of the relations between labor and capital. In 1931, Pius XI in *Quadragesimo Anno* (On reconstructing the social order), widening the scope to take in the national economy's failure to provide employment and just wages, addressed the "reconstruction of the social order" within a nation. In the 1940s and 1950s, Pius XII wrote extensively about issues of war and peace. Near the end of his papacy in the late 1950s, he began to address international issues of justice. But it was the 1961 encyclical of John XXIII, *Mater et Magistra* (On Christianity and social progress), which first recognized that the "social question" had become worldwide.[6]

In that letter John XXIII reviewed the social teachings of his predecessors, beginning with Leo XIII, and set forth the foundation of his own teaching in the basic principles of human dignity, social responsibility, and subsidiarity. Describing the realities of the world as he saw them, he identified the imbalance between rich and poor nations as the most pressing problem of the modern world, one for which all must share responsibility because of our common membership in the human family and because of the growing interdependence among nations.[7] This theme was reiterated in John's next encyclical, *Pacem in Terris* (Peace on earth), and in the Vatican Council document *Gaudium et Spes* (On the Church in the modern world).

Pope John, who in the early 1960s "opened the windows" of the Catholic Church to look out on the world as it really was and to let the real world in, was optimistic about the possibility of human collaboration once people understood the need for it, and about the potential of capitalism on the Western model to bring about a more just and humane world for all peoples.[8] In this, he reflected the time in which he lived. The belief that a rising tide would lift all boats was widely shared in the early 1960s. Through "welfare state" programs the democratic capitalist nations of Europe and North America seemed capable of ameliorating the ill effects of the free market on the citizens it marginalized. Economic development on the Western model, it was assumed, would soon be experienced by the poor nations as well. Pope John therefore relied on the promise of gradual reform and did not criticize the structures of capitalism as his successors would.

Nonetheless, Pope John did direct Catholic social teaching into new paths. He restated the Church's long tradition regarding the rights of private property—that ownership does not confer absolute rights, since "in the right of private property there is rooted a social responsibility." In a much controverted passage about "socialization" he recognized the "multiplication of social relationships" in the ever more complex interdependence among persons and nations. He accepted the need for state intervention in the economy to a greater degree than had his predecessors, and he recommended initiatives by public authorities to remedy the imbalances within and between nations.[9] Donal Dorr, surveying one hundred years of Vatican social teaching, concludes that in *Mater et Magistra* John XXIII set a new direction by clearly and publicly putting the weight of the Church "on the side of a policy of social reforms in favor of the poor and deprived both within each country and at the international level."[10]

Prior to John XXIII the popes had focused on the evils of socialism, but he began the process of calling into question the structures of both capitalism and socialism in the light of the experience of their effects on persons and on the human community.[11] This had profound political implications, since it broke with a papal stance that had previously weighed in on the side of the established order of Western society. Economic and political elites had always been able to invoke papal authority in opposition to all calls for systemic reform.[12] Paul VI and John Paul II, reflecting on the worsening situation of the world's poor over the succeeding twenty-five years, would draw out the moral implications of this reality and sharpen the critique of capitalist structures. Each new papal document would call with increasing urgency for change and what has come to be known, since its formulation by the Latin American bishops, as the "preferential option for the poor."

Vatican II's *Gaudium et Spes* built on Pope John XXIII's contributions. It was a watershed statement regarding the relationship of the Church to the modern world, placing the Church solidly *in* the world and at the service of humankind. It emphasized the right, in justice, of the poor to share in the goods of the earth, asserting that this right put a claim on the superfluous goods of the rich. Note that this is a claim of justice, not of charity. It envisioned a new international economic order in which the earth's goods would be shared more equitably, and it recognized that expropriation of property would be legitimate in some cases.[13]

Paul VI's 1967 encyclical, *Populorum Progressio* (On the progress of peoples), specifically addressed the problem of global poverty and called for "bold transformations" of the way the international order was/is structured.[14] It laid the ground for the specific critique of the international economic system. This papal letter and those of John Paul II (two of which are discussed at length by Gregory Baum in Chapter 3), along with the documents produced by the bishops' gatherings mentioned above, are used extensively in this chapter as the basis for theological reflection on seven specific "structures of sin" in the current global economy.

First, however, it is necessary to make some introductory comments on the basic neoclassical economic assumptions which not only fail to solve but help to cause the underlying systemic sin in the international economy.

INTERDEPENDENCE AND
THE RULES OF THE MARKETPLACE

Global interdependence is the reality in today's world economy, yet the structures are still those of a period when national autonomy was a reasonable economic and political arrangement. In an interdependent world the current structures are clearly dysfunctional. We live in an age in which the power to destroy the planet is dispersed among many. Massive flows of capital ordered by invisible investors can dramatically shift the resource and employment base of nations. Transnational enterprises transfer technology, production, products, and capital from place to place without taking responsibility for the effects on either those left behind or those at the new site. Existing political systems, still based on principles of national sovereignty and atomized markets, have proved incapable of dealing with global interdependence.

The markets of the world economy are dominated by the rules of the game of capitalist market systems. This fact results from two historical realities: the enduring legacy of colonialism in Africa, Asia, and Latin America; and the decision of the socialist nations to hold themselves apart from world markets so as to build their economies according to socialist principles. As these socialist nations have entered world markets in recent years, they too have participated according to the rules of the capitalist market game.[15]

In neoclassical orthodoxy the rules of the marketplace are rooted in a set of three assumptions about human nature and social interactions.

1. If everyone takes care of him- or herself, everyone will be taken care of. This is the principle of basic self-interest, coming out of utilitarian philosophy. It assumes that every individual will seek those things that she or he believes (according to her or his own values) are good (that is, will bring satisfaction or utility) and avoid those that are not. In economic theory it is assumed that the nation as an economic unit will also act in its own self-interest.

2. Everyone has access to marketable resources with which to earn a living and participate in exchanges that will be mutually beneficial. This assumption posits that all individuals and nations have some natural,

168

human, or manufactured resource that someone else is willing and able to buy at a price that will enable the sellers to satisfy their wants and continue to provide the resource in the future. The freely made choices of the individuals or nations who buy and sell in the markets will lead to the greatest good for the greatest number—they will be mutually beneficial. Through the interaction of free individuals or nations, all of whom have freedom of movement and equal access to markets, the best possible social outcome will be achieved as well as the best outcome for individuals. This belief in the "invisible hand" of markets is the root of conservative opposition to a positive role for government in the economy. For conservatives, government can only interfere with the natural order of things.

The principle of comparative advantage holds that in international markets each nation has some good or service that it can produce and sell to others at a price and in quantities that will enable it to benefit from trade. International specialization will benefit all nations and ultimately equalize the returns to trade. Such is the assumed "magic of the market."

3. Economic units are equal in bargaining power and none has power to control the outcomes in the markets. Through competition among equals, price and quality will be maintained, and exploitation of one by another will be prevented. Thus, competitive markets are assumed to be self-regulating.

These three assumptions—motivation in self-interest, coordination through the price mechanism, and regulation through competition—form the basics of the capitalist market rules of the game as applied to local, national, and international markets. The degree to which the failures of these market rules are judged remediable aberrations or inherent flaws differentiates various schools of thought among economists.[16]

The actual effects of the workings of international markets, governed though they may be by the "rules of the game" just described, hardly present a picture of the mutually beneficial outcomes predicted by neoclassical economic theory. As Ann Seidman demonstrates in Chapter 6, the operation of market forces in Africa has contributed to starvation there because the mass of people have been shut out from any gains from trade. Analyses of such effects by economists of various perspectives over some twenty years have demonstrated certain systemic factors contributing to the inability of the poorest countries to overcome their poverty.

The functioning of international markets is not the only cause of impoverishment. In addition, seemingly intractable internal factors in the poor nations hinder their ability to provide for the poor among them. These include

- internal political realities such as control of government by a wealthy oligarchy and/or the military, tribal or ethnic or religious division or civil war, bureaucratic inefficiency and/or corruption;
- the historic class divisions between rich and poor, with the ownership of land and other resources controlled by the rich, who are insensitive to the poor majority and who enrich themselves by exploiting the labor of peasants and workers and using their market power to capture for themselves the gains from trade which accrue to the country;
- lack of education and of the skills needed to use new technology in agriculture or to gain employment in industry or services;
- unchecked population growth, causing absorption of potential savings in consumption rather than in investment in future crops or equipment to enhance production to increase living standards;
- lack of basic infrastructure such as water supply, roads, and communication systems, particularly in rural areas;
- wide cultural and technological gaps between modern cities and primitive areas, which hinder implementation of nationwide development strategies;
- massive environmental damage cause by both the unrestrained greed of local elites and the desperation of the poor whose traditional livelihoods have vanished, leaving their survival to the mercies of the market.

Each of these internal factors deserves detailed consideration in itself, but this chapter focuses on seven aspects of the international economic system: the international trading system; private investment capital in poor nations; public funds in the form of foreign aid; the debt crisis; the drain of skilled persons from poorer to richer countries; the impact of the arms race; and obstructionist U.S. policies in the global arena. Each of these contributes to the systematic marginalization of poor nations and can be considered one of the "structures of sin" that John Paul II speaks of in his recent messages.[17] An economic analysis of each of the seven elements is followed by theological reflection based on selected passages from papal documents and other Vatican and regional and national Catholic sources. The chosen passages reflect the orientation of Catholic social teaching as it has developed since John XXIII.

PATTERNS OF INTERNATIONAL TRADE

Contrary to the easy assumption that access to markets is equal and mutually beneficial, the poorest nations of the world have experienced patterns of world trade that have systematically kept them in a dependent relationship. As Paul VI said in *Populorum Progressio*, "Free trade is not fair trade when the partners are too unequal."[18]

Concrete historical and geopolitical realities of our times condition the way the markets work and negate for the poorest countries the presumed benefits of pursuing their "comparative advantage"—a concept suggested nearly two hundred years ago by David Ricardo as an argument for participation in trade: the free flow of products between countries would enable each to use its resources most efficiently and thus lead to more wealth for all nations and to the "greatest good for the greatest number."

Modern advocates of comparative advantage theory argue that poor nations, by earning income through specializing in crops and products for export markets, can obtain far more of other goods and services than could be produced domestically with the same inputs. The thrust of the policies advocated by the World Bank and the International Monetary Fund (IMF) as economic advisers to the poor nations has been toward this export orientation as a stimulant of economic development.[19]

An examination of the experience of the poor nations in recent decades shows that trade based on comparative advantage has in fact been a powerful "engine of growth" for some, specifically the seven newly industrialized countries, or NICs: Taiwan, South Korea, Hong Kong, Singapore, Brazil, Mexico, India. This has also been true for the thirteen oil-exporting countries of the Organization of Petroleum Exporting Countries (OPEC), who organized themselves into a cartel in order to take advantage of their collective domination of world petroleum supplies.

But the same strategy is being pursued by another twenty to thirty nations—dubbed "would-be NICs" by Robin Broad.[20] Their success rate is far less impressive. These countries struggle to compete in markets dominated by the first NICs with the same "comparative advantage": large numbers of unskilled workers for labor-intensive manufacturing of apparel and shoes and for electronic component assembly. Also, the slowing of growth in the world economy is reducing the growth in demand necessary to provide customers for the goods produced by additional suppliers. Further, the debts incurred to build the infrastructure required to entice multinational corporations to set up factories impose heavy burdens, which are choking off new investment and requiring painful austerities.

Studies of Brazil and the Philippines reveal that export-oriented industrialization requires large imports that reduce the gain to the domestic economy to as low as 25–40 percent of the total export revenue. When the industry is set up by a transnational corporation, the direct repatriation of profits reduces the proportion even further.

To make matters worse, the revenues gained from the export of food grown as a cash crop support the import of consumer luxuries for the small elite class of owners and professionals who profit from capitalist development. Importing food for the poor, who no longer produce in subsistence agriculture, is simply not profitable, because the poor cannot afford to participate in the market sufficiently to satisfy their basic needs.[21]

In addition to seven NICs, twenty to thirty would-be NICs, and thirteen OPEC countries, the nations of Africa, Asia, and Latin America include nearly a hundred that are less fortunate: sixty less developed countries (LDCs) whose economies are still based primarily on the export of agricultural products and other raw materials, though some small industries have been set up; and the thirty to thirty-five that are called the "least developed countries" or the Fourth World—the world's poorest nations, with few natural resources and little capacity to export goods.

Such categorizations are not rigid and include vast diversity. But what all these nations have in common is that they participate in a world economy dominated by the rich nations. While talking free trade, rich nations can change the rules and move capital and production freely around the world in ways that have profound impact on the smaller, poorer nations seeking to gain from trade in world markets. How does this dependency relationship operate in international trade?

First, colonialism's legacy remains in the technological gap between rich and poor nations and between modern and primitive sectors within poor nations. The products that the poorest countries have to sell in world markets tend to be primarily in their raw, unprocessed state; thus the producers do not share in the returns to the later stages of processing.[22] The 1980s saw a continuing slump in the markets for primary commodities, contrary to what would be expected in a time of "recovery" such as that experienced in the United States and other developed nations in the post-1982 period.[23] Commodity markets, in short, were not behaving as the orthodox theory asserts they should, participating in the good times and the bad. The products of the world's poorest nations did not share in the improvements.

Second, when poor nations enter world markets, they find barriers to trade erected by rich nations to protect their own producers. For example, sugar producers face quotas and tariff barriers intended to protect U.S. sugar beet farmers; rice exporters can sell their unprocessed rice duty-free to rich nations but must pay import duties if they try to capture some of the processing gains by exporting milled rice. When poor nations have tried to have such barriers lowered or to get preferential treatment for their products, the United States in particular has obstructed any change.[24] This response stands in sharp contrast to U.S. complaints about Japanese trade barriers and subsidies, when the shoe is on the other foot.

Third, prices for primary products are volatile because they respond to changes in supply and demand much more directly than manufactured products do. The undifferentiated nature of primary products, the difficulty of storing agricultural products, the dependence on the vagaries of the weather all contribute to the producers' inability to control either supply or price. (OPEC in the 1970s was one singular exception; the breakdown of discipline in that cartel in recent years has been more typical.) The dramatic shifts in commodity prices in the 1970s and 1980s have affected most adversely the countries most dependent on exported commodities for their income. The effects have been worst in those countries whose basic self-sufficiency in food and other necessities has been undermined by development strategies premised on the efficacy of export-led growth. To the extent that income is generated, the imported consumer goods it goes to pay for tend to be luxuries for the small elite of owners, professionals, and political figures—not food for the poor.

Fourth, the net result of the asymmetry in world markets for commodities and those for manufactured goods exposes the poorest nations to a "double whammy" of declining prices for what they sell and rising prices for what they buy. Economists call this "the declining terms of trade." The Queen in *Through the Looking Glass* called it having to run faster and faster just to stay in the same place.

Nicaraguan leader Daniel Ortega described this scissors effect to the UN in terms of the increase in what Nicaragua had to exchange in world markets for a U.S. tractor: in 1977 it had to produce and sell 98 units of coffee; in 1981, 248 units—a 145 percent increase in the price in real terms over just four years.[25] In 1985 the prices of nonfuel primary products compared with the prices of manufactured exports reached their lowest level in the postwar period; in the 1980s the ratio declined an average of 3.8 percent per year.[26]

This prevailing system of trading relations was challenged by Paul VI in *Populorum Progressio*, which calls it neocolonialist.[27] Pope Paul points out that imbalances in power relationships cause injustice in trade and negate the advantages that can flow from international exchange when there are not excessive inequalities between the parties involved. After noting the reliance of poor nations on trade in primary products, and the "wide and sudden" fluctuations in their prices, he concludes:

> The poor nations remain ever poor while the rich ones become still richer. In other words, the rule of free trade, taken by itself, is no longer able to govern international relations. Its advantages are certainly evident when the parties involved are not affected by any excessive inequalities of economic power. . . . But the situation is no longer the same when economic conditions differ too widely from country to country: prices which are "freely" set in the market can produce unfair results. One must recognize that it is the fundamental principle of liberalism, as the rule for commercial exchange, which is questioned here. . . . Freedom of trade is fair only if it is subject to the demands of social justice.[28]

Pope Paul advocates not abolishing the competitive market but establishing limits to make its effects just, moral, and humane. He points out that the conditions for equality of bargaining power, assumed by the theory of free market competition, do not exist between rich and poor nations. He then calls for international agreements to restore some measure of equality in international trade relations, specifically to "establish general norms for regulating certain prices, for guaranteeing certain types of production, and for supporting certain new industries."[29] In their 1986 pastoral letter, *Economic Justice for All*, the U.S. bishops reiterate the same concern for the inequities of international trade and call for international action to redress them.[30]

In his 1988 encyclical, *Sollicitudo Rei Socialis*, John Paul II urges reform of the international trade system, which "frequently discriminates against the products of the young industries of the developing countries and discourages the producers of raw materials." He goes on to point to the role of transnational corporations in this system:

There exists too a kind of international division of labor whereby the low-cost products of certain countries which lack effective labor laws or which are too weak to apply them are sold in other parts of the world at considerable profit for the companies engaged in this form of production, which knows no frontiers.[31]

PRIVATE FOREIGN INVESTMENT
AND TRANSNATIONAL CORPORATIONS

Because private investors seek to maximize their returns, the poorest nations—with their underdeveloped infrastructure, relatively inexperienced labor force, volatile political environments, and inadequate support services—confront unequal competition for private foreign investment when they seek to industrialize. More attractive to investors than the neediest nations are the NICs or would-be NICs. In addition, the developed economies of both East and West (most particularly the United States) have been inviting foreign investments in recent years. Thus, the bulk of investments of transnational corporations goes to the "have" nations, according to the UN Center on Transnational Corporations.[32]

Just after World War II, when considerable economic activity focused on natural resource extraction and exploitation and then on textiles, steel, and construction, transnational enterprises sought out the poor nations. Their untapped natural resources, relatively low wages, and political and economic naiveté made them profitable places to invest. Now, however, transnational enterprises are concentrating their investments in high-tech, capital-intensive industries such as chemicals and electronics—sectors in which citizens of the poorest nations have little attraction except as assemblers.

The data do not support the generalization that the presence of foreign investors is universally harmful to poor nations; the debate continues on this point. Those who judge transfers of technology and modernization of the economy critical to the development of an ability to provide for the needs of the people see private foreign investment as one necessary source of resources. Those who argue for development rooted in self-reliant production to meet basic human needs, however, consider private foreign investment inherently inimical to this goal.[33] Of course, country-specific and company-specific analysis is required to identify which transnational corporations are exploitive.

Since the early 1970s the United Nations has developed codes of conduct for transnational enterprises (TNEs) and has assisted poor nations in developing mutually beneficial arrangements. This has been one of the positive outcomes of the ill-fated call of the Third World nations for a New International Economic Order (NIEO) during the 1960s and 1970s.[34]

In her analysis of the economic realities of the Philippines, Robin Broad describes the dynamic set of interrelationships linking transnational clients in poor nations with technocrats in the multilateral institutions—such as the World Bank and IMF—that serve as advisers to those nations' governments, and with the transnational business people and bankers who are being courted to invest in infrastructure or new industries. Both the state and private business sectors are thus divided into nationalist and transnationalist factions, allowing for pervasive outside influence on policy-making. The common schooling and corporate culture of both the poor country's transnationalists and the representatives of multilateral institutions and transnational corporations and banks create the climate for new linkages between elites in rich and poor nations.[35] Since the economic strength of the two parties is so unequal, these relationships usually constitute a new form of dependency.

In his 1971 letter, *Octogesima Adveniens* (A call to action), Paul VI noted with concern the breaking-down of national frontiers and the emergence of the transnational corporations as new economic powers, largely independent of national governmental authority. He cautioned that these can lead to a new and abusive form of economic domination on the social, the cultural, and even the political level. He called for the movement "from economics to politics" to bring the economic realm under the control of political power, "which is the natural and necessary link for ensuring the cohesion of the social body which must have for its aim the achievement of the common good."[36] John Paul II, in his encyclical *Laborem Exercens* (On human labor), implicates the policies and practices of the transnational companies in the poverty of the poor nations and their individual workers, calling them causal factors.[37]

In *Economic Justice for All*, the U.S. bishops reflect the 1980s view of the role of multinational enterprises. They advocate an increase in direct foreign investment in developing countries, since it provides needed capital, technology, and managerial expertise. But they go on to warn against investing in ways that "create or perpetuate dependency," "sustain or worsen inequities," "help maintain oppressive elites in power," or "increase food dependency by encouraging cash cropping at the expense of local needs." The bishops also call foreign investors to consider the implications for jobs in their own country and for workers' rights in the host country. They advocate products and technology that will benefit all the consumers in the host country and will not contribute to displacement of labor. They support mandated adherence to the UN codes for transnational enterprises.[38]

PUBLIC FUNDS FOR FOREIGN AID

In addition to private foreign investment, transfers of public resources, called foreign aid, have become a feature of the international economy.

Since the Marshall Plan of the 1940s, it has been part of the public policy of rich nations to transfer aid to poor nations. From the initial period of public generosity in the United States, however, the history of foreign aid has been stormy. Moreover, from the perspective of the poor nations, the aid has come in ever more restrictive forms and in trickles ill matched to the magnitude of the need.

Aid has come with political strings attached, with requirements that purchases be made in the donor country and that repayment be in the currency of the donor. Most recently, it has come more often as military assistance than as economic assistance. Because it has been channeled through the government of the recipient nation, it has often failed to reach the people whose needs prompted the transfer from the donor nation.

Channeling multilateral aid through organizations such as regional development banks or UN agencies has avoided some of these problems, but the unwillingness of the United States and other nations to fund these multilateral agencies adequately has hampered their ability to assist. The International Monetary Fund and the World Bank are controlled by the rich countries, and the poor nations have complained of policies unresponsive to their real needs. The austerity (structural adjustment) programs that the IMF has required as a condition for new loans in the 1980s have been especially costly for the heavily indebted nations, and having the inevitable mandated by the rich nations has made it all the more unpalatable.

In the 1960s the nations of the world proclaimed the First Development Decade. Economists projected that if the rich nations committed 1 percent of their GNP to foreign aid, it would provide enough added resources to move the majority of poor nations onto the path of self-reliant growth by 1990—but the rich nations did not meet that goal in either the First or the Second Development Decade.

It should be noted, however, that the "success stories" of the 1970s and 1980s—the newly industrialized nations—are those that did receive large amounts of foreign aid from the West. India reached food self-sufficiency in the 1970s, and it too had garnered a lion's share of foreign assistance. The poorest nations have received the smallest share of foreign assistance.

There are those who argue that all foreign aid should be discontinued because it has created a dependency pattern, has enriched corrupt elites instead of the people, and has distorted the natural development of the poor nations.[39] More of those focusing now on the needs of the poorest are seeking to channel the assistance through nongovernmental agencies (NGOs) such as the churches and their programs. These groups have a track record of effective use of resources, have developed delivery systems in rural and remote areas, and are close to the people themselves.[40]

In *Mater et Magistra,* John XXIII roots the call for assistance to the poor nations in the solidarity of the human race. He advocates emergency assistance and scientific, technical, and financial cooperation. All of this, he cautions, is to be done "without thought of domination," so that the poor nations will eventually be in a position to progress on their own initiative. This would permit the shaping of "a community of nations wherein each will have regard for the common good of all."[41] Pope John's basic optimism about the possibility of human cooperation is apparent here. The same optimism is evident in *Gaudium et Spes,* written a few years later. Christian people as well as their governments are urged to give assistance "out of the substance of their goods, and not only out of what is superfluous." Young persons are exhorted to consider giving service.[42]

In *Progressio Populorum,* Paul VI also puts the call on a personal level, exhorting each individual to be willing to contribute in the form of higher taxes and higher prices on commodities imported from poor nations.[43]

The obligation of sharing-based human solidarity exists for nations as well as individuals. Paul VI challenges:

Given the increasing needs of the under-developed countries it should be considered quite normal for an advanced country to de-vote part of its production to meet their needs and to train teachers, engineers, technicians and scholars prepared to put their knowledge and their skill at the disposal of less fortunate peoples.[44]

He goes on to call for a World Fund—made up of part of the money now spent on arms—to be fitted into a framework of worldwide collabo-ration that would avoid the pitfalls of neocolonialism possible in bilateral aid and thereby assist in better allocation. Less optimistic than John XXIII about human cooperation, Pope Paul, writing in 1967, urges "consis-tent, constant and courageous efforts," recognizing that peace within and among nations is at stake.[45]

Two decades later the U.S. bishops, in *Economic Justice for All*, reflect on the reality of the 1980s: U.S. commitment to development assistance, when measured as a percentage of GNP, is one-tenth of what it was dur-ing the Marshall Plan; the United States is still the largest donor but lags proportionately behind other donor nations; U.S. bilateral aid in-creasingly takes the form of military assistance; and U.S. contributions to multilateral agencies have been reduced or postponed. The bishops express particular regret over the last point "because these institutions are often better able than the bilateral agencies to focus on the poor and reduce dependency in developing countries." They also deplore the U.S. abdication of positive leadership in international organizations such as the UN: "A more affirmative U.S. role in these institutions, which we took the lead in creating, could improve their performance, send an en-couraging signal of U.S. intentions and help reopen the dialogue on the growing poverty and dependency of the Third World."[46]

John Paul II in his 1987 letter, *Sollicitudo Rei Socialis*, decries the effects of East-West polarization and its implications for poor nations seeking to establish their own identity and needing "effective and impartial aid" from all the richer nations. He links the internal divisions in poor nations to the ideological conflicts between East and West that have often been played out in granting or refusing to grant foreign aid.[47]

Increasing realism about the geopolitical realities of the world of the 1980s and the learnings of the previous thirty years is apparent in the

1987 encyclical. Aid is advocated, but the realities of external political pressure and the experience of internal misallocation are recognized. John XXIII's optimism has given way to greater realism.

Debt Burden

The combination of need and greed generated a crushing debt burden of over $1 trillion carried by the poor nations in the 1980s. The need to buy ever more costly oil in the 1970s and to purchase necessary equipment and supplies in world markets where the terms of trade were adverse led the poor nations to borrow heavily. Commercial bankers in the rich nations, flush with the invested earnings of OPEC countries, in their greed paid insufficient attention to the prospects of poor nations for generating the income necessary to make payments. In addition, the lenders negotiated loans with variable interest rates, which rose even as commodity prices fell in the 1980s.

The decline in the prices of primary products on world markets has meant ever greater diversion of real resources to external creditors at the expense of basic human needs. Prices of necessities have skyrocketed as imports have been cut and as production for export rather than for internal needs has dominated the economies of the debtor nations.

IMF assistance with debt rescheduling has required structural adjustment programs that include reduction of government subsidies and social services, freezes on local wages, and devaluation of the currency—all at the expense of the poorest segments of the population. Even under the best of circumstances, the servicing of the debt will impose heavy burdens on poor nations, burdens that will dominate their economies and the world economy for decades to come. Through its dampening effect on imports, the debt of poor nations contributes to the slowdown of world trade and thus adversely affects all nations.[48]

At present the flow of debt payments from the poor nations to the rich nations exceeds all flows in the other direction. So much for the equalizing tendencies of the international market system.[49]

Catholic social teaching's emphasis on the priority of the claim of human needs on the resources of the earth, on the social responsibility inherent in ownership, and on the obligations of distributive justice undergird the theological reflection on the debt crisis.

As early as 1967, Paul VI in *Populorum Progressio* called for "dialogue between those who contribute wealth and those who benefit from it" so that the response of rich nations would be based on the real needs of poor nations:

> Developing countries will thus no longer risk being overwhelmed by debts whose repayment swallow up the greater part of their gains. Rates of interest and time for repayment of the loan could be so arranged as not to be too great a burden on either party, taking into account free gifts, interest-free or low-interest loans and the time needed for liquidating the debts. Guarantees could be given to those who provide the capital that it will be put to use according to an agreed plan and with a reasonable measure of efficiency, since there is no question of encouraging parasites or the indolent. And the receiving countries could demand that there be no interference in their political life or subversion of their social structures.[50]

Here we find the elements of a vision of "a system of cooperation freely undertaken . . . carried out with equal dignity on either side, for the construction of a more human world."[51]

This world vision underlies all the subsequent exhortations of popes and bishops regarding the debt crisis. The U.S. bishops, in *Economic Justice for All*, cite the indebtedness dominating the economic agenda of the poor nations in the 1980s as evidence of the asymmetry and dependency relationships in the international economic order. They identify the major international actors who share responsibility for the crisis and point to the inability of the global financial system established by the 1944 Bretton Woods Conference to deal with the situation. Specifically, they remind the people of the United States that the structures of the IMF, the World Bank, and the GATT (General Agreement on Tariffs and Trade) do not adequately represent Third World debtors, and their policies are not dealing effectively with problems affecting poor nations.[52]

The bishops become quite specific regarding what is needed. Having described the effects on the poor of IMF-required austerity programs, they issue an urgent call for action to lift the debt burden, suggesting moratoria on payments, conversion of dollar-denominated debt to local currency debt, discounting of loans, capitalization of interest payments, or outright cancellation.[53]

In *Sollicitudo Rei Socialis* John Paul II recalls that the reason the poor nations borrowed was to invest in development projects, something desirable in itself. But circumstances have changed within both the debtor nations and the international capital markets. Thus, "the instrument chosen to make a contribution to development has turned into a counter-productive mechanism . . . the means intended for the development of peoples has turned into a brake upon development instead." He calls for "an effective political will" to bring about the necessary reforms of the "structures of sin" in the international economic and social order.[54]

THE DRAIN OF SKILLED PERSONS TO RICHER NATIONS

The inexorable working of the markets shows itself in another perverse effect on the poor nations—the "brain drain," the way in which the best and the brightest are "creamed off" through the workings of the market system, past and present. The most promising young people are sent abroad to study in universities in First World countries, where the curricula and life-styles are literally worlds apart from their own experience; where theory and practice reflect the resource endowments, organizational patterns, cultural mores, contemporary issues, and economic and political histories of the host country; where the pressing problems of the Third World are hardly known, much less addressed. Graduates of U.S. or European universities returning to their own countries find themselves both over- and undereducated as they seek employment. With expectations raised by the life-styles they enjoyed as students, they find the living conditions at home unattractive and seek better for themselves and their children.

As early as 1972, Jan Tinbergen pointed out the drain of resources that such a pattern entails—hardly the equalizing flows predicted by conventional economic theory. He estimated that from 1960 to 1972 the imputed value of the skill of technicians who migrated from poor nations to the United States, the United Kingdom, and Canada was $50.9 billion—compared with a total of $46.3 billion in foreign aid over the same period from the same three nations.[55] The net drain of $4.6 billion—a systemic flow of specialized resources in the direction of rich nations—was both effect and cause of the continuing poverty of poor nations.

No comment appears in the papal writings about the "brain drain"; however, encouraging skilled persons from developed nations to go to the assistance of Third World nations is a constant theme. Young Christians are also exhorted to give some portion of their time in poor nations, as a way of expressing their membership in the human community and their concern for justice in the world.

Paul VI, in *Populorum Progressio*, quotes Vatican II to remind the rich nations of their responsibility: "Advanced nations have a very heavy obligation to help the developing peoples."[56] Even the generous response to papal appeals for hunger relief, Paul reminds Catholics, is not enough: "Let each one examine his conscience, a conscience that conveys a new message for our times. Is he prepared . . . to leave his country if necessary and if he is young, in order to assist in this development of the young nations?"[57]

Once again, the obligation of human solidarity is normative both for nations and for individuals. Far from enticing skilled persons to leave poor nations, the wealthier nations should be encouraging a flow in the other direction.

THE ARMS RACE

The continuing arms race victimizes the poor nations in particular. In a militarized world, sophisticated weaponry becomes the badge of nationhood. In countries ruled by military dictatorships, expenditures on arms assume special legitimacy. Areas torn by age-old tensions and modern rivalries are armed by nations peddling weapons in international markets.[58]

The production and purchase of arms is particularly detrimental to the poorest nations because of what is displaced by the use of resources for military purposes. In the thirty poorest countries of the world (as measured by their infant mortality rates), the median figures for 1986–87 show 6 percent of government expenditure allocated to health, 12 percent to education, and 9 percent to defense.[59] In these countries the median percentage of the urban population which is absolutely poor is 45 percent; of the rural population, 65 percent (1977–87). Clearly, basic subsistence-level needs are being sacrificed to military expenditures.[60]

The diversion of scarce resources to military purchases or service contributes to inflation and worsens unemployment. As development of such infrastructure as irrigation systems, roads, and storage facilities is postponed or inadequately funded, for example, food production is constrained, which contributes to inflation in staple food prices. Scarce foreign exchange is used to buy weapons instead of job-creating technical assistance, technology, or infrastructure development. Yet in the early 1980s the Food and Agriculture Organization estimated that allotting half of 1 percent of the world's military expenditures to improvements in agricultural technology for poor nations would be enough to eliminate the food deficit by 1990.[61]

The link between the arms race and world poverty has been made consistently in Catholic social teaching for three decades. John XXIII described the arms race and world poverty as two conflicting trends that are distortions of the Creator's purpose and an expression of mutual distrust in the world.[62] In *Pacem in Terris* he condemns the arms race for absorbing intellectual and economic resources of the rich nations and thus depriving the poor nations of "the collaboration they need in order to make economic and social progress."[63]

The Council Fathers of Vatican II reiterate the link between the arms race and world poverty, calling the arms race "an utterly treacherous trap for humanity, and one which injures the poor to an intolerable degree."[64] They go on to call for international action to avoid war and to build up the international community, two other persistent themes in Catholic social teaching.

Paul VI strongly condemns the arms race, reiterating the theme that basic human needs must take priority in budgetary decisions: "When so many people are hungry, when so many remain steeped in ignorance, when so many schools, hospitals, and homes worthy of the name remain to be built, all public or private squandering of wealth, all expenditure prompted by motives of national or personal ostentation, every exhausting armaments race, becomes an intolerable scandal."[65] In an often quoted section of *Populorum Progressio*, Paul develops a theme from *Gaudium et Spes* which links peace and justice (in the sense of structural transformation): "Peace cannot be limited to a mere absence of war, the result of an ever precarious balance of forces. No, peace is something that is built up day after day, in the pursuit of an order intended by God, which implies a more perfect form of justice among men." At the end of the same encyclical is his famous statement: "The new name for peace is development."[66]

In the document of their 1971 Synod the bishops of the world speak of a crisis of world solidarity because of age-old divisions between nations and empires, races and classes, which possess new instruments of destruction.[67] This point is made even more strongly in the 1976 Vatican Statement to the United Nations, which called the arms race "an act of aggression against the poor because it causes them to starve."[68]

John Paul II in his first encyclical, *Redemptor Hominis* (Redeemer of man), provided the foundation of his later teaching, reiterating the centrality of the dignity of the human person as the basis for justice in the social order. In this document he observes that modern "development" is destroying humanity rather than promoting true progress and that the institutions on which the world economic order rests "have proved incapable of remedying the unjust social situations inherited from the past or of dealing with urgent challenges and ethical demands of the present." He cites as one example the arms race, which squanders resources that could have been used to overcome poverty.[69]

In *Sollicitudo Rei Socialis*, written to observe the twentieth anniversary of *Populorum Progressio*, John Paul II speaks more strongly about the ways in which the arms buildup has impeded progress toward a more just world order. He observes the tendency in both rich and poor nations to utilize huge sums for stockpiles of weapons, a tendency antithetical to development: "If 'development is the new name for peace,' war and military preparations are the major enemy of the integral development of peoples." This letter specifically condemns trade in arms with an "even more severe" moral judgment, characterizing it as "a trade without frontiers, capable of crossing even the barriers of the blocs," and as contributing to the debt crisis.[70]

Consistently and with ever more specificity, the popes have recognized the link between poverty and the arms race and, with ever more stridency, have condemned it, joining their voices to those of other world leaders alarmed by the threat to the common security of humankind that is posed both by the stockpiling of nuclear arms and the worsening of the poverty of the majority of the world's people.[71]

The U.S. bishops in two pastoral letters, *The Challenge of Peace* and *Economic Justice for All*, echo the message of the popes and draw out the implications for U.S. policy. In the peace pastoral they note that the contrast between U.S. expenditures on arms and on development assistance reflects a shift in national priorities away from meeting human needs and presents a "massive distortion of resource allocations." That letter specifically draws out the connections between peace and development.[72] In *Economic Justice for All* the bishops specifically call us as a nation "to go beyond economic gain or national security as a starting point for the policy dialogue." They see the impact of the U.S. role in promoting the arms trade and call for leadership in arms reduction: "Rather than promoting U.S. arms sales, especially to countries that cannot afford them, we should be campaigning for an international agreement to reduce this lethal trade."[73]

Opposition to the arms race on grounds that it harms the poor of the world as well as endangering peace is a consistent theme in Catholic social teaching, both from Rome and from the U.S. bishops.

OBSTRUCTIONIST U.S. POLICIES

During the 1980s U.S. policy toward the Third World has been obstructionist. Little wonder that the United States is referred to as the "elephant in the boat." The escalation in the buildup of U.S. military might, coupled with supply-side economics tax cuts for the wealthy, caused unprecedented U.S. borrowing to fund federal deficit spending. In order to attract investors, interest rates were kept high, and the United States drained capital from the rest of the world.

The posture of U.S. diplomats in international forums was self-interested in the narrowest sense and obstructionist from the perspective of other nations. Initiatives by the poor nations and U.S. allies to address the pressing global economic issues were met with hostility. We failed to sign the Law of the Sea treaty and voted against initiatives for trade liberalization, the codes of conduct for transnational enterprises, and covenants to protect the environment. We opposed preferential tariff treatment for poor nations, which was supported by Western European nations. It appears that even while recognizing that no one nation can any longer dominate the world economy, the United States determined to use its economic power to prevent any change that would benefit those left behind by the markets. In his meetings with world leaders, Ronald Reagan kept stressing reliance on the "magic of the market," a magic that has worked well for a small minority of nations but left the majority of the world's people behind.

Catholic social teaching's vision of what ought to be is quite different. From the definition of the human person as a member of a human family comes the consistent call for international collaboration to regulate the international markets and organize the international order for peace and development for all peoples. The necessity of collaboration was foundational in John XXIII's view of the world.[74] The Vatican Council advocated a new global economic order based on the bonds of mutual dependence and responding to "modern obligations, particularly with reference to those numerous regions still laboring under intolerable need."[75]

Pope Paul VI, in his 1965 address to the United Nations, called for the establishment of a "world authority capable of acting effectively in the juridical and political sectors." Two years later, in *Populorum Progressio*, he urged "concerted planning" for assistance of "developing" nations by "advanced" ones.[76] In 1971 he called for a revision of international relationships in light of the realities of mutual dependence:

> Thus it is necessary to have the courage to undertake a revision of the relationships between nations, whether it is a question of the international division of production, the structure of exchanges, the control of profits, the monetary system—without forgetting the actions of human solidarity—to question the models of growth of the rich nations and change people's outlooks, so that they may realize the prior call of international duty, and to renew international organizations so that they may increase in effectiveness.[77]

John Paul II, in *Redemptor Hominis*, recommends a "programmed" global economy, making more explicit the proposals of Paul VI in *Populorum Progressio*.[78] Economic progress must be planned if it is to be at the service of people and in accord with the solidarity of all. His 1987 letter, *Sollicitudo Rei Socialis*, acknowledges the need for a review of the operations of existing international organizations and calls for "the overcoming of political rivalries and the renouncing of all desire to manipulate these organizations, which exist solely for the common good." He begins with recognition that the existing organizations and institutions have benefited the peoples of the world, but he adds: "Nevertheless, humanity today is in a new and more difficult phase of its genuine development. It needs a greater degree of international ordering, at the service of the societies, economies and cultures of the whole world." He goes on to urge regional collaboration among the developing nations themselves in the production, monetary, and financial sectors as a way to make themselves less dependent on the more powerful nations.[79]

The realities of our time, he asserts, require transcendence of the barriers that divide nations and peoples:

> We are all called, indeed obliged, to face the tremendous challenge of the last decade of the second millennium, also because the present dangers threaten everyone: a world economic crisis, a war without frontiers, without winners or losers. In the face of such a threat, the distinction between rich individuals and countries and poor individuals and countries will have little value, except that a greater responsibility rests on those who have more and can do more.[80]

This emphasis on the special obligations of those with economic power underlies the U.S. bishops' treatment of the U.S. relationship to the poor nations of the world. "The pervasive U.S. presence in many parts of our interdependent world . . . creates a responsibility for us to increase the use of U.S. power—not just aid—in the service of human dignity and human rights, both political and economic." They recognize that the international economic order, like many aspects of the U.S. economy, is in crisis and that the United States "represents the most powerful single factor in the international economic equation." They see this as both an opportunity and an obligation for their country "to launch a worldwide campaign for justice and economic rights to match the still incomplete, but encouraging, political democracy we have achieved in the United States with so much pain and sacrifice."[81]

The bishops quote John Paul II's speech during his 1979 visit to the United States in which he commended the generosity of its people and called on them to match this generosity with an equally convincing contribution to the establishment of a world order that can create the necessary economic and trade conditions for a more just relationship between all the nations of the world. They remind us of the need to pursue the international common good as well as the common good of each nation, recalling that "equity requires, even as the fact of interdependence becomes more apparent, that the quality of interdependence be improved in order to eliminate 'the scandal of the shocking inequality between the rich and the poor' in a world divided ever more sharply between them." They join in the call for review and reform of the existing international agencies and urge the United States to support United Nations efforts to move in the direction of an "international political entity . . . with the responsibility and power to promote the global common good," expressing regret that such an entity does not now exist.[82]

They observe that in recent years U.S. policy toward Third World development has been increasingly dominated by an "East-West assessment of North-South problems, at the expense of basic human needs and economic development," making national security "the central policy principle." They remark that the rest of the world has come to expect the United States to assume an adversarial posture in discussions of Third World development. They call the nation to its responsibility: "The U.S. approach to the developing countries needs urgently to be changed; a country as large, rich and powerful as ours has a moral obligation to lead in helping to reduce poverty in the Third World." They go on to specify what this means in the areas of aid, trade, finance, and investments.[83]

The bishops conclude with a summary statement of the moral principles that should direct U.S. policy toward the pursuit of global justice and peace: "We call for a U.S. international economic policy designed to empower people everywhere and enable them to continue to develop a sense of their own worth, improve the quality of their lives and ensure that the benefits of economic growth are shared equitably."[84]

In reality, this statement is a summary of Catholic social teaching on what ought to be in the international economic order. It gives first place to meeting human needs, states the right of peoples to shape their own destiny, calls for international equity of distribution, and advocates active public policy to achieve these goals. Commitment to these goals and the people-centered means to achieve them is shared by radical political economists.

CONCLUSION

What seems clear from a review of Catholic social teaching regarding the global economic order is that the Church has come to take its official stand, at least in word, on the side of the poor. The effects of this, Donal Dorr has suggested, may turn out to be the most important shift since the time of Constantine.[85] The coming together of the insights of radical economists and leaders of churches is one of the hopeful signs of our time that social change in favor of the poor of the world may be possible. Though those sharing these insights must struggle against powerful established forces in church and society, they are seeds for change in the global order.

John Maynard Keynes reminded the people of his time that "the power of vested interests is greatly exaggerated compared with the gradual encroachment of ideas."[86] Margaret Mead is said to have observed: "Never doubt that a thoughtful, committed minority can change the world. Indeed it is the only thing that ever has."

Change in the direction of social justice has taken place when church groups, labor groups, peace groups, and women's groups have organized for change. The stark realities of our times seem to be adding farsighted industrialists and diplomats, scientists questioning the conventional uses of science, environmentalists concerned about the fate of the earth, and other creative minorities to the groups of those advocating change. Religious people call it the movement of the Spirit; radical political economists see it as the inevitable crisis of capitalism. Whatever it is, we may yet learn to live together as brothers and sisters on this planet. That is our challenge and opportunity.

NOTES

1. John Paul II, *Sollicitudo Rei Socialis, Origins* 17, no. 38 (1988): 641–60, n. 36 (hereafter cited as *SRS*).

2. Note that there are efforts to discredit this branch of the field by those who find the neoclassical orthodoxy adequate. See Deepak Lal, *The Poverty of Development Economics* (Cambridge, Mass.: Harvard University Press, 1985), for a readable summary of the position.

3. Gunnar Myrdal, *The Challenge of World Poverty* (New York: Pantheon Books, 1970), p. 25. Myrdal points out that it is necessary to identify one's viewpoint and value premises at the stage of developing economic theory, since "what one sees depends on where one stands."

4. Cf. Peter Henriot, SJ, and Joe Holland, *Social Analysis: Linking Faith and Justice* (Maryknoll, N.Y.: Orbis Books, 1983); Rita Hofbauer, Dorothy Kinsella, and Amata Miller, *Making Social Analysis Useful* (Washington, D.C.: Leadership Conference of Women Religious, 1983). The foundation of the method is summarized in Paul VI, *Octogesima Adveniens* (1971), in David J. O'Brien and Thomas A. Shannon, eds., *Renewing the Earth: Catholic Documents on Peace, Justice, and Liberation* (Garden City, N.Y.: Doubleday, 1977), pp. 352–83, n. 4 (hereafter cited as *OA*).

5. Michael Harrington, *The Vast Majority: Journey to the World's Poor* (New York: Simon & Schuster, 1977).

6. For a review of Catholic social teaching and introduction to the period beginning with *Mater et Magistra*, see O'Brien and Shannon, *Renewing the Earth*, pp.

1–49; David Byers, ed., *Justice in the Marketplace: Collected Statements of the Vatican and U.S. Catholic Bishops on Economic Policy, 1891–1984* (Washington, D.C.: U.S. Catholic Conference, 1985), pp. 110–13; Donal Dorr, *Option for the Poor: A Hundred Years of Vatican Social Teaching* (Maryknoll, N.Y.: Orbis Books, 1983), pp. 87–116; David Hollenbach, "Modern Catholic Teaching Concerning Justice," in *The Faith That Does Justice*, ed. John Haughey (New York: Paulist Press, 1977), pp. 207–31.

7. John XXIII, *Mater et Magistra* (1961), in O'Brien and Shannon, *Renewing the Earth*, pp. 50–116, nn. 157–59 (hereafter cited as *MM*).

8. See Dorr, *Option for the Poor*, chap. 5.

9. *MM*, nn. 19, 59–60, 116–17, 120, 128–41, 157–65.

10. Dorr, *Option for the Poor*, p. 112.

11. In the early 1930s Pius XI had called for a new "corporatist" social order (cf. *Quadragesimo Anno*, in Byers, *Justice in the Marketplace*, pp. 91–97) but this was an exception in the otherwise continuous support of capitalism by the popes prior to John XXIII. See Dorr, *Option for the Poor*, chap. 3.

12. For a nuanced treatment of the links between papal teaching and the political right in the period between Leo XIII and John XXIII, see Dorr, *Option for the Poor*, pp. 107–16. For a right-wing Catholic view of Catholic social teaching on Third World development issues, see George Weigel, *Catholicism and the Renewal of American Democracy* (New York: Paulist Press, 1989), chap. 10, pp. 171–90. Another source from the same perspective is Michael Novak, *Catholic Social Thought and Liberal Institutions: Freedom with Justice*, 2d ed. (New Brunswick, N.J.: Transaction Publishers, 1989), esp. chap. 7, "The Development of Nations: John XXIII and Paul VI," and chap. 12, "International Economics."

13. See Dorr, *Option for the Poor*, chap. 6 and pp. 256–57. Also see O'Brien and Shannon, *Renewing the Earth*, pp. 171–77.

14. Pope Paul VI, *Populorum Progressio* (1967), in O'Brien and Shannon, *Renewing the Earth*, pp. 311–46 (hereafter cited as *PP*).

15. At the same time, they have begun to introduce elements of market orientation into their own economies. Note that despite popular perceptions to the contrary, it is appropriate to distinguish the modes of decision-making in an economy as market, command, tradition; to distinguish the ownership patterns as private (i.e., capitalist), and government (i.e., socialist); and to distinguish between Communist political parties and communism as an economic system in which ownership would be held in the hands of the people as a whole.

16. The neoclassical school believes that the market, left to itself, will be self-correcting over time; any interference by nonmarket forces is predicted to be less beneficial than the market approach. Keynesian economists believe that government fiscal and monetary policy can be used as tools to stabilize the economy at the macroeconomic level, thus eliminating the most harmful inequities that would flow from pure market approaches. Neo-Marxists argue that the primary focus of the economy should be on meeting human needs; structures and public policy should focus on enablement of the people rather than on the macroeconomic level. For a collection of articles on these various approaches, see the papers in Charles K. Wilber, ed., *The Political Economy of Development and Underdevelopment*, 3d ed. (New York: Random House, 1984).

17. John Paul II, *Redemptor Hominis* (1979), excerpted text reprinted in Byers, *Justice in the Marketplace*, pp. 285–87, n. 16. See also *SRS*, n. 36.

18. *PP*, n. 58.

19. Critique of the World Bank and IMF export-oriented policies in terms of their effects on the poor is widespread. See Robin Broad, *Unequal Alliance: The World Bank, the International Monetary Fund, and the Philippines* (Berkeley: University of California Press, 1988); Cheryl Payer, *The Debt Trap: The International Monetary Fund and the Third World* (New York: Monthly Review Press, 1974); and Payer, *The World Bank: A Critical Analysis* (New York: Monthly Review Press, 1982). See also the analysis by Walden Bello, "Confronting the Brave New World Economic Order: Toward a Southern Agenda for the 1990's," *Alternatives* 14 (1989): 135–67.

20. Broad, *Unequal Alliance*, pp. 4–6.

21. Ibid., p. 192.

22. John W. Sewell, Richard E. Feinberg, and Valeriana Kallab, eds., *U.S. Foreign Policy and the Third World: Agenda 1985–86* (Washington, D.C.: Overseas Development Council, 1985). Also see Independent Commission on International Development Issues (chaired by Willy Brandt), *North-South: A Program for Survival, 1980* (Cambridge, Mass.: MIT Press, 1980), pp. 141–42. Most of the Third World's export earnings come from primary products: 57 percent in 1978, or 81 percent if oil is included; these commodities are 50–60 percent of the total GNP of some countries. The Overseas Development Council (Sewell, Fineberg, and Kallab, *U.S. Foreign Policy*, p. 195) reports that in 1979–81, developing countries supplied over 90 percent of the world's exports of coffee, cocoa beans, and bananas, for example. Cocoa was 20 percent of the exports of Ghana; bananas were 17 percent of those of Honduras; and coffee was 18 percent of the exports of Brazil, where iron ore constituted another 22 percent.

23. See UN Department of International Economic and Social Affairs, *World Economic Survey, 1986: Current Trends and Policies in the World Economy* (New York: United Nations, 1986), pp. 48–50 (Doc. No. E/1986/59-ST/ESA/183).

24. See Steve Lande and Craig Van Grasstek, "Trade with the Developing Countries: The Reagan Record and Prospects," in *U.S. Foreign Policy and the Third World: Agenda 1985–86, U.S.–Third World Policy Perspectives*, vol. 3 (Washington, D.C.: Overseas Development Council, 1985); and William R. Cline, ed., *Policy Alternatives for a New International Economic Order* (New York: Praeger, 1979).

25. Daniel Ortega, address to the UN General Assembly, October 8, 1981, in UN General Assembly, 36th Session, *Provisional Verbatim Record of the Twenty-ninth Meeting* (Doc. No. A/36/PV. 29, 8 October 1981), p. 11.

26. UN Department of International Economic and Social Affairs, *World Economic Survey, 1986*, pp. 78–79.

27. *PP*, nn. 7–9, 52.

28. *PP*, nn. 56–59.

29. *PP*, n. 61.

30. *Economic Justice for All: Catholic Social Teaching and the U.S. Economy* (Washington, D.C.: National Conference of Catholic Bishops, 1986), p. 269 (hereafter cited as *EJFA*).

31. *SRS*, n. 43.

32. Nicholas D. Kristof, "Curbs Give Way to Welcome for Multinational Companies," *New York Times*, May 11, 1985, pp. 1, 33.

33. See Frances Moore Lappé and James Collins, *Food First: Beyond the Myth of Scarcity* (Boston: Houghton Mifflin, 1977).

34. The codes specify mutual rights and responsibilities to be incorporated into agreements between host countries and private foreign investors. Methods of protecting the host country against exploitation and of protecting the foreign investor are included. The UN Center on Transnational Corporations also conducts programs to assist host countries in negotiations. For the fate of the NIEO, see, e.g., John P. Lewis, "Development Promotion: A Time for Regrouping," in *Development Strategies Reconsidered: U.S.–Third World Policy Perspectives, No. 5*, ed. John P. Lewis and Valeriana Kallab (Washington, D.C.: Overseas Development Council, 1986), pp. 3–33.

35. See Broad's insightful analysis, "Newest International Division of Labor," in her *Unequal Alliance*, pp. 6–9.

36. *OA*, nn. 44, 46.

37. John Paul II, *Laborem Exercens* (1981), in Byers, *Justice in the Marketplace*, pp. 290–337, n. 17 (hereafter cited as *LE*).

38. *EJFA*, pp. 278–79, 280.

39. See Frances Moore Lappé, Joseph Collins, and David Kinley, *Aid as Obstacle: Twenty Questions about Our Foreign Aid and the Hungry* (San Francisco: Institute for Food and Development Policy, 1980).

40. See the policy statement of the International Campaign Coalition, convened by World Hunger Year of New York and Development GAP of Washington, D.C.; summarized in *Center Focus* 86 (September 1988), published by Center of Concern, Washington, D.C. See also "Through a Barefoot Revolution: An Interview with Bertrand Schneider," *Development Forum* 14, no. 2 (1986): 1, 6. Schneider is secretary general of the Club of Rome.

41. *MM*, nn. 155, 163–65, 171–74.

42. Second Vatican Ecumenical Council, Pastoral Constitution on the Church in the Modern World, *Gaudium et Spes* (1965), in O'Brien and Shannon, *Renewing the Earth*, pp. 178–284, nn. 85, 88 (hereafter cited as *GS*).

43. *PP*, n. 47.

44. *PP*, n. 48.

45. *PP*, nn. 51–55.

46. *EJFA*, pp. 265–66.

47. *SRS*, n. 21.

48. UN Department of International Economic and Social Affairs, *World Economic Survey, 1986*, pp. 86–87.

49. E.g., in the Philippines, one of the most favored countries in terms of aid, annual payments of interest and principal due are $3.6 billion annually from 1987 to 1992; the most optimistic estimates of official development assistance from bilateral and multilateral sources total $3.5 billion annually.

50. *PP*, n. 54.

51. *PP*, n. 54.

52. *EJFA*, pp. 271, 272–73, 277.

53. *EJFA*, p. 274.

54. *SRS*, nn. 19, 35–43.

55. Jan Tinbergen, *Reshaping the International Order: A Report to the Club of Rome* (New York: Dutton, 1976), p. 36.

56. *GS*, n. 86, cited in *PP*, n. 48.

57. *PP*, n. 47.

58. The Reagan administration made the arms trade one of its instruments of foreign policy from the outset. Brazil and other newly industrializing nations became active exporters of military hardware in the 1980s. In 1975 developing nations exported 4.06 percent of the arms in world trade; by 1982 their share was 12.03 percent. See Sewell, Feinberg, and Kallab, *U.S. Foreign Policy and the Third World*, p. 196.

59. UN Children's Fund, *The State of the World's Children, 1990* (New York: Oxford University Press, 1990), table 1, p. 86.

60. See successive editions of Ruth Leger Sivard, *World Military and Social Expenditures*, published annually by the World Policy Institute, Washington, D.C.

61. Cited in Independent Commission on International Development Issues, *North-South*, p. 14.

62. *MM*, nn. 198, 69, 204.

63. *Pacem in Terris*, in O'Brien and Shannon, *Renewing the Earth*, pp. 124–70, n. 109 (hereafter cited as *PT*).

64. *GS*, n. 81.

65. *PP*, n. 53.

66. *PP*, nn. 76, 87.

67. *Justice in the World*, in O'Brien and Shannon, *Renewing the Earth*, pp. 390–408, chap. 1, n. 4.

68. Vatican Statement to the UN Ad Hoc Committee on the Review of the Role of the United Nations in the Field of Disarmament, 1976; excerpted in Virginia M. Sixeas, "Voices for Peace," *Network* 10 (May–June 1982): 11–12.

69. John Paul II, *Redemptor Hominis*, in *The Papal Encyclicals, 1958–81*, comp. Claudia Carlen, IHM (Wilmington, N.C.: McGrath, 1981), pp. 245–73, n. 16 (hereafter cited as *RH*).

70. *SRS*, nn. 10, 24.

71. Independent Commission on Disarmament and Security Issues Staff, *Common Security: A Blueprint for Survival* (New York: Simon & Schuster Touchstone Books, 1982); excerpted in Olof Palme et al., "Military Spending: The Economic and Social Consequences," *Challenge* 25, no. 4 (1982): pp. 4–21.

72. National Conference of Catholic Bishops, *The Challenge of Peace: God's Promise and Our Response*, Pastoral Letter on War and Peace (Washington, D.C.: U.S. Catholic Conference, 1983), pp. 259–73.

73. *EJFA*, pp. 260, 289.

74. See Dorr, *Option for the Poor*, pp. 89–91.

75. *GS*, n. 84; see nn. 83–89 for development of the theme.

76. *PP*, n. 78 (quoting his 1965 UN address) and n. 50.

77. *OA*, n. 43.

78. *RH*, n. 16. Cf. Dorr, *Option for the Poor*, p. 221.

79. *SRS*, nn. 43, 45.

80. *SRS*, n. 47.

81. *EJFA*, pp. 288, 290.

82. *EJFA*, pp. 291, 252, 273, 277, 261.

83. *EJFA*, pp. 262–63, 264–92.

84. *EJFA*, p. 292.

85. Dorr, *Option for the Poor*, p. 263.

86. John Maynard Keynes, *The General Theory of Employment, Interest, and Money* (New York: Harcourt, Brace, 1936), pp. 383–84.

8

CLASS AND POVERTY IN
THE U.S. ECONOMY

Michael Zweig

From its beginnings, liberation theology has focused attention on the problems of the poor. In one important document of the movement, Latin American bishops enunciated the "preferential option for the poor,"[1] through which the church is urged to commit itself first and foremost to the needs of the poorest members of society. This formulation has now become widespread. In asserting such an option, church leaders are drawing on a long Christian tradition of concern for the poor, which is also found in Jewish religious practice through the ages and in virtually all other religions as well.

When this assertion is considered in the North American context, it also touches broad concerns of social policy. At least since the publication of Michael Harrington's *The Other America*,[2] a special focus on the poor has been a hallmark of U.S. secular politics. First captured in "the war on poverty" of the 1960s, it continues to the present in debates over programs for the homeless and the so-called "safety net" for the poor.

Yet liberation theology goes far beyond the traditional religious urging to perform acts of charity, which in so many ways is also embodied in government poverty programs, designed as they are to dispense social alms to the "truly needy." Liberation theology is a call to inspect the social structures that produce poverty and human degradation, so that those structures can themselves be changed.

It is the thesis of this chapter that the structural problems of the poor, whether economic or political, can better be understood and corrected if we approach them in the context of a broader class analysis of society.

POVERTY IN THE UNITED STATES

Poverty is a complex phenomenon, the product of interaction among class, race, gender, and many economic and social dynamics. To get at the problem, let us begin with some basic information about poverty and poor people in the United States. The economist Mollie Orshansky devised the first government definition of poverty at the Social Security Administration in 1964.[3] On the basis of her work, the government has collected and published data on "poor people" since the 1960s.

For example, the federal government defined the poverty-level income for a family of four in the United States in 1987 as $11,611. A single individual was defined as "poor" if he or she had an income no more than $5,788, or $5,909 if the person was over sixty-five years old. At the other end of the spectrum, a family of nine could make no more than $23,105 to be considered officially poor.[4] Such numbers are often published but are difficult to appreciate. To get a sense of what standard of living a maximum poverty income will provide, let's see how far income for a family of four will go toward buying basic household goods and services.

The U.S. government regularly monitors the prices of nearly four hundred goods and services that people normally buy—everything from cars to bacon to laundry soap, household appliances, babysitting, and various kinds of clothing. It also collects information through surveys of consumer spending about how important each item is in the average consumer budget. Meat, for example, accounts for $2.50 of every $100 spent by urban wage earners, while eggs account for only $0.22 of every $100.[5] We can get an idea of the living standard of a "poor" family, then, by comparing what it can buy on its income if it tries to buy what the average family buys.

As we saw, a family of four in 1987 could receive no more than $11,611 and be considered poor. After deducting 6.5 percent of that for the average federal income tax paid on such an income that year, and 7.15 percent more for social security tax,[6] the family is left with $10,000 to spend. If this family tries to live like the average wage-earning family, it will have $250 for the entire year to spend for meat. That's $1.20 per week per person, stark evidence that the poverty budget provides a family no more than "an even chance of . . . a diet meeting 2/3 of the recommended dietary allowances of the National Research Council."[7]

Taking all food and beverage together, this family will have available $1,965 for the year, or $1.35 per person per day. It might of course spend

---

more, but then it would have less available for other items in the budget, which are no less tight already. The basic budget allows $212 a month for rent, $26 a year for cosmetics, and $54 a year for admission to all movies and concerts for the entire family. All transportation must be had for $1,902 a year, which involves car payments of $72 a month, $241 a year for insurance, and $114 a year for all public transportation for the entire four-person family.

These amounts from a *maximum* budget of a poor family begin to suggest the conditions of grinding poverty experienced by those included in the official measure of the poor. Many people who are not counted as poor by the official definition nonetheless lead very straitened lives far from the advertised norms of "the American way." We will return to this point later, when we consider the position of the working class in the United States. But let's consider first who it is who lives in official poverty.

Table 8.1 shows the number of poor people in the United States, and their percentage of the total population, over three decades. Even using the stringent standard of the official definition, there were more than 32 million poor people in the United States in 1987, 13.5 percent of the population.

At the end of the 1950s, over one-fifth of all people in the United States were poor, and well over half of all Black people were poor. Significant reductions in these rates were accomplished through the economic boom of the mid-1960s and especially through the implementation of a host of programs that constituted the "war on poverty." By 1978, despite a weak economy, poverty rates were at their lowest, but even then more than 30 percent of all Black people were poor. Since that time, poverty rates have risen dramatically, approaching the level of the 1960s.

Table 8.1 clearly shows that poverty has consistently been more prevalent among Blacks and Hispanics than among whites. But it is also more prevalent among women than among men. In 1984, for example, 15.9 percent of all women but 12.8 percent of men were poor, and women constituted 57 percent of all poor people in the United States.[8] Further, while 13 percent of all families lived in poverty in 1986, and 15 percent of all families with children, 46 percent of all families headed by a single woman were poor.[9]

Poverty is also concentrated among the young and the very old. Table 8.2 shows the percentage of poor people in different age groups in 1985, for all age groups where the poverty rate was greater than the aver-

TABLE 8.1
PERSONS BELOW POVERTY LEVEL, 1959–1987

	Number of Persons (millions)				Percent below Poverty Level			
	All Races	White	Black	Hisp.	All Races	White	Black	Hisp.
1959	39.5	28.5	9.9	na	22.4	18.1	55.1	na
1966	28.5	20.8	8.9	na	14.7	12.2	41.8	na
1970	25.4	17.5	7.5	na	12.6	9.9	33.5	na
1975	25.9	17.8	7.5	3.0	12.3	9.7	31.3	26.9
1978	24.5	16.3	7.6	2.6	11.4	8.7	30.6	21.6
1980	29.3	19.7	8.6	3.5	13.0	10.2	32.5	25.7
1982	34.4	23.5	9.7	4.3	15.0	12.0	35.6	29.9
1984	33.7	23.0	9.5	4.8	14.4	11.5	33.8	28.4
1986	32.4	22.2	9.0	5.1	13.6	11.0	31.1	27.3
1987	32.5	21.4	9.7	5.5	13.5	10.5	33.1	28.2

SOURCE: *Statistical Abstract of the United States* (Washington, D.C.: U.S. Bureau of the Census, 1989), table 734.

age rate for the racial/ethnic group as a whole. Even in the mid-1980s nearly half of all Black children younger than ten lived in families whose budgets were *at best* the meager standard of living described above; this fact stands in sharp contrast to the American dream. That one in seven white children were in similar circumstances shows that all racial groups suffer a heavy burden of poverty.

Governments at all levels in the United States collect volumes of data on the poor.[10] They are counted and measured over a great variety of characteristics. While it is important to have this wealth of information, there are pitfalls in looking at the poor strictly in terms of their own characteristics.

For example, we saw in Table 8.1 that poverty is concentrated among Blacks and Hispanics. Because so much attention has been given to the influence of racism in society, especially as a cause of poverty, most people make an easy identification between poverty and people of color. Yet the great majority of poor people in the United States are white. In fact, by official measures about two-thirds of all poor people are white, and two-thirds of all Black people are not poor.[11]

TABLE 8.2
POVERTY RATES BY RACE/ETHNICITY AND AGE, 1985

Age	White (and other) non-Hispanic	Black non-Hispanic	Hispanic
0 to 4	15.7	46.9	41.6
5 to 9	13.6	47.2	41.8
10 to 14	12.8	39.6	37.7
15 to 19	11.5	35.8	37.1
—			
75 to 79	12.4	36.0	31.0
80 to 84	14.7	33.6	23.0
85 plus	16.0	41.6	23.8

SOURCE: Thomas Gabe, "Income, Wealth, Poverty, and the Life Cycle," in *Retirement Income for an Aging Population* (Washington, D.C.: Committee on Ways and Means, U.S. House of Representatives, 1987), pp. 265–66.

Confusion about these facts has important political consequences. In a thorough study of the attitudes and life circumstances of a large group of industrial workers in New Jersey, David Halle found that about 75 percent of working men display a "lack of sympathy" for the poor. "There are two main reasons for the widespread hostility toward the poor. First, a number of workers equate them with the Black and Hispanic population. As a result, their attitudes toward the poor are flavored with any racial or ethnic stereotypes they have." The second reason is a widespread belief that everyone can achieve the American Dream.[12] It is of course important to address the racism extant among working people. But it will be easier to do so, and easier to confront poverty on a realistic basis, if we proceed from the fact that poverty is an overwhelmingly white phenomenon.

Working-class resentment toward the poor also arises from the fact that millions of working people are "near poor," earning somewhat more than the official poverty income but still living far from comfortable lives. These "near poor," counted by the government as those with incomes up to 125 percent of official poverty, are typically not eligible for relief programs aimed at "the poor." In 1987 they numbered 11 million people, in addition to the more than 32 million people with incomes at or below the poverty level.[13] Their suffering is unabated, and their resentment is too often turned toward those officially counted as poor.

The stereotyping of people in poverty is often connected with a tendency to see poor people as suffering from a weakness in their own makeup or person. The poor are poor because of who *they* are; there's something wrong with *them*, and their poverty is their own fault. To improve the condition of the poor person, one must then focus on changing one or more of his or her characteristics. While this may result in certain beneficial programs, blaming the victim poisons the undertaking.

Such an approach does, however, conform both with the individualism that dominates our thinking and with the whispers of "There but for the grace of God go I" that motivate a great deal of charitable behavior. The stereotyping also feeds on the currents of racism and male chauvinism so deeply embedded in U.S. society. But this approach misses entirely the social structures which shape people's individual circumstances, which generate and reproduce poverty, and which assign and evaluate personal characteristics such as education, skill, employment, or family structure.

Responding to poverty does involve addressing racism, male chauvinism, "ageism," and other ideological characteristics of mainstream society which facilitate the marginalization of whole groups of people simply by virtue of some supposed defect shared by their members. Because oppressive ideologies do in fact help to shape the contours of social marginalization and poverty, it is important to confront them, not least in order to challenge the blame-the-victim paternalism of conservative political economy. But attention to ideological and political issues is best undertaken in conjunction with attention to the class component of poverty.

CLASSES IN U.S. SOCIETY

There is a host of competing definitions and understandings of class. In the popular culture there is a widespread view that class is nonexistent in U.S. society, or irrelevant because of social and economic mobility. Before looking at the connection between class and poverty, let us look more closely at classes in U.S. society.

It is quite commonly believed that poor people themselves constitute a class. This belief is most often reflected in references to a broad division of U.S. society into a vast "middle class," flanked by the rich and the poor as somewhat marginal classes. In this view, Rockefeller, Trump, and Wall Street brass are the rich; the poor are the homeless and the chronically unemployed "underclass" typically associated with people of color, a connection that reinforces the racist conception of the poor that Halle observed among working men; and the middle class comprises all the ordinary working people who hold steady jobs, raise families, and have to worry about how to make ends meet. Within this scheme, most people think of themselves as middle class and believe that the middle class is the overwhelming majority of the population.

This view is also widespread in American political thinking. Two typical examples of popular political analysis illustrate the point. Discussing Michael Dukakis's strategy in his 1988 presidential campaign, Elizabeth Drew wrote that "there has been an accelerated and disciplined effort to show Dukakis as the candidate talking about programs that would help the middle class (the poor, who are out of fashion these days, get a few crumbs)."[14] The full class spectrum was invoked by Geraldine Ferraro in her response to a U.S. Supreme Court decision limiting access to abortion; she observed that the decision "will have little impact on the middle class or wealthy women [who] will continue to have safe abortions available to them. . . . But what of the poor?"[15]

In a society so focused on money, it is natural enough to divide people according to their income. Indeed, there are rich, there are poor, and there are as many in the "middle" as one might want to put there. But the popular view of classes based on income stratification is again misleading and in fundamental ways counterproductive to understanding poverty. To see why this is so, it is necessary to consider more carefully what a social class is.

To begin with, a social class is a number of people who share certain common attributes and life circumstances that distinguish them from other people who can be grouped separately. Most of the vast sociological literature on class seeks to identify just which attributes may be used to define social class, and which are the most important. Among the main elements usually taken to position a person in one class or another are the amount of income and its source, occupation and the prestige that society confers on it, length and place of education, place of residence, network of social connections, and the subjective association of the person with others in society.[16]

Whatever particular combination of factors one settles upon, all approaches that seek to define class simply by the shared characteristics of class members suffer a common fault: defining a class strictly in terms of its members results in a tautological aspect to the definition and an arbitrariness to the distinctions made between classes.

Further, these isolated strata stand only in ordinal relation to one another; a class is higher or lower in income or prestige or general social standing as its members have more or fewer of the characteristics taken to define classes. So "the division of society into classes or strata, which are ranged in a hierarchy of wealth, prestige, and power, is a prominent and almost universal feature of social structure."[17] Such an ordinal ranking of isolated strata succeeds in carrying the principle of individualism to a higher level.

It is natural enough to hold with sociologist Bernard Barber that "stratification systems may be assumed to be a continuous hierarchy" of standing, in which somewhat arbitrary lines are drawn between upper, middle, and lower classes or such further refinements as upper-middle class and other borderline cases.[18] Certainly our experience is of hierarchies of power and prestige, associated with hierarchies of income and wealth. Still, there is something missing in these formulations of class.

We must acknowledge that people are social beings. We are individuals, of course, but we must enter into social relationships in order to survive. Economic activity in particular is thoroughly social, so a proper analysis of economic status has to go beyond the individual and investigate how the person is enmeshed with others in society—indeed, how the person is in significant degree constituted by these social relationships. This important insight, articulated by Karl Marx in his economic and social theory, is discussed by Herbert Gintis and Samuel Bowles in Chapter 9.

As has been noted by two sociological scholars of class: "In the Marxist perspective, classes are not, as Barber would have it, 'divisional units within systems of social stratification.' Classes constitute common positions within social *relations* of production."[19] That is, for Marx and for most in the Marxist tradition, classes are not defined in and of themselves; they are defined by the relations established among people as they undertake the social process of producing goods and services.

Marx developed a holistic approach to social science and human experience. He proceeded from the existence of society, in which people live in relation to one another. He rejected individualism but developed an analysis of individuals nonetheless. For Marx, a person exists and is constituted in a complex social web, within which individual creative powers are exercised in a complex amalgam of freedom and social and historical constraint.[20]

In the Marxist framework,[21] there is a mutuality among classes in that a person's class is determined by what she or he does *in relation to* others in the economy. This relationship is an intimate one, one in which the various people are involved with one another across class lines. As Marx put it, "Society is not merely an aggregate of individuals; it is the sum of the relations in which these individuals stand to one another. . . . Being a slave or a citizen is a socially determined relation between an individual A and an individual B. Individual A is not as such a slave. He is only a slave in and through society."[22]

Slaves may be poor. Slaves may be people of one or another specific race or nationality. Slaves may have many specific characteristics, but slaves are not slaves "as such," are not slaves because of their own personal attributes. Rather, slaves are slaves because they have a special relation in society to their owners. The various attributes of the slave—possession of few resources, little education, membership in a particular racial or ethnic group—derive from the relation of subordination in which the slave exists, not from the inherent nature of the slave "as such." And this relation also defines the owner as part of a different class whose members have quite different attributes, associated with life in a dominant social position. Class is an intimate relation, a mutually defining relation, not simply an ordinal relation (although, of course, the slave owner is "above" the slave in the hierarchy of most social characteristics).

Neither are the poor a class "as such," whether we measure them by income, education, race, or family status. By promoting tautological conceptions of class, the standard sociological and popular literatures mask the *connections* among people, which are the important features that define true status in society. The poor of course constitute a large group in the United States, but to understand their class position, we need to look at the relations people enter into in the social processes of production. In doing so, we will get a better appreciation of the way capitalist economic dynamics generate poverty.

In capitalism, the two classes whose interdynamics dominate social development are the capitalists and the working class. As a first approximation to the meaning of these terms, the capitalists own the means of production—the factories and capital equipment used to produce goods and services. Working-class people do not own means of production. Therefore, in order to produce anything and derive income they must sell their productive abilities to some owner-employer in exchange for a wage. These two classes are intertwined in the everyday course of production and are defined in their relation to one another.

There are also middle strata, which taken together can be called a "middle class" but not in the colloquial sense. The middle class is defined not in terms of its income but in terms of the structural relation of its members to the capitalist and working classes.

Marx also defines a *lumpenproletariat*, those people who are not absorbed into mainstream capitalist society and are therefore forced to exist on its margins.[23] The *lumpen* tend to live in poverty, often the most abject poverty. Even though they are not directly engaged in capitalist production, their existence as a group, and the poverty in which they live, derive in important measure from the dynamics of capitalism and the relations between the capitalist and working classes. I will return to this point.

While the central attribute of a class is its relation to the means of production, it would be simplistic to leave the matter there. For class is a relation among people and conveys the authority and control one group possesses (or is subject to) in relation to others. Ownership of means of production is one basis of control, and in some sense the most fundamental, but it does not fully determine class relations.

Owning the means of production gives the owner control over the labor process—the organization of work, its content, purpose, and pace. What is more, through the application of labor in production, additional wealth is produced and can be accumulated as additional capital, which is, after all, the entire point of the labor process for those who control it.

Marx's economic analysis is devoted to exploring the origins of capital and the social and historical implications of capital accumulation. Capital arises out of the productive labor of workers yet is kept by the capitalists solely because they own the means of production, means that are themselves the product of labor. In this way, Marx not only describes the process of economic exploitation in the capitalist economy; he demonstrates that capital itself is a *social relation*.[24] While the means of production take on a material form as factories, machinery, buildings, and equipment, these objects are not simply objects. They are the product of specific social relations. Both in the way capital is produced and in the way it is then used by its owners to continue to subjugate and control labor, the means of production are embodiments of relations among people.

This is a well-known conclusion of Marx. But the same view is also forcefully enunciated by Pope John Paul II in his encyclical *Laborem Exercens* (On human work) as a foundation of his assertion of "the priority of labor over capital."[25] Gregory Baum explores this theme in Chapter 3, and I return to it toward the end of this chapter as well.

Even though the ownership of capital can carry with it an exploitative control of labor, it is not true that *lack* of legal ownership of the means of production, through actual title in shares or proprietorship, consigns one to the working class. Many people who own no means of production nevertheless exercise a more or less significant degree of control over the labor process—as supervisors or managers of other people's work, or as independent professionals or proprietors. It is from these people that the "middle class" is drawn.

Understood in this way, the middle class is not defined by its income, even though the income of people in the middle class does generally fall between that of people in the capitalist class and the much lower income of those in the working class. The middle class is in the middle because the people in it engage in the social processes of the economy in such a way as to carry aspects of both capitalist and working classes simultaneously. They are in what Erik Olin Wright calls "contradictory locations" in the economic process.[26]

Consider, for example, an office supervisor or shop foreman. This person typically works for a wage or salary, as does a worker, and is controlled by higher levels of management. But his or her social task is to exercise direct control over workers on behalf of that higher management and ultimately the owners of the capital, who employ workers and supervisors alike.

In this regard, the supervisor or foreman is not part of the working class, a reality codified in collective bargaining law, which requires such employees to be represented in different bargaining units from those of production workers. It is also reflected in the well-known fact that being a supervisor or foreman is an extremely stressful job because of the contradictions experienced by these people at work. They are neither workers nor owners; they are caught in the middle.

The middle class also includes professional people, family farmers, and other small business people often called the "petit bourgeoisie." These small capitalists are not workers (even though they work), insofar as they are not employed by another capitalist. But even those who are employed, such as a corporate lawyer, university professor, or engineer, are not members of the working class, because they tend to have a degree of control and authority over their own work and the work of others which places them in a social relation at work quite different from that experienced by working-class employees of the firm. They also have skills that sustain a culture of personal job mobility in this stratum, giving these people some resemblance to individual entrepreneurs, even though they work for a salary. The fact that the middle class is structurally caught between the working class and the capitalists contributes to the vacillating political and ethical beliefs of the middle class, described by Norman Gottwald in Chapter 2.[27]

Just as it is true that being an employee does not make a person a worker, so owning some capital does not make one a capitalist. Many workers (though far from a majority) own shares in one or another company, perhaps the one at which they are employed, or own a small amount of rental property. But despite this formal ownership, they exercise no control whatever over capital or labor on the basis of their holdings, nor do they derive any significant share of their income from their property. Their social existence remains defined by their life as workers.

Even among capitalists it is important to distinguish between the millions of owners of small businesses, often unincorporated "mom and pop" operations, and the relatively few "captains of industry and finance" who dominate the major industrial and financial wealth of the country. Although in a formal sense the owner of the local deli is a capitalist, a part of the bourgeoisie, these small entrepreneurs are part of the middle class, insofar as they too often share some of the interests and experiences of working people as well as those of large capitalists.

Because class at root conveys information about social relations, class is a political concept as well as an economic one—political not simply, or necessarily, in terms of electoral politics but in the sense that class involves relations of control, subordination, and relative degrees of personal autonomy at work. When analysts recognize the profound political dimension of production relations in the economy per se, many seek to extend the familiar democratic demands of electoral politics into demands for economic democracy in the arena of production itself.[28]

The political aspect of class extends beyond control of the labor process. The owners of capital use their accumulated wealth to influence profoundly, if not control entirely, the institutions of state power and the larger political and cultural conditions of society. Political and military leaders are sometimes drawn into the bourgeoisie as a ruling class, even if they own no capital, insofar as their social activity serves significantly to support the owners of capital. The same is true of major religious leaders. While that subject is quite beyond the scope of this chapter, many liberation theologians who criticize the role of the church in perpetuating capitalist-class domination in society are alert to this broader play of class forces.[29]

Because class has a relational basis, a person's nominal occupation is not always a reliable indicator of class. A carpenter, for example, is a worker if he or she owns few tools and works for a contractor, but is in the middle class if self-employed. Truck drivers who own their own rigs are in the petit bourgeoisie, but a truck driver for a transport company is in the working class. A salesperson (clerk) in a discount store is in the working class, but a salesperson (broker) in a commodities trading firm is in the middle class. For any given occupational title, one must look at the particular content of the work to assess the relational character of the job and, from that, to determine its class standing.

Table 8.3 presents the approximate class composition of the civilian employed labor force in the United States in 1986. Over 60 percent of the labor force is in the working class, if we take that to include those who are employed by others, do not supervise others, and have little autonomy over their work. The table probably underestimates the size of the working class because it does not count those in military service or the unemployed, people disproportionately drawn from the working class. Furthermore, people with the relatively lower levels of income and formal education common in the working class tend to have larger families. We can conclude that about two-thirds of the U.S. population is in the working class. The United States is not a middle-class society.

To divide gross occupational categories into class groups, one can look at the more detailed occupational titles, in hopes of better assessing the work relations involved. Among the "technical, sales, and administrative support" personnel recorded in Table 8.3, for example, supervisors, proprietors, commodities traders, and sales representatives for finance and business services are likely to be outside the working class, whereas cashiers, licensed practical nurses, secretaries, and computer operators are likely to be in the working class (computer programmers and analysts are counted as professional employees). Among "managerial and professional" occupations, dentists, lawyers, and natural scientists are professionals generally in the middle class. But most nurses and hospital therapists have working-class positions, even though they are officially counted as professional people. The table reflects these rough distinctions. Similarly, farm proprietors and managers should be excluded from the working class, but not farm workers or nonsupervisory employees in

TABLE 8.3.
OCCUPATIONAL AND CLASS COMPOSITION OF EMPLOYED
CIVILIAN U.S. LABOR FORCE, 1986

Occupation	Total Employed (000)	% of Total	Working Class (000)	Other Classes (000)
Managerial and professional	26,554	24.2	2,026	24,528
Technical, sales, and administrative support	34,354	31.3	25,550	8,804
Service	14,680	13.4	13,682	998
Precision production, craft, and repair	13,405	12.2	8,756	4,649
Operators, fabricators, and laborers	17,160	15.7	16,582	578
Farm, forestry, and fishing	3,444	3.1	2,107	1,337
Total	109,597	100.0	68,703	40,894
Percentage of Total	100		62.7	37.3

SOURCE: *Statistical Abstract of the United States*, 1988, table 627, and author's calculations. See text for derivation of class distributions.

the logging and fishing industries. Self-employed people in the "service" and "operators, fabricators, and laborers" categories are not counted as working class.[30]

Similarly, as an approximation in Table 8.3, half of all mechanics and construction trades employees (included in the "precision production" category) are taken to be outside the working class, and no engineer, writer, or teacher is taken to be in the working class. These latter are grouped by the Department of Labor with other professional and managerial occupations, such as financial managers, doctors, and business executives. While the specific divisions shown in the table remain somewhat arbitrary, because almost any occupational classification contains a variety of work relations within it and some misclassification is bound to occur, the overall estimates are consistent with other findings and support the conclusion that the American people are largely a working-class people.[31]

As we have seen, income is not the basis of class. But income differences are certainly related to class differences. In 1986, for example, the occupational group containing the smallest proportion of working-class people (see Table 8.3), "managers and professionals," had the highest median income ($505 per week), and median income fell as the proportion of nonfarm working-class people increased. Managerial and professional income was more than twice the income of "service" workers ($223), and 70 percent higher than that of "operators, fabricators, and laborers" ($301), the two occupational categories in which the working class is concentrated.[32]

These income differences are actually even more substantial when we consider that the income data cited are for full-time work only. Working-class jobs are more frequently part time than are professional, managerial, and executive jobs, so the actual differences in class income are greater than those shown above. The differences are further exacerbated by the fact that property income and capital gains income, not counted in occupational earnings, go overwhelmingly to people in the top income strata, who are not in the working class.[33]

Income inequality among families in the United States is clearly revealed in the distribution of family income measured by the U.S. Bureau of the Census. In 1985 the richest 20 percent of families received 43 percent of all income, while the poorest 20 percent received only 5 percent. The 60 percent of the population at the low end of society, corresponding roughly to the working class, accounted for just one-third of all income. Meanwhile, the richest 5 percent of families, corresponding roughly to the capitalist class, garnered 16 percent of all income, as much as the income received that year by the bottom 40 percent of families in the United States.[34]

The inequality in distribution of income in the economy is striking, but personal wealth is far more unequally distributed. If we account for the gross value of all real estate, stocks, bonds, and other financial assets held by American families in 1983, we find that the top ½ percent of all families owned 32 percent of the wealth, while the bottom 90 percent of families owned 33 percent. If we remove housing from the picture and look at net worth in all other assets (after subtracting all debts outstanding), wealth is even more concentrated: the richest ½ percent owned half of it all, while the bottom 90 percent held less than 10 percent.[35]

Against this backdrop, it seems preposterous for people to continue to claim that "the egalitarianism of modern America represents the essential achievement of the classless society envisioned by Marx."[36] Yet such claims are regularly made and widely believed. All evidence is to the contrary.

Assessing the returns that different people in society can expect to experience from increased levels of education, Andrew Levison found that "the class differences between workers and employers are considerably greater than the differences between men and women or Blacks and whites within the working class."[37] While the differences in income and economic and political status between Blacks and whites and between men and women are widely known, the even greater differences between classes are regularly overlooked.

In 1986 in the United States, men working full time earned 1.4 times as much as women working full time, while whites working full time earned 1.3 times as much as Blacks. But the earnings of managers and professionals were 1.6 times those of technical, sales, and administrative support personnel, 1.7 times those of precision production and related personnel, and 2.3 times the earnings of service workers.[38]

My crude division between working class and everyone else still masks the great differences between the middle class and the capitalists. The category "managers and professionals" includes capitalists, but it includes very many more people whose class position is in the middle, as discussed above. The difference between workers and capitalists, therefore, is certainly much more pronounced than is indicated by the income data cited and is more closely suggested by the distribution of wealth.

THE CLASS CONTENT OF POVERTY

Poverty in the United States is concentrated in the working class. At the start of the "war on poverty" in 1963, "more than 1 in 3 of all men at the head of a family in poverty . . . were never out of a job all year. . . . the primary cause of poverty [was] a history of an erratic series of short-term jobs or a spell of uninterrupted employment at low pay, coupled with a large number to be supported out of the family income."[39] During the 1980s there was a worsening in living conditions of the working class, precisely as part-time employment proliferated and low-paying full-time work came to supplant many relatively well-paid industrial jobs.[40] For a family of five in 1987, even two full-time, year-round jobs earning minimum wage couldn't bring the family above the poverty line.

The fact that poverty is closely associated with conditions of employment is further reflected in the transitory experience of poverty for great numbers of Americans. One study tracked a representative sample of Americans from 1967 to 1976. During this period, fully 40 percent of the people experienced poverty for at least one year. Ten percent were poor for most of the period and could be thought of as the long-term or hard-core poor, while 30 percent experienced poverty during a year within the period and could be thought of as the transitory poor.[41]

If 30 percent of the population experiences transitory poverty at some time during a decade, poverty is surely a regular feature of life for a large section of the American working class. Poverty is not a condition of a fringe population. Even though hard-core poor are the majority of the poor *at any one time,* the experience of poverty over time is borne primarily by the working class.

What is it about being a worker that makes one especially vulnerable to poverty? Unemployment and employment at low wages or for part-time work are conditions concentrated in the working class. Working-class people have few resources to cushion times without work. When the steel mills close, the steel workers are the most vulnerable. The owners and management aren't reduced to minimum wage, and their communities don't lose vital social services. Quite simply, it is the working class that is without wealth, and without the power and security that wealth provides.

The importance of low wages for much of the working class should not be underestimated. In 1987 almost half of all poor families were headed by someone who worked during the year, and 15 percent worked full time all year. Nearly 20 percent of all households in poverty had two or more people working during the year. Of those poor people over age fifteen who did not work at all, more than 40 percent were disabled, retired, or in school. In short, a large fraction of the poor work for their poverty.[42]

For individual workers, upward social mobility is possible in the United States. Belief in this possibility is firmly implanted in the popular culture and such achievements are regularly presented as evidence of the meaninglessness of class distinctions for individual life. But social structures drastically limit the number of success stories in the saga of personal uplifting. Small businesses go broke almost as fast as they are created, wiping out hard-won savings and throwing the hopeful worker-entrepreneur back into the working class.

The working class is also effectively restricted from access to the professional middle-class strata, "all those people whose economic and social status is based on education, rather than on the ownership of capital and property."[43] The educational system on which people must rely for the foundation of class transcendence provides class-based training largely designed to reproduce the class structure of society.[44] Children in working-class families receive schooling that guides them into working-class lives, while children of middle-class and bourgeois families receive a very different training, more suited to the future wealth and authority they are expected to wield.

There can be no capitalism without the working class, which must be reproduced from generation to generation *as a class* by the institutions of capitalist society. While some individuals do escape upward, upward mobility as a social phenomenon is simply impossible within the bounds of capitalist society because the working class as a whole must continue to exist, and the conditions of its existence expose millions to poverty.

To understand and confront poverty in capitalist society, therefore, one must understand the position and experience of the working class. To do this, one must confront the class relations of capitalism and the economic and cultural structures that reproduce them. For it is in the very process and logic of capital accumulation that the working population is rendered vulnerable and regularly consigned to poverty. This is one of the central findings in Marx's economic analysis.

Even the *lumpenproletariat,* sometimes called the underclass in large urban centers in the United States, is understandable in terms of the logic of capital.[45] These are people who have been entirely cast off as unnecessary from the point of view of capital accumulation. Capital has no need for them, so they and their communities are allowed, even forced, to degenerate. Wasted and thrown out, they are then alternately pitied and reviled. As we have seen, the great majority of the adult poor have more or less steady work experience or are out of the labor force because of disability or retirement. The poor are overwhelmingly part of the working class. But the same economic engine that defines and limits the condition of the working class also consigns some people to abject poverty outside even the limited life of working people.

The importance of class analysis should not obscure the fact that the working class is constituted in the midst of the pervasive influence of racism and male chauvinism, which locate women and minorities disproportionately in the working class and, further, within low-paying, part-time, and temporary positions. The fact that poverty is disproportionately experienced by women and minorities is consistent with the fact that the working class itself is largely composed of women and minorities. White men are a minority of the working class.[46] Capitalism renders workers vulnerable to poverty, but racism and male chauvinism concentrate that burden among women and people of color. Pamela Brubaker addresses these connections in Chapter 4.

Even though class is central to the existence of poverty, then, class considerations alone are not sufficient to comprehend the problem. To confront poverty, one must confront racism and male chauvinism as well as the forces of capital accumulation as such, which steadily press down on working people regardless of race, gender, or national origin.

It is true, if perhaps somewhat ironic, that Pope John Paul II's formulation "priority of labor over capital" is more appropriate as a point of departure for addressing poverty in the United States than is the Latin American bishops' formulation "preferential option for the poor." As Gregory Baum explains in Chapter 3, the Pope, despite his many conservative teachings and his rejection of antagonistic class struggle, has identified the class basis of social degradation and in so doing has provided a fruitful direction for study, reflection, and social action.

Because class entails interpersonal relations and not simply an ordinal hierarchy, class realities support a kind of claim upon resources different from claims based on income differentials alone. Without the connection of class, the poor have claim to the resources of the rich only through resort to charity in some form or other, perhaps based on an ethic of equality drawn from an abstract commitment to community. This is conveyed in the very notion of an "option," which may or may not be picked up.

Because he relies on the relational nature of class, and in particular on the fact that capital is the product of labor, the Pope asserts a "priority" that has its foundation in the material processes of production, not just in an arbitrary moral code. "All these means [of production] are the result of the historical heritage of human labor. . . . There is a need for ever new movements of solidarity of the workers and with the workers. This solidarity must be present whenever it is called for by the social degrading of the subject of work [the worker], by exploitation of the workers and by the growing areas of poverty and even hunger. The Church is firmly committed to this cause."[47]

Hierarchical notions of class suggest some redistribution of income as a response to inequality. But relational notions of class promote more basic economic and social restructuring. The claim of the poor on the rich for simple redistribution of income is often an attempt to implement a subjective egalitarian principle (even if it involves structural change to force the rich to share their income and wealth). Such redistributional claims are regularly rejected as inappropriate.

When classes are understood in relational terms, however, the claim of the worker on capital is a material claim for what they have already created as workers. However insistently the conservative political and economic analysts seek to dismiss redistributional programs as unjustified taking of property, if we keep in mind the class basis of property itself, and with it also the class basis of poverty, we can secure the claim of working people and the poor among them. This claim is not for simple redistribution of income but for the redistribution of control over capital, as capital is the labor-created social wealth from which income is in turn created.

It is of course true that such consciously class-based politics does not operate in the United States. This is consistent with the fact that class is not recognized as a meaningful social category. Many reasons are proposed in the generous literature exploring the lack of class consciousness in American politics.[48] Still, class is a reality. Liberation theologians are no strangers to class analysis. In response to those critics, including Pope John Paul II, who fear that a class analysis will foment unnecessarily divisive social unrest, Gustavo Gutierrez has pointed out that "those who speak of class struggle do not 'advocate' it—as some would say—in the sense of creating it out of nothing by an act of (bad) will. What they do is recognize a fact and contribute to an awareness of that fact. . . . To build a just society today necessarily implies the active and conscious participation in the class struggle that is occurring before our eyes."[49]

NOTES

1. See the "Final Document" of the Latin American bishops' 1979 meeting in Puebla, Mexico, in *Puebla and Beyond: Documentary and Commentary*, ed. John Eagleson and Philip Scharper (Maryknoll, N.Y.: Orbis Books, 1979), p. 264.

2. Michael Harrington, *The Other America* (New York: Macmillan, 1962).

3. The definition is based on the cost of food in the cheapest food plan devised by the U.S. Department of Agriculture. The official poverty income is three times the money needed to buy this minimum amount of food. See Current Population Reports, ser. P-60, no. 163 (Washington, D.C.: U.S. Bureau of the Census, 1988), p. 156.

4. *Money Income and Poverty Status in the United States: 1987*, Current Population Reports, ser. P-60, no. 161 (Washington, D.C.: U.S. Bureau of the Census, 1988).

5. *Handbook of Methods,* Bulletin 2285 (Washington, D.C.: U.S. Bureau of Labor Statistics, 1988), p. 187.

6. *Statistical Abstract of the United States* (Washington, D.C.: U.S. Bureau of the Census, 1989), tables 507, 576.

7. Mollie Orshansky, *The Measure of Poverty: Documentation and Background Information and Rationale for Current Poverty Matrix,* Technical Paper 1 (Washington, D.C.: U.S. Department of Health, Education and Welfare, 1977), p. 234.

8. Lowell Gallaway and Richard Vedder, *Poverty, Income Distribution, the Family, and Public Policy* (Washington, D.C.: Joint Economic Committee of the U.S. Congress, 1986), p. 10, table I-5.

9. *Statistical Abstract of the United States,* 1989, table 741.

10. The fullest sources of information from the federal government are the annual surveys published in Series P-60 of Current Population Reports by the U.S. Bureau of the Census.

11. *Statistical Abstract of the United States,* 1989, table 735.

12. David Halle, *America's Working Man* (Chicago: University of Chicago Press, 1984), pp. 212–13.

13. *Money Income and Poverty Status,* tables 16, 17.

14. Elizabeth Drew, "Letter from Washington," *New Yorker,* October 10, 1988, p. 107.

15. Geraldine Ferraro, "Abortion: The Issue Can't Be Ducked," *New York Times,* July 15, 1989, p. 15.

16. See, e.g., Richard Centers, *The Psychology of Social Classes* (Princeton, N.J.: Princeton University Press, 1949); W. Lloyd Warner, Marchia Meeker, and Kenneth Eells, *Social Class in America* (Chicago: Science Research Associates, 1949); Bernard Barber, *Social Stratification* (New York: Harcourt, Brace & World, 1957); Milton M. Gordon, *Social Class in American Sociology* (Durham, N.C.: Duke University Press, 1958); G. William Domhoff, *The Higher Circles* (New York: Random House, 1970).

17. T. B. Bottomore, *Classes in Modern Society* (New York: Random House, 1966), p. 3.

18. Barber, *Social Stratification,* p. 78.

19. Erik Olin Wright and Luca Perrone, "Marxist Class Categories and Income Inequality," *American Sociological Review* 42 (February 1977): 33.

20. Karl Marx, *The German Ideology* (New York: International Publishers, 1966); and Karl Marx, *Economic and Philosophical Manuscripts of 1844,* reprinted in *The Marx-Engels Reader,* 2d ed., ed. Robert Tucker (New York: Norton, 1978), pp. 66–125; Frederick Engels, *Anti-Dühring* (New York: International Publishers, 1977); Bertell Ollman, *Alienation: Marx's Conception of Man in Capitalist Society* (Cambridge: Cambridge University Press, 1970).

21. Even though class is a central concept in Marx's writing, there is no single place where he elaborates his concept of class. Rather, there are scattered discussions, and a number of elaborations by subsequent theoreticians in the Marxist tradition. See, e.g., Karl Marx, *Selected Writings in Sociology and Social Philosophy,* ed. T. B. Bottomore (New York: McGraw-Hill, 1964); Maurice Dobb, *Studies in the Development of Capitalism* (New York: International Publishers, 1964); Bottomore, *Classes in Modern Society;* Harry Braverman, *Labor and Monopoly Capital* (New York: Monthly

Review Press, 1974); and Erik Olin Wright, *Class, Crisis, and the State* (London: New Left Books, 1978).

22. Karl Marx, *Grundrisse*, excerpted in Marx, *Selected Writings*, pp. 96–97.

23. No economic system is pure. Within capitalism there are often vestiges of prior economic systems, whether semifeudal sharecropping, landed aristocracy, or even slavery. This chapter ignores the presence of noncapitalist economic and class forms, which no longer play a significant role in the United States. Class analysis is more complex in Latin America and other areas where capitalism still operates in the midst of significant remnants of older societies.

24. Karl Marx, *Capital*, vol. 1 (New York: International Publishers, 1967), esp. pt. 7.

25. John Paul II, *Laborem Exercens* (Washington, D.C.: U.S. Catholic Conference, 1981), pp. 25–27. See also Gregory Baum, *The Priority of Labor: A Commentary on Laborem Exercens* (New York: Paulist Press, 1982).

26. Wright, *Class, Crisis, and the State*, pp. 61–63. See also Erik Olin Wright, David Hachen, Cynthia Costello, and Joey Sprague, "The American Class Structure," *American Sociological Review* 47 (December 1982): 710.

27. For an excellent analysis of the socioeconomic position, uncertainty, and political vacillations of the middle class in the United States, see Barbara Ehrenreich, *Fear of Falling: The Inner Life of the Middle Class* (New York: Pantheon Books, 1989).

28. See, e.g., Samuel Bowles and Herbert Gintis, *Democracy and Capitalism: Property, Community, and the Contradictions of Modern Social Thought* (New York: Basic Books, 1986); and Chapter 9 in this volume.

29. See, e.g., Leonardo Boff, *Church: Charism and Power* (New York: Crossroad, 1985); and Gustavo Gutierrez, *A Theology of Liberation* (Maryknoll, N.Y.: Orbis Books, 1973).

30. See *Statistical Abstract of the United States*, 1989, table 627.

31. See, e.g., Andrew Levison, *The Working Class Majority* (New York: Coward, McCann & Geoghegan, 1974); and Wright et al., "The American Class Structure," pp. 709–26.

32. *Statistical Abstract of the United States*, 1989, table 651.

33. See, e.g., Gallaway and Vedder, *Poverty*, pp. 116–17.

34. Howard Wachtel, *Labor and the Economy*, 2d ed. (New York: Harcourt Brace Jovanovich, 1988), p. 156.

35. *The Concentration of Wealth in the United States* (Washington, D.C.: Joint Economic Committee of the U.S. Congress, 1986), table 2, p. 24.

36. Francis Fukuyama, "Witnessing the End of Political History," *San Francisco Chronicle*, August 9, 1989; excerpted from *National Interest* 16 (Summer 1989). When he wrote the article, Fukuyama was deputy director of the U.S. State Department's Policy Planning Staff.

37. Levison, *The Working Class Majority*, p. 53.

38. *Statistical Abstract of the United States*, 1989, table 651.

39. Mollie Orshansky, "Who's Who among the Poor: A Demographic View of Poverty," *Social Security Bulletin* 28 (July 1965); reprinted in Orshansky, *The Measure of Poverty*, p. 63.

40. See Bennett Harrison and Barry Bluestone, *The Great U-Turn* (New York: Basic Books, 1988), esp. chap. 2, "Zapping Labor."

41. Lee Rainwater, "Persistent and Transitory Poverty: A New Look" (Working Paper no. 70, Joint Center for Urban Studies of MIT and Harvard University, June 1981), p. 14.

42. *Money Income and Poverty Status, 1987*, tables 18, 19. See also Bradley R. Schiller, *The Economics of Poverty and Discrimination*, 4th ed. (Englewood Cliffs, N.J.: Prentice-Hall, 1984), pp. 42–73.

43. Ehrenreich, *Fear of Falling*, p. 12.

44. Samuel Bowles and Herbert Gintis, *Schooling in Capitalist America: Educational Reform and the Contradictions of Economic Life* (New York: Basic Books, 1976).

45. See Braverman, *Labor and Monopoly Capital*, esp. pt. 5.

46. Wright et al., "The American Class Structure," pp. 722–24.

47. John Paul II, *Laborem Exercens*, pp. 26, 19.

48. An excellent review and analysis is provided in Mike Davis, *Prisoners of the American Dream* (London: Verso, 1986).

49. Gutierrez, *A Theology of Liberation*, p. 274.

IV

POLITICAL IMPLICATIONS

9

THE ECONOMY PRODUCES PEOPLE: AN INTRODUCTION TO POST-LIBERAL DEMOCRACY

Samuel Bowles and Herbert Gintis

One of the hallmarks of the revival of progressive theological concern with social problems is the insistent demand that the economy conform to moral precepts. But are such precepts capable of fulfillment? Does the "ought" of social justice imply the "can" of economic policy?

The moral criteria the economic system is called upon to satisfy are often demanding indeed. For instance, the Pastoral Letter on Catholic Social Teaching and the U.S. Economy, *Economic Justice for All*, affirms that the dignity of the human person, realized in community with others, is the criterion against which all aspects of economic life must be measured.[1] Similarly, the United Church of Christ statement on the economy holds: "Far from being confined to the allocation of scarce resources or to the analysis of prices and wages, among Christians the sphere of economic concerns encompasses issues central to the well-being of the individual, [and] the integrity of the community."[2]

Elementary economic theory informs us, by contrast, that in the production of goods and services, economic growth and material progress dictate efficiency (measured by net product produced per unit of input), not freedom (the dignity of the human person, or social participation), as the central evaluative criterion in economic life.

The Catholic bishops further assert that "commutative justice calls for fundamental fairness in all agreements and exchanges between individuals or private social groups."[3] Once again, however, elementary economic theory affirms the efficacy of market exchange and the sanctity of contractual agreement according to the principle of self-interest rather than "fundamental fairness." According to this view, in the absence of coercion, as long as the exchange was "chosen" by each party to it, it cannot be deemed unfair, no matter what its terms involve.

In this chapter we argue that it is by no means unreasonable to hold economic life to the demanding criteria of fundamental fairness, the dignity of the human person, and enhanced social participation. Our argument has two parts. First, we hold that "justice" and "fairness" are best understood, and the prospects for their satisfaction best assessed, when translated into the notion of democratic accountability and human rights. Not equality but freedom is our moral anchor; we support the former because it promotes the latter. Instead of discussing how the pie should be divided up, we want to discuss who gets to decide on the division. Second, we maintain that traditional economic theory, long known as the "dismal science" because of its predilection to rule out the possibility of achieving such "utopian" goals as "fairness," vastly understates the possibilities for progressive change.

We begin by arguing that the dominant philosophical tradition in the modern capitalist world—which we shall call liberalism—is so preoccupied with "choice" that it has become blind to the fact that human dignity and well-being depend as much on what we *are* as what we *have*. We yearn not only to *get* that which we lack but to *become* what we are not. "Learning" as much as "choosing" is central to our economic well-being, and it is in the sphere of learning and personal development that the notions of dignity, freedom, and community must be grounded.[4]

We thus go on to argue that the economy produces people as much as goods and services. We can evaluate economic arrangements not only for what things they help us acquire but for what people they help us become. This human development perspective on the economy will lead us to argue that the democratization of economic life is a prerequisite to the full personal development of the human individual. Our analysis does not lead to the rejection of either individual choice or market exchange but rather suggests that the multidimensional social reality of community and workplace, as the "schools" through which individuals become who they are, must be made arenas of popular accountability and personal liberty as a prerequisite to the attainment of economic justice.

We are thus led to propose a vision of a new economic order—"post-liberal democracy"—in which dignity and community are achieved by fostering the growth of democratically controlled firms and economically powerful communities. These institutions, we suggest, can provide the solidarity and meaning required to offset the anonymity of the abstract individual, the power that wealth conveys, and the power of both the state and the global corporation in modern capitalism.

Simply put, the goal of a post-liberal democracy is to let all of us, as people and as a people, become more nearly the authors of our own history. We seek to do this by turning right side up the inverted morality of the capitalist age: rather than economic development being the end and human development the means, we propose the reverse. Let us decide who we would like to become, and then fashion an economy that will foster rather than impede our individual and group projects of becoming.

LEARNING AND CHOOSING

Among liberalism's most enduring contributions is its rich conception of individual action. Whatever its defects, the liberal conception of the individual has served and will continue to serve as a key point of departure in democratic theory.

But the liberal conception of the individual has one defect that renders its model of choice incompatible with modern democratic theory. This is the assumption that the individual chooses on the basis of given goals—hatching, as it were, fully grown with all his or her capacities and desires in place. The liberal tradition is not prone to ask how we come to want what we want. The "preferences" of neoclassical economics and the "interests" of political science are simply assumed.

Thus, where considerations of liberty and democratic accountability apply, individuals can be taken as given. This handy fiction makes the argument for individual liberty extremely simple and elegant. Consider, for instance, the following well-known passage from John Stuart Mill's On Liberty: "The only purpose for which power can be rightfully exercised over any member of a civilized community against his will is to prevent harm to others. His own good . . . is not a sufficient warrant."[5] But by the same token, taking the individual's objectives as given, this justly celebrated defense of liberty undermines the defense of popular sovereignty. For the fiction of given tastes and desires, while allowing us to recognize democracy's contribution to the proper aggregation of wants, obscures the essential contribution of democratic institutions to human development—the unique capacity of democratic participation to foster in people the ability to control their lives intelligently and creatively.

Liberalism tells us that people make decisions. But the liberal conception of the individual must be transcended to recognize that decisions also make people.

Of course the liberal model of action recognizes that people are formed somewhere. Its error is to assume that where individuals are in the process of becoming, problems of choice are absent. For instance, Mill's famous proclamation of the inviolability of individual preferences quoted above is followed immediately by the following less frequently cited proviso:

> It is, perhaps, hardly necessary to say that . . . we are not speaking of children or of young persons below the age which the law may fix as that of manhood or womanhood . . . [who] must be protected against their own actions. . . . For the same reason we may leave out of consideration those backward states of society in which the race itself may be considered as in its nonage. . . . Despotism is a legitimate mode of government in dealing with barbarians, provided the end be their improvement.

Mill here erects an opposition between what we may term "choosers" on the one hand and "learners" on the other, and he justifies a system of relations of domination and subordination between the former and the latter. This opposition is characteristic of liberalism: choosers are the knights in shining armor, while learners represent a residual category—individuals whose status does not include and whose behavior does not support (be it temporarily or *in perpetuum*) the right of free choice; in short, they are those who are not deemed to be rational agents.

The status of "chooser" has always applied in liberal discourse to educated, propertied, white male heads of households, and variously through history to others as well. The status of "learner" has always applied in liberal discourse to children, prisoners, the insane, and the "uncivilized." It has also applied variously to women, servants, and workers, as well as to specific races and cultures which, by virtue of their biological constitution or social station, are deemed to be more or less permanently denied the status of rational agent.

Liberalism thus exempts cultural institutions—those that make us who we are—from democratic scrutiny; it does not invite us to evaluate schools, churches, families, neighborhoods, and other institutions essential to our formation as human beings according to the principles of rational agency, freedom, and choice. Since such favored institutions of learning as patriarchal families and race- and class-biased schools are not required to be accountable to their participants, central forms of domination governing personal development are obscured. Within liberal political philosophy one does not ask, for instance, whether schools are democratic.

Moreover, liberalism relegates choice to an arena of personal autonomy ostensibly devoid of developmental potential. Although the favored liberal institutions of choice—the market and the ballot box— are praised as sensitively attuned to record the wills of consumers and citizens, this sensitivity fails to extend to a most central area of personal control: the choice as to how we are to develop our wants, our capacities for social participation, and our abilities to make critical and informed choices.

Liberalism claims that market and ballot box allow people to get what they want. But it fails to tell us how people get to be what they want to be, and how they get to want what they want to want.

This defect in the liberal model of action helps us understand how the nineteenth-century golden age of free trade and the democratic revolution in the late eighteenth and nineteenth centuries also saw the birth of systems of institutional dependence (such as compulsory education) and social control (such as conscription) and incarceration (asylums, prisons) to an extent unparalleled in human history. Our point here is hardly to mourn some fictitious idyllic past when mythical popular forces impressed upon society a free and democratic structure of personal development. We suggest, rather, that it is in the nature of the liberal learning/ choosing partition systematically to obfuscate the issue of domination in learning.

In our view, learning and choosing represent polar forms of a more general form of social action. In place of the archetypal "child" and "adult" of liberal theory, we use the notion of the individual constituting him- or herself by developing personal powers through acting in the world. This model supplements Mill's liberal vision of the rational chooser with Marx's conception of the formative power of action. For it was Marx who stressed that labor is "a process going on between man and nature, a process in which man, through his own activity, initiates, regulates, and controls the material reactions between himself and nature. He confronts nature as one of her own forces. . . . By thus acting on the external world and changing it, he at the same time changes his own nature."[6]

Using a becoming-by-acting model, schools, families, workplaces, the electoral process, playgrounds, town meetings, markets, and hospitals can all be assessed according to the same criteria: those of liberty, popular accountability, and contribution to personal development.

Our unification of learning and choosing, in rejecting the traditional status of the child, also thereby rejects the status of adult. Those traditional liberal defenses of liberty based on the sanctity of individual preferences are thus severely compromised. When individuals are at once choosers and learners, the boundaries between liberty, popular sovereignty, and authority become blurred. However convenient, the old defense of liberty is uncompelling and unwittingly provides the door through which domination over human development becomes an aspect of liberal society—a result all the more pernicious for being invisible through the lens of liberal political philosophy.

The clarity introduced through the use of a becoming-by-acting model of individual choice provides post-liberal democratic theory not with a set of ready-made political slogans but rather with a challenging intellectual enterprise: how might the centrality of individual choice and the commitment to liberty and popular sovereignty be preserved and, at the same time, the myths of the autonomous individual and the fully formed chooser be rejected?

We handle this problem by recognizing that personal development is in general best served through an interaction of two strategies: exercising one's freedom to choose, independent of collective sentiment; and entering into mutual, reciprocal, and participatory action with others to achieve commonly defined goals. These two strategies are precisely Albert Hirschman's twin notions of "exit" and "voice."[7]

The critique of the liberal model of action in terms of exit and voice is then simply stated. By taking preferences and interests as given, liberalism equates agency with exit: one's power is simply the power to walk away. Individuals exercise their rights through either the market or the ballot box. Both present a menu of alternatives, of which the preferred can be chosen by the individual in social isolation. The power of the chooser, then, is limited to his or her ability to abandon a product or a political party—that is, to "exit." The capitalist economy and the liberal democratic state, then, stress exit to the virtual exclusion of voice, and representation to the virtual exclusion of participation.

But voice—participation in decisions, not simply choosing from a set menu—is essential to a democratic culture. If "freedom" is reduced to choosing items from a menu—as it often is in a capitalist society—the balance of exit and voice upon which personal development depends is not permitted to develop.

EXIT, VOICE, AND MARKET EXCHANGE

Traders make trades, but trades also make traders. Though the fact is unrecognized by economists, exchanging goods in markets is not altogether unlike exchanging greetings, kisses, or blows. Goods and services are indeed allocated through market exchange, but the exchanging parties are themselves transformed or reproduced in the process. The becoming-by-acting model treats exchange as an interaction between subjects shaping human development. Indeed, there is a strong analogy between exchange and language in that both represent forms of social interaction that shape who we are and who we might become.

The point is a familiar one to anthropologists. Marshall Sahlins writes: "If friends make gifts, gifts make friends . . . the connection between material flow and social relations is reciprocal. A specific social relation may constrain a given movement of goods, but a specific transaction—'by the same token'—suggests a particular social relation . . . the material flow underwrites or initiates social relations."[8]

Exchanges do much more than allocate goods and services. Indeed they may not even do that at all. Again Sahlins: "Sometimes the peace-making aspect [of exchange] is so fundamental that precisely the same sorts and amounts of stuff change hands: the renunciation of opposed interest is in this way symbolized. On a strictly formal view the transaction is a waste of time and effort. . . . They do, however, decidedly provision society: they maintain social relations, the structure of society."[9]

The exchange process need not cement social unity, however. It may as well be an explosive centrifugal force, eroding social relationships and courting social dissolution. Karl Polanyi took this view of what he called the "disembedded" market economy of the nineteenth-century European capitalist nations:

The disembedded economy of the nineteenth century stood apart from the rest of society, more especially from the political and governmental system. In a market economy, the production and distribution of material goods in principle is . . . governed by . . . the so-called laws of supply and demand, and motivated by fear of hunger and hope of gain. Not blood-tie, legal compulsion, religious obligation, fealty or magic creates the sociological situations which make individuals partake in economic life. . . . Such an institution could not exist for any length of time without annihilating the human and natural substance of society.[10]

A constitutive conception of exchange must therefore reject the shibboleth of materialism, according to which what economic life is about is the production of things—how, by whom, for whom, and for whose benefit. The economy is no less about the production of people. A theory of exchange adequate for a just and democratic society must address not only the question, who gets what and why? It must also ask, who gets to *become* what and why? A theory that focuses exclusively on the production of things runs the risk of seeing economic activity as simply a process of getting rather than also a process of becoming. A democratic theory of the economy must thus encompass learning as well as labor, the production and reproduction of people as well as the production of things.

THE ECONOMY PRODUCES PEOPLE

Once the given nature of people's tastes, capacities, and goals is rejected, it is clearly inconsistent to consider as democratic a society in which the rights of democratic determination and individual choice do not extend to the social relations through which people themselves are formed.

Philosophical critiques of the liberal treatment of the economy have, reasonably enough, centered on questions of distributional justice and allocational efficiency. The capitalist economy, it is rightly claimed, is both unfair and wasteful. The learning/choosing partition, however, sheds additional light on the shortcomings of the liberal justification of capitalism. For liberal discourse clearly presents the economy not only as a set of private as opposed to public institutions but as a sphere of social life within which "choosing" rather than "learning" occurs. This notion is sanctified in liberal economic theory, the very definition of which is, following the liberal economist Lionel Robbins, "the study of the allocation of scarce means towards the satisfaction of given ends." Whence the common-sense but misleading notion of the economy as a process that produces things according to the preferences of its participants.

But the economy does more than allocate "scarce means." It produces people. The experiences of individuals as economic actors is a major determinant of their personal capacities, attitudes, choices, interpersonal relations, and social philosophies; individuals develop their needs, powers, capacities, consciousness, and personal attributes in part through the way they go about transforming and appropriating their natural environment. Moreover, individuals and groups regulate their own development to the extent that they succeed in controlling their projected interventions in the transformation of nature. Thus, under ideal circumstances, education forms an essential and intentional element of production itself.

To the extent that the experiences of production constitute an important learning environment, then, the despotic character of the capitalist economy obstructs the ability of liberal democratic capitalism to foster generalized popular control over personal development. Since the work environment is generally unaccountable to its participants, these participants will not possess the social power to control their own development as workers or, insofar as development through work suffuses their total personality, as citizens and family members either.

By democratic culture we mean the broadest possible diffusion among the citizens of politically relevant information, skills, and attitudes of political effectiveness, as well as the availability of forms of discourse conducive to the effective functioning of democratic institutions. It is often claimed that modern capitalism promotes precisely such a democratic culture. Such claims, based on arguments dating back to Alexis de Tocqueville and Thomas Jefferson, cannot be dismissed. The discourse of individual rights, the near-universal spread of literacy, the extension of social interaction to ever wider circles of contact, the consequent destruction of many forms of patriarchy, parochialism, and political deference are all integral to democratic culture and, at least in some measure, promoted by the ethic of market exchange.

But we find the claim that capitalism supports the generation and regeneration of democratic culture not altogether persuasive. Our first two arguments for a critical reconsideration of this view concern the division of labor within the capitalist enterprise and the market, respectively; our third concerns the structure of liberal discourse itself.

Consider, first, the experience of production as it may affect the formation of people and communities. Our analysis of the organization of the labor process within the capitalist enterprise suggests that it may be antithetical to the production of a democratic culture. Alexis de Tocqueville and Adam Smith foresaw similar dangers well before the birth of the Marxian tradition.

A modern restatement of the argument may begin by noting that under conditions of capitalist production the division of labor within the enterprise quite generally exhibits four relevant characteristics: the minute fragmentation of tasks, the separation of conception from execution, the hierarchical control of the labor process, and the assignment of persons to positions on the basis of race, sex, age, or academic credentials. These four characteristics would appear to promote precisely the opposite of a democratic culture, as they concentrate information, information processing, and decision-making at the narrow pinnacle of a pyramidal structure. At the same time the structure of capitalist production promotes a sense of political ineffectiveness and assigns to racial, sexual, and other differences a set of hierarchical meanings that are as inconsistent with tolerance and respect as they are hostile to the forms of solidarity and cooperation necessary for effective political intervention.

But can these antidemocratic effects be traced to the specifically capitalist structure of production? Each of the four characteristics noted above might well be taken as a lamentable manifestation of the technically or genetically determined requirements of efficient production. They would then presumably appear in any system and would thus present natural rather than social limits to democratic accountability.

If labor were a commodity like any other, these counter-claims would be compelling. But labor is not a commodity, since the relationship between employer and worker is composed of social understandings and implicit commitments that are incapable of contractual enforcement. This noncontractual dimension simultaneously explains the four characteristics of the labor process and forces a divergence between efficiency and profitability even under competitive conditions.

The minute fragmentation of tasks and the separation of conception from execution make individual workers dispensable (and hence susceptible to the threat of dismissal) by restricting the areas of production involving high levels of skill and expertise; in addition, fragmentation renders the worker's activities more susceptible to measurement and supervision. The hierarchical control of the labor process, whatever its technical properties, is required to enforce the delivery of labor services, and the assignment of persons to positions on the basis of race, sex, age, or academic credentials serves to legitimate the hierarchical division of labor and divide workers against one another. On this basis we claim that the hierarchical structure of the labor process is consistent with a competitive equilibrium of profit-maximizing, noncolluding capitalists, but it is not reducible to the imperatives of technical efficiency in production.[11]

If the antidemocratic nature of the labor process has traditionally been all but ignored, the other major facet of economic coordination in capitalist society—competitive markets—has provided its foundation. It is true, to be sure, that few liberal theorists since Tocqueville have made much of the relationship between markets and culture. Where the issue has been raised, as in Milton Friedman's classic defense of markets (*Capitalism and Freedom*, 1962), it has been to assert that markets inhibit discrimination and the arbitrary use of power. This argument, which may be traced to Montesquieu, is an attractive but only partial truth. The strength of the argument lies in the anonymity and range of choice offered in markets, which explain, to cite Friedman's example, why the consumer of bread does not care whether it was produced by "a Negro, a Jew, or a Communist." The shortcoming of the argument consists in overlooking the relationship between markets, political participation, and the formation of a democratic culture.

Demonstrating this shortcoming is quite straightforward. A democratic culture is produced and reproduced through the activities that people undertake. Perhaps the most important of these activities is democratic politics itself. John Stuart Mill expressed this familiar point: "This discussion and management of collective interests is the great school of that public spirit, and the great source of that intelligence of public affairs, which are always regarded as the distinctive character of the public of free countries."[12] Under what conditions will people engage in such a "discussion and management of collective interests"? Clearly, where such opportunities exist and where there are incentives to participate. The incentives to participate will be greater where something important is at stake or, to put it differently, where the opportunity cost of not participating is high.

Markets minimize the cost to the individual of not participating in democratic political practices. For markets promote exit over voice and hence provide an alternative to political participation as a means toward acquiring desired ends. The exclusive reliance upon markets thus undermines a democratic culture. For if most important social outcomes

are generated by market processes, the stakes of democratically constituted decision processes are severely circumscribed. That markets might
undermine democratic political participation through limiting the stakes
and reducing the opportunity costs of not participating is perhaps not
surprising. For it is precisely this reduction in the "need" for collective
decision which is so much applauded in liberal social theory.

In short, the issue of market versus nonmarket decision-making, which
is traditionally seen as an "economic" debate, is also political. Indeed,
it is an instance of the age-old dilemma of liberty versus popular sovereignty. The issue cannot be resolved in favor of one or the other, we
submit, for the same reason that a reasonable political philosophy does
not choose between liberty and popular sovereignty.

POST-LIBERAL DEMOCRACY

Liberal capitalism has banished serfdom and slavery; it has reined in the
pretensions of the absolutist state; but it has failed to inaugurate freedom, to ensure human dignity, or to achieve social justice. Its promise of
the material security and liberty on which freedom and dignity depend
has not been wholly empty. But neither has it been fulfilled. The liberal
era has thus seen neither freedom itself nor its nemesis; at best it may
be considered, to borrow a phrase from Alexis de Tocqueville, freedom's
apprenticeship: "Nothing is more fertile in marvels than the art of being
free, but nothing is harder than freedom's apprenticeship . . . liberty
is generally born in stormy weather, growing with difficulty amid civil
discords, and only when it is already old does one see the blessings it has
brought."[13]

The liberal vision of people effectively controlling their lives is not a
hollow promise, doomed by defects in human nature and the dictates of
modern technology. Liberalism's fault lies not in overstating the possibilities for human freedom but rather in failing to identify the roots
of domination—those that lie in economic dependency and patriarchal
authority chief among them—and in elevating a radically individual conception of autonomy to the detriment of a conception of community that
might form the basis of democratic empowerment.

As a result, liberal theory has justified a social order whose precious
accomplishments have been gained at the cost of a historically unprece-

dented accumulation of unaccountable economic power and an unconscionable degree of inequality of wealth.

Liberal capitalism has flourished by undermining rather than supplementing venerated sources of personal and collective autonomy. The sense of communal belonging, the center of the sense of self in precapitalist times, was at least metaphorically traded for the vote. The control of the land and the tools of one's livelihood—the foundation of autonomy in the thought of Thomas Jefferson—was traded for a wage.

Post-liberal democracy promises to reverse this development, to continue the expansion of citizen rights and thus to render the exercise of both property rights and state power democratically accountable. It affirms the traditional democratic forms of representative democracy and individual liberty, and proposes novel forms of social power independent of the state: democratically accountable, chartered freedoms in community and work. These aspects of economic democracy, including the democratic control of investment and production, are not only desirable in their own right; they are also an increasingly necessary condition for the viability of democratic control of governments.

Democracy is a relationship among free people, and economic dependency no less than personal bondage is the antithesis of freedom. The hardheaded seventeenth-century advocates of representative government thus had a point in opposing the extension of suffrage to "servants": they claimed that employees had exchanged their autonomy for a wage. The Jeffersonian synthesis of property and democracy addressed the issue of economic dependency by proposing its elimination through the extension of ownership. But Jefferson's vision was against the capitalist grain: property was not to become more generally shared but the reverse.

The eclipse of small ownership by the large-scale employment of wage labor has rendered Jefferson's solution archaic. The Marxian conception of socialism as common ownership and collective control of productive property suffered a similar fate, for just as Jefferson had underestimated the corrosive power of the capitalist accumulation process, Marxists typically failed to take account of the impressive ability of the coercive state to thwart democratic accountability.

Post-liberal democracy may be considered a synthesis of the Jeffersonian and Marxian visions, affirming both the Jeffersonian commitment to decentralized control of the productive apparatus and the Marxian recognition that because production is social, its decentralization cannot take the form of individual property ownership. The post-liberal democratic commitment to democratic control of the workplace thus amounts to a rejection of the Jeffersonian attempt to make property ownership universal and the Marxian attempt to make property ownership collective. It proposes, rather, that property rights should simply be demoted and citizen rights elevated.

We conceive of post-liberal democracy as more than a new set of rules of the game. It encompasses as well a set of human purposes, embracing a broad vision of human development as its guiding principle. If for liberalism the archetypal human activity is choice and for Marxism it is labor, post-liberal democratic theory represents people as learners for whom both choice and labor are indispensable means toward personal development. We thus follow John Stuart Mill in celebrating Wilhelm von Humboldt's profession of Enlightenment faith: "The grand, leading principle, towards which every argument unfolded in these pages directly converges, is the absolute and essential importance of human development in its richest diversity."[14]

In contrast to traditional liberal doctrine, which supports a society of acquisition based on the exchange of property claims, post-liberal democracy is a vision of a society based on learning governed by citizen rights. It thus presents a profound reorientation of our normative grid, an inversion of the relationship between human development and economic organization allowing economic activity to be considered not as an end but as a means toward democratically determined forms of human development. The legitimation of this model—as well as its sense of history—is based not on capital accumulation but on learning, not on the ever widening appropriation of nature in the interests of economic development but on the continuing process of personal and social transformation, human development.

Thus a new model of economic growth no less than a new model of democracy is implied. The Canadian political philosopher C. B. Macpherson expressed this notion as follows: "As soon as democracy is seen as a kind of society, not merely a mechanism of choosing and authorizing governments, the egalitarian principle inherent in democracy requires not only 'one man, one vote' but also 'one man, one equal effective right to live as fully humanly as he may wish.'"[15] Although this vision of a post-liberal democracy is unmistakably the product of the aspirations of the liberal era itself, it breaks sharply with the liberal tradition in two respects: it represents the individual as an intrinsically social being actively engaged in the continual transformation of his or her own and others' capacities, sentiments, and attachments; and it represents the private ownership of concentrated productive property not as a salutary barrier to the pretensions of the state but as the bedrock of economic dependency and an obstacle to popular sovereignty.

By stressing workplace and community empowerment as opposed to state expansion, the vision of post-liberal democracy avoids one of the great dead ends encountered in the expansion of citizen rights and simultaneously addresses a key weakness of social democracy. By stressing that the extension of democracy is not synonymous with the extension of state power, post-liberal democracy affirms the sentiment that neither the centralized state nor the capitalist enterprise will be the vehicle of human liberation.

Moreover, as we shall see presently, there is an economic logic that may propel elements of the post-liberal democratic vision to prominence. Just as the technical and economic environment of the early modern period of European history generally favored the expansion of commerce and the encroachment on feudal hegemony, new technical and organizational demands being made upon economic life today may favor a radical extension of democratic principles to the economy. The continuing growth of output and the shift from goods production to services, the democratic erosion of hierarchical authority, the growing centrality of knowledge as the sine qua non of economic dynamism, and the increasingly costly predation of nature have combined and will continue to combine to raise the costs of maintaining the status quo. Correspondingly, we argue, these developments may propel more democratic and egalitarian economic institutions from being little more than post-scarcity utopias to the status of practical means of addressing the not soon to be banished problem of scarcity.

PREFACE TO THE POLITICAL ECONOMY OF A POST-LIBERAL DEMOCRACY

Our vision of a post-liberal democracy is based on the following propositions. First, a coherent conception of democracy requires that the powers conferred on individuals and institutions in the capitalist economy be subject to democratic accountability.

Second, lack of secure access to basic material needs is a form of dependency which renders individuals fundamentally powerless. The exploitation of economic dependency—whether the economic dependence of women on men, unemployment induced by macroeconomic policy to discipline the labor force, or the threat of dismissing "insubordinate" workers—arbitrarily limits individual choices and erodes democratic accountability even where it is formally secured. Economic dependency is thus antithetical to both liberty and popular sovereignty.

Third, the economy, like the family, produces people. The lifelong development of capacities, sentiments, and personal identities results from an interaction between genetic potential and structured social practices. The impact of social structure on human development ranges from the relationship between the sexual division of labor and what Nancy Chodorow calls "feminine personality"[16] to the connection between the hierarchical structure of work and the value that parents place on obedience in their children, to the effect of the decline of residential neighborhoods on civic orientations. Because the growth and effectiveness of democratic institutions depend on the strength of democratic capacities, a commitment to democracy entails the advocacy of institutions that promote the development of a democratic culture.

Fourth, learning or, more broadly, human development is a central and lifelong social activity of people. Hence there is no coherent reason for exempting the structures that regulate learning—whether they be schools, families, neighborhoods, or workplaces—from the criteria of democratic accountability and liberty.

We do not intend to derive specific institutional prescriptions from these four quite general propositions. But they do point unmistakably toward the democratization of the economy, the attenuation of economic inequality, the democratization of the learning process, and the promotion of what Hannah Arendt called "new public spaces for freedom."[17]

The main imperatives of the democratization of the economy are clear—workplace democracy, democratic economic planning, and community access to capital—but the relationships among them are complex at best and possibly contradictory. The logic of the democratic workplace is that democratic decision-making in production units will replace unaccountable hierarchy with democratic participation and commitment. One might hope thereby to contribute to a more effective system of production through reduced enforcement cost, as well as to support a participatory learning environment and an autonomous democratic community.

By democratic economic planning we mean the socially accountable determination of the broad outlines of the pattern of economic structure and its evolution. Accountability entails collective deliberation and control over investment decisions, for concentrated control over the accumulation process places the present and future technological, spatial, environmental, sectoral, and other aspects of economic evolution beyond the realm of popular will.

While the central position of democratic control of investment is clear, the instruments by which the overall accountability of the economy might most effectively be achieved cannot be prejudged. The debate on the merits of centralized planning and direct allocation of resources relative to the use of markets is a practical matter to be decided by study of the associated costs in particular cases. Our analysis does not favor one over the other but rather poses new criteria for the evaluation of each: the evaluation of apparently specialized economic institutions such as markets or systems of economic planning must balance the claims of democratic and other valued forms of human development against the more traditional claims based on liberty, the alleviation of scarcity, and the like. Similarly, the question of public or private ownership may be variously answered under differing particular conditions according to the norms of liberty, efficiency, equity, and democratic accountability.

Our concern with democracy leads us to a political critique of economic inequality. We propose that the access to a socially acceptable standard of living be considered a human right, for depriving a person of the means to satisfy basic needs is as contrary to the notion of personal dignity as depriving a person of liberty.

A society which, as a part of its ordinary functioning, allows many of its members to live in material distress expresses a degree of indifference toward its members that fortifies social division. As the distinguished political theorist Michael Walzer has observed:

> The idea of distributive justice presupposes a bounded world within which distributions take place: a group of people committed to dividing, exchanging, and sharing social goods, first of all among themselves. That world . . . is the political community. . . . Membership is important because of those things the members of a political com-

munity owe to one another and to no one else, or to no one in the same degree. And the first thing they owe is the communal provision of security and welfare. This claim might be reversed: communal provision is important because it teaches us the value of membership. If we did not provide for one another, if we recognized no distinctions between members and strangers, we would have no reason to form and maintain political communities.[18]

Yet this mutual commitment to material security raises economic problems. Capitalist societies rely heavily on economic insecurity as a major if often implicit disciplining and motivating device, and we doubt that any society will dispense altogether with the need to motivate work. If the post-liberal social order is to guarantee economic security, it must simultaneously alter the meaning of work so that work no longer appears to so many as an alien imposition.

Our commitment to the right to a livelihood does not mean, of course, that good work cannot be rewarded but only that the stakes should not be so high and the penalties should not include the loss of an acceptable living standard. More important, democratic work groups in an environment of economic security will be pressed to develop means of eliciting good work from their members; participation in decision-making and the equitable sharing of the net revenues of the production unit would undoubtedly be augmented by a wide range of recognitions, and sanctions, drawing more heavily on the capacity of work team members for pride and shame than on their economic insecurity.

The attenuation of economic inequality and the democratization of the economy would represent a major step toward a more democratic society and would contribute to the democratization of human development as well. Economic necessity is today one of the most binding constraints on educational choices over the course of one's life. The guarantee of an acceptable livelihood would open up a more ample menu of educational choices by eliminating the threat of economic calamity as a possible consequence of wrong choice. More directly, the democratization of the economy would constitute itself a major step toward a positive learning environment.

The democratization of learning is not without its problems. Any philosophically self-conscious viewpoint must grapple with the difficult issues of choice, authority, and social ends which are necessarily bound up in the analysis of learning. But the apparent intractability of these

THE ECONOMY PRODUCES PEOPLE

issues within the liberal framework may stem more from the characteristics of liberal thought than from the peculiar difficulties to which the
educational encounter gives rise. Philosopher Amy Gutmann identifies
the key contradiction of liberalism as an educational philosophy in this
way: "Utilitarians and . . . rights theorists . . . agree on one point about
the education of children: at least in principle they both are committed
to providing an education that is neutral among substantive conceptions
of the good life."[19]

We do not share this liberal neutrality concerning the good life. Nor,
we suspect, do many liberals in their daily activities as parents, teachers, friends, and citizens. It is true that people ought to learn what they
choose to learn when they make choices in a general environment of liberty, community, and popular sovereignty. We do not know what people
would choose to become under these conditions: our moral commitment
is to try it and see. Many educational choices are not now made under
these conditions. But enough are made under sufficiently auspicious conditions that we envision the possibility of a democratic learning dynamic,
one that would progressively transform ever wider circles of social life
toward democratic ends.

DEMOCRACY, AGENCY, AND HISTORY

Whether rooted in the indomitable human spirit, the growth of reason, or the civilizing character of science and technology, the idea that
time is on the side of liberty and equality is deeply ingrained in post-
Enlightenment culture. It appears in the liberal notion of modernization
as a passage toward affluence, tolerance, and the pluralist commonwealth,
and in the Marxian vision of Communism as the first society in which
the freedom of each is the prerequisite for the freedom of all.

No such faith comforts us. The indomitable human spirit can be bro-
ken. Reason is a cruel master. And modern science ever refines the tools
for dominating not just nature but people as well. Not the inevitability of
freedom but rather its existence against great odds is the true monument
to the human spirit.

Democracy may be, quite simply, an accident of history—an exotic
social variety heady with possibilities but of questionable survival capacity. The question the democrat must face is simply this: what condi-

tions contribute to its survival power, and how may our understanding of these conditions allow us to extend and deepen democratic institutions?

We answer that democratic institutions tend to survive and flourish because the systemwide costs incurred in enforcing democratically arrived-at rules are less than the costs of enforcing authoritarian solutions. In addition, both modern consciousness and modern technology tend increasingly to lessen the relative costs of democratic enforcement.

The costs of enforcing any set of rules, whether they be contractual exchanges, town meetings, patriarchal sex-gender systems, or bureaucratic hierarchies, depends intimately on the constitution of the actors— on their skills, sentiments, and understandings. If the rules appear legitimate, the enforcement costs will be low; if on the other hand the rules appear unfair, resistance will mount, and resort to costly forms of coercion is likely to be frequent. The foremost Marxian historian of slavery, Eugene Genovese, comments: "Ruling classes differ, and each must rule differently. But . . . each must confront the problem of coercion in such a way as to minimize the necessity of its use."[20]

Moreover, enforcement costs depend critically on the activities being regulated. Some activities are most suitably regulated by market exchange, others by bureaucratic authority, and yet others by communal relationships. It is perhaps illustrative of the manner in which the nature of the activity itself favors particular types of social organization that even in the most diverse cultures babies are raised in what we call families; and, to take a quite different example, that throughout the nineteenth century around the world, sugar was raised on plantations and tobacco was grown on small owner-operated farms, even (as in Cuba) where these crops were part of a single economy and social system.

The central flaw in modern capitalism is this: rather than being an efficient solution to the problem of scarcity, the unaccountable economic power and high stakes of the game characteristic of capitalism foster increasingly wasteful authoritarian social relationships. Contemporary human needs and (as we will argue presently) modern technology develop in ways increasingly unamenable to bureaucratic authority. At the same time, inegalitarian bureaucratic systems appear increasingly illegitimate, in part because of the expansionary nature of the logic of citizen rights.

The result of these technological, economic, political, and cultural developments is a growing mismatch between needs and consciousness on the one hand and the demands of bureaucratic hierarchy on the other.

Modern capitalism thus incurs growing levels of resistance and hence is burdened with mounting enforcement costs.

Hierarchy replaces market exchange, according to liberal economic theory, when the transaction costs of exchange exceed the enforcement costs of hierarchy. Transaction costs tend to be high where the good or service being exchanged is costly to measure with precision. Where measurement costs are low—as for example in monitoring the flow of electricity from a seller to a buyer—market transactions will have low transaction costs, even where the exchanging parties have sharply conflicting interests. This will be the case because, given the low cost of measurement, attempts to take advantage of one's exchange partner will be easily detected and rectified, if necessary by recourse to a court of law. The case of low measurement cost is essential for the concept of private property as a claim readily enforceable by resort to external authority.

But what about the reverse case, when the activities being exchanged are difficult to measure? If conflicts of interest between the exchanging parties remain severe, some suitably costly form of organization will result: either litigious markets or the proliferation of surveillance activities within a bureaucratic authority. Modern capitalism favors them both.

Two general developments in the liberal democratic capitalist societies are likely to render this solution increasingly costly. The first development tending to raise the costs of hierarchical order concerns people's orientation toward work itself and the manner in which work is organized. In traditional economic theory the "propensity to shirk" is the result of a natural dislike of work on the part of a self-interested actor. Thus, "opportunism is a key attribute of human agents," observes Oliver Williamson.[21]

Liberal economic theory is surely right to focus on how systems of organization can induce people to do things they would otherwise not do, for it is unlikely that any social order will ever banish unpleasant necessities. But it seems considerably more plausible to posit that people's attitudes toward their work depend on how the work is organized, how the rewards are distributed, and how they personally are treated at work, as well as on the more general structure of social relationships, including those of the family and the state. More pointedly, a society that elevates self-interested behavior as a privileged form of rational action, and at the same time fosters high levels of inequality and conflict of interest, should not complain if it finds itself faced with unusually severe problems of malfeasance and burgeoning costs of enforcement.

The second reason to expect mounting costs of the modern capitalist solution concerns the structure of the economy itself. With economic growth, people are changing the manner in which they seek to meet their needs. Most obviously, services—ranging from education, health, and entertainment to finance, insurance, and psychiatric advice—are replacing goods as the main product of labor, now accounting for well over half the output of some advanced economies. Services, however, are generally more difficult to measure than are goods, simply because they are intangible.

Equally important, the nature of production itself is changing. Technical innovation and information have had an increasingly important effect on economic performance. Economic systems that falter in the management of technical change and the production and distribution of knowledge will be increasingly unable to take advantage of possibilities readily exploited by more adept social systems.

Knowledge is difficult to exchange for the converse reason: because it is so easily stolen or shared. The costs of reproducing it are so low compared with the costs of producing it that excluding others from its use is nearly impossible and attempts to do so are almost always irrational from a societywide standpoint. Kenneth Arrow, one of the preeminent students of information and technical change, concludes:

> We expect a free enterprise economy to underinvest in invention and research (as compared with an ideal) because it is risky, because the product can be appropriated only to a limited extent, and because of increasing returns in use. This underinvestment will be greater for more basic research. Further, to the extent that a firm succeeds in engrossing the economic value of inventive activity, there will be an under-utilization of that information as compared with an ideal allocation.[22]

The import of these observations concerning the direction of technology and economic development is clear enough. The old ways of doing business are not only morally repugnant; they are increasingly unworkable, or workable only at the cost of increasingly hierarchical and wasteful structures of enforcement. Recasting the economy as the servant of human development rather than its master, through the progressive democratizing of autonomous communities and workplaces, is more than an attractive vision. It is a feasible journey that we ought to begin.

NOTES

1. *Economic Justice for All: Catholic Social Teaching and the U.S. Economy* (Washington, D.C.: National Conference of Catholic Bishops, 1986), p. 15.

2. Audrey Chapman Smock, ed., *Christian Faith and Economic Life* (New York: United Church Board of World Ministries, 1987), p. 4.

3. *Economic Justice for All*, p. 35.

4. For a more expansive treatment of these issues, see Samuel Bowles and Herbert Gintis, *Schooling in Capitalist America: Educational Reform and the Contradictions of Economic Life* (New York: Basic Books, 1986); Samuel Bowles and Herbert Gintis, *Democracy and Capitalism: Property, Community, and the Contradictions of Modern Social Thought* (New York: Basic Books, 1986).

5. John Stuart Mill, *On Liberty*, in *The Philosophy of John Stuart Mill*, ed. Marshall Cohen (New York: Modern Library, 1961), pp. 185–320.

6. Karl Marx, *Capital* (New York: Vintage Books, 1977), p. 283.

7. Albert Hirschman, *Exit, Voice, and Loyalty* (Cambridge, Mass.: Harvard University Press, 1970).

8. Marshall Sahlins, *Stone Age Economics* (Chicago: Aldine Press, 1972), p. 187.

9. Ibid.

10. See Karl Polanyi, *The Great Transformation* (New York: Farrar & Rinehart, 1944), pp. 3–4; Karl Polanyi, Conrad Arensberg, and Harry W. Pearson, *Trade and Market in the Early Empires* (New York: Free Press, 1957), p. 68.

11. See Herbert Gintis, "The Nature of the Labor Exchange and the Theory of Capitalist Production," *Review of Radical Political Economics* 8, no. 2 (1976); Samuel Bowles, "The Production Process in a Competitive Economy: Walrasian, Neo-Hobbesian, and Marxian Models," *American Economic Review* 75, no. 1 (1985): 16–36; Herbert Gintis and Tsuneo Ishikawa, "Wages, Work Discipline, and Unemployment," *Journal of Japanese and International Economies* 1 (1987): 195–228.

12. Mill, *On Liberty*, pp. 197–98.

13. Alexis de Tocqueville, *Democracy in America* (Garden City, N.Y.: Doubleday, 1969), p. 240.

14. Epigraph facing title page of Mill's *On Liberty*.

15. C. B. Macpherson, *Democratic Theory: Essays in Retrieval* (Oxford: Clarendon Press, 1973), p. 51.

16. Nancy Chodorow, *The Reproduction of Mothering* (Berkeley: University of California Press, 1978).

17. Quoted in Michael J. Sandel, *Liberalism and the Limits of Justice* (Cambridge: Cambridge University Press, 1982), p. 240.

18. Michael Walzer, *Spheres of Justice: A Defense of Pluralism and Equality* (New York: Basic Books, 1983), pp. 31, 64–65.

19. Amy Gutmann, "What's the Use of Going to School?" in *Utilitarianism and Beyond*, ed. Amartya Sen and Bernard Williams (New York: Cambridge University Press, 1982), p. 261.

20. Eugene Genovese, *Roll, Jordan, Roll: The World the Slaves Made* (New York: Vintage Books, 1976), p. 26.

21. Oliver Williamson, "Organizational Form, Residual Claimants, and Corporate Control," *Journal of Law and Economics* 26 (June 1983): 351–66.

22. Kenneth Arrow, "Economic Welfare and the Allocation of Resources for Invention," in National Bureau of Economic Research, *The Rate and Direction of Inventive Activity* (Princeton, N.J.: Princeton University Press, 1962), pp. 609–25.

10

INDIVIDUAL AND COMMUNITY
IN SOCIETY AND NATURE

Frances Moore Lappé and J. Baird Callicott

The contemporary, post-1960s ecological vision began as an extension of the progressive political vision. The broad, popular environmental movement was born in the 1960s—at an intensely political moment in American history. The same capitalist-military-industrial machine that was bombing Hanoi and the Ho Chi Minh trail, searching and destroying South Vietnam—with Black and white working-class American youth as the cannon fodder—was also defoliating Southeast Asian rain forests, building nuclear power plants as well as nuclear weapons at home, and mining and polluting North American soils and waters. Progressive political and ecological movements coalesced in response.

The intellectual sources of both the progressive political and ecological visions are deeply ethical. The lasting appeal of Marx rests on his moral outrage at the human misery and gross social injustice produced by the Industrial Revolution. John Muir, Aldo Leopold, and Rachel Carson were equally outraged by the heartrending destruction of nature brought about by the same historical phenomenon.

The ethical vision and critique of capitalism shared by these two movements have a common root. Both progressive political and ecological movements find individual meaning within community—human society and its several classes on the one hand, and the "biotic community" and its several species on the other.

Their emphasis on the whole, not the individual, sets both ecological and progressive political visionaries apart from the classical liberal tradi-

This article is drawn from a talk given to the Seventh Congress of the International Federation of Organic Agricultural Movements: Global Perspectives on Agroecology and Sustained Agricultural Systems (University of California, Santa Cruz, 1986). A differently edited version appeared in *Tikkun* 2, no. 4 (1987).

tion, which has so shaped Western political and economic thought. Liberalism, from the days of Thomas Hobbes, John Locke, and Adam Smith, places ontological and axiological emphasis on individuals. The liberal tradition proposes an "atomistic" world in which individual appetite is the inertial momentum of each social atom. Each person is imagined to have an inner life or consciousness and to maintain only "external" relations with other similarly insular egos. The liberal vision imagines, further, that an orderly society will shake out of the random collisions of self-seeking individuals or social atoms, as if designed by an "invisible hand."

Traditional liberals attack the left for subordinating the interests and autonomy of individuals to the interests and authority of the social whole, which they see as a spectral menace, threatening the inherent worth, rights, and "freedom" of individuals. Political movements and postcapitalist societies based on Marxist conceptions of class and social organization have indeed typically overemphasized the social whole to the detriment of the individual—and thereby ultimately also to the detriment of the working class, society, or whatever social aggregate has been taken as preeminent. We recognize that ecological holism too often involves inappropriate subordination of the individual to the biota. Yet the individualism of classical liberalism provides no satisfactory basis for social organization either.

Consider, for example, the central problem of individual freedom so dear to the liberal, and to us as well. The progressive political and ecological notions of freedom contrast dramatically with the liberal notion, classically expressed at midcentury by Isaiah Berlin (*Two Concepts of Liberty*, 1958): "The essence of the notion of liberty . . . is the holding off of something or someone—of others, who trespass on my field or assert their authority over me—intruders or despots of one kind or another." In the liberal's world where we social atoms bounce about in limited space, freedom is merely what's left over after others have established their turf—"my freedom ends where your nose begins."

The progressive political and the ecological vision, however, share a concept of freedom different from this literal liberal notion of elbow-room. Both share a more positive and systemic understanding of freedom and responsibility. The political progressive sees the multitudinous ways in which an economic and political structure can indirectly limit or enhance freedom. How many choices do the jobless have when unemployment rates are high? they ask. Freedom cannot flourish unless it is understood to include active responsibility for developing social structures ensuring opportunity to all.

Similarly, the ecological visionary, understanding our systemic links to the entire natural world, expands our responsibility. Our task is not just to refrain from directly harming nature ourselves—an extension of the liberal view. Rather, we should strive to be active "stewards," responsibly safeguarding the well-being of the biosphere.

Such common values open up, we believe, the possibility that the ecological and progressive political movements can reinforce each other and contribute insights concerning the relation and proper balance between individual and community.

The ecological vision offers a reinterpretation of the fundamental concepts of individuality and society which can give new life, meaning, and appeal to the progressive political tradition. Ecological science focuses attention on *relationships*. Indeed, the textbook definition of ecology is the study of the relationships of organisms to one another and to the inorganic environment. Ecology stresses symbiosis in the most general sense of the term. Ecology reveals that organisms are not only mutually related and interdependent; they are also mutually defining. In general, species adapt to a "niche" in the biotic community, to a role or profession in the "economy of nature." The fluctuations of temperature and rainfall and hours of daylight and darkness, the peculiarities of predators and prey, and hundreds of other variables all sculpt the outward and inward forms and structures of Earth's myriad species (*Homo sapiens* not excepted). For example, the polar bear lives in the extremely cold Arctic climate. Its size, intelligence, stealth, white fur, swimming skills, and digestive track are all adaptations to its predatory life way in a world of ice, fish, marine mammals, and frigid sea water.

A species is thus "internally related" to its habitat. That is, its completely unique and identifying characteristics are determined by its network of relationships. It is what it is because of where and how it lives. From an ecological point of view, a species is the intersection of a multiplicity of strands in the web of life. It is not only located *in* its context or related *to* its context; it is literally constituted *by* its context.

When one views the human microcosm through the lens of ecology, a new picture of the relationship of individuals to society snaps into focus. The individual is no longer simply an elemental unit with society taken as either an emergent or an artificial abstraction. Rather, the social whole appears as the organic and enduring matrix that gives form and substance to individual human lives.

From this point of view the modern classical picture of a "state of nature" as drawn by Thomas Hobbes, in which fully formed human beings once lived as solitaries in a condition he described as a "war of each against all," is patently absurd. Not only is it impossible to imagine human beings to have evolved in the absence of an intensely social environment; it is impossible to conceive of a fully formed human "person" apart from a social milieu.

Rather, a person's individuality is constituted by the peculiar concatenation of relationships the person bears to family, friends, neighbors, colleagues, and coworkers. As the polar bear, from an ecological point of view, is internally related to its environment—possessed of its distinctive characteristics by virtue of coevolution with other species within its biotic community—so a person is properly also defined by his or her unique social relationships and interactions.

Compared with the modern monadic paradigm, such a conception of personal identity is more authentic and more involving. We are free to *be* our social roles instead of feeling that they are external to our essential selves and therefore phony or artificial. Our understanding of human happiness can shift from material accumulation and self-indulgence, as the basis of human definition, toward community involvement and social participation.

Since we are ultimately interdependent, from the perspective of a social ecology, it is wrong to pit individual welfare against individual welfare in a zero-sum game. And it becomes equally ridiculous to think in terms of tradeoffs between social integrity and the individual's unfettered pursuit of happiness. The health and integrity of the social whole is literally essential to a socially constituted individual's well-being. Active involvement in a multiplicity of interactions not only enriches and enhances an individual's personal life; it more closely knits together the fibers of the social fabric considered as a whole. Individual welfare and happiness and socially responsible activity thus become one and the same thing. Acknowledging such a vision of individuality, drawn from ecology, would free the progressive political vision both from the destructive social atomism of classic liberalism and the equally chilling reification of class interests long associated with the left.

Once the ecological paradigm—interdependent, synergistic, dynamic—is applied to human society, we can understand freedom differently.

Within the liberal tradition, freedom is a self-possessed and individual characteristic. But if individuality is realized in large part through relationships, then how can freedom be conceived independently of these connections? It cannot. Historically, both visions have been saddled with seemingly burdensome restrictions—social and ecological, respectively—on individual freedom. Now, however, these "restrictions" reappear as opportunities for personal expansion and enhancement.

For example, the responsibility not to pollute or otherwise degrade the environment—a limitation on freedom of action from the reductive point of view—becomes something very like the opportunity to brush one's teeth or put on fresh clothes: activity one can look forward to doing. Similarly, the responsibility to restructure social rules so as to end poverty—a seemingly impossible burden—in the doing becomes, on the contrary, an incredible weight lifted from our shoulders.

Imagine walking through any neighborhood of any city in our country and basking in the vibrant street life with no fear of assault—either psychic or physical—by human misery and deprivation. Or, from the opposite approach, imagine the total deflection of your own energy were you to be handed a pink slip tomorrow with no hope for reemployment. Such positive and negative images may help us grasp the magnitude of the human potential stolen from us by endemic poverty—and thus the incredible potential to be released by its eradication.

More positively still, by letting go of a zero-sum concept of freedom we can see the obvious—that creative human endeavors mutually enhance rather than compete with one another. Each expression inspires, challenges, and provokes the expression of others in an ever changing cultural dynamic.

Consider an example of human activity that immediately involves people in both economic and ecological networks: agriculture. Based on their integrative visions, the movements we have described challenge capitalist agriculture, characterized by large-scale monoculture and the intensive use of energy, chemical inputs, and wage labor. Gone also are the days when political progressives were enamored of the large state-owned or collective model of agricultural organization, efficiently employing the latest technology to free peasants from the land. Thus, both communities have awakened to the problems inherent in the industrial agricultural mode, whether U.S. or U.S.S.R.

The ecologically sensitized focus particularly on how industrial agriculture necessarily *exploits soil and water resources;* the politically sensitized focus on how industrial agriculture *exploits people*, dispossessing peasant producers or family farmers and taking advantage of wage workers. The politically motivated see in large landholdings in the Third World a most grotesque example of such exploitation—peasants starving while good land grows luxury export crops that enrich only a few. Thus both the ecological and the political agree on the need for reform, for distributing control of the land among the majority.

Specifically, three essentials of capitalism undermine a benign agricultural ecology.

First is the market system's glaring omission: *it simply cannot provide the information needed if we are to protect the land and the people who farm it.* The only information the market offers is price. Yet prices—to which all producers in a capitalist market must respond in order to stay in business—do not incorporate the true *resource* or *human* costs of production. Prices of farm commodities do not inform us that their production entails the erosion of topsoil, for example—that now on one-third of U.S. farmland, topsoil is being eroded faster than nature can rebuild it. Neither is the reduction of groundwater reserves registered in the market price. Because the market omits such critical information, it deludes us. What nature makes, we come to see as "free." The market price cannot incorporate the price to be paid by later generations for whom providing food will be more difficult on land with impoverished topsoil and depleted groundwater.

Like the prices of farm commodities, prices of farm inputs—fertilizers, pesticides, machinery—also send farmers false signals. They too fail to incorporate long-term costs or consequences. Following the market's cues, farmers will purchase manufactured inputs as long as they can estimate (hope) that market prices for their crops will be high enough to cover the input costs, plus turn a profit *this year*. The market cannot warn the farmer that the choice of inputs this year may be generating a dependency that will threaten the farmer's very survival on the farm when the prices of these inputs double—as a result of economic forces perhaps unrelated to agriculture altogether. Nor can the market signal health risks from exposure to pesticides, for example.

Most simply put, farming choices guided exclusively or even centrally by the market will be ecologically destructive because the market is blind to costs that cannot be quantified. It assumes *no* cost to nature's supplies—topsoil, natural fertility, groundwater. It assumes less than the real cost of inputs—pesticides, herbicides, fossil fuels, and fertilizers.

And it "externalizes" such costs as environmental pollution and ecological degradation.

Second, within the market system, farmland—like washing machines or waffle irons—is in one sense merely another commodity to be bought and sold in the marketplace. But because the supply of land, especially good farmland, is limited, it is also a *speculative* commodity. People buy it as an investment.

As a speculative commodity, farmland thus acquires a value dissociated from the body of knowledge and skills that are the product of generations on the land. Wealth, not land wisdom, becomes the criterion for ownership. Farmland ownership becomes disconnected from the culture of agriculture.

Third, in the market economy, labor is a commodity as well. And as farmland becomes increasingly the domain of the wealthy, with absentee landlords buying up acreage, more and more farm work is done by workers selling their labor to landowners. In the Third World this process is far advanced. And now, for the first time in American history, most of the work on American farms is done by those who themselves do not live on a farm.

But agriculture dependent upon hired labor belies the vision of agroecology just as much as does heavy use of petrochemical inputs. Agroecology is necessarily knowledge-intensive, dependent on *all* the faculties of the farmer. As agroecology replaces simple monocropping with a mix of crops and animals, farmers must understand the many subtle interrelations of their chosen mix in order to enrich the soil and minimize pest damage.

Thus agroecology depends upon a specific kind of *relationship of the farmer to the land*. It must be enduring, for only over time can the necessary information be acquired. And the farmer must feel a personal stake in the welfare of the land in order to call forth not just the physical exertion required but the mental alertness needed to observe and record subtle changes and interactions over decades. Where land and labor remain mere commodities, such a relationship of the farmer to the land will be the rare exception.

Agroecology and capitalist economic rules, then, are in direct conflict. The market is an insufficient and often even misleading guide to land use. And land and labor treated as commodities dissociate agriculture from its sustaining culture.

Integrating the principles of genuine democracy and economic justice into our economic decision-making will allow us effectively to tame the market—without throwing it out altogether. Only by unflinchingly addressing capitalism's essential rules will true agroecology be possible.

Ecologically destructive practices continuing today in "revolutionary" *non*capitalist societies might seem to put the lie to what we have just said. They do not. The mistakes of noncapitalist society, often inherited from the dominant practice of capitalist society itself, do not alleviate the weaknesses of capitalism. But such sad developments do demonstrate that challenging the dictates of the market, however necessary, is not a *sufficient* step to effect the transition from industrial agriculture to agroecology. Values, attitudes, and specific policies must change, too, as the ecological voices so eloquently remind us. Our point here, however, is that to realize their vision agroecologists cannot retreat from the more controversial, emotionally charged arena of debate on *economic structure* beyond the strictly agronomic questions.

In sum, advanced capitalist society poses a mortal threat to individuals and to the social and natural ecology of the planet. Whether our concern is for the individual in society or for entire species, for human society or for the global environment, we are led to grapple with the dynamic codetermination of individual and whole. The lessons of ecology are in many ways relevant to social organization. Our understanding of how we as individuals are shaped in social and economic contexts, and in turn create those contexts, allows us to push beyond individualism to a more fully human society. It allows us to become more truly respectful of the individuals in it, as well as to appreciate the social and natural structures upon which we all depend and for which we are all responsible.

CONTRIBUTORS

GREGORY BAUM is Professor of Religious Studies at McGill University in Montreal. He is editor of *The Ecumenist* and author of *The Priority of Labor*, *Theology and Society*, and (with Duncan Cameron) *Ethics and Economics*.

SAMUEL BOWLES and HERBERT GINTIS, Professors of Economics at the University of Massachusetts, Amherst, are the authors of *Schooling in Capitalist America: Educational Reform and the Contradictions of Economic Life* and *Democracy and Capitalism: Property, Community, and the Contradictions of Modern Social Thought*. They are now working on the theory and practice of economic democracy.

PAMELA K. BRUBAKER is Assistant Professor of Religious Studies at Cleveland State University and the author of *She Hath Done What She Could: A History of Women's Participation in the Church of the Brethren*.

J. BAIRD CALLICOTT is Professor of Philosophy and Natural Resources at the University of Wisconsin at Stevens Point and author of *In Defense of the Land Ethic*.

NORMAN K. GOTTWALD is Professor of Biblical Studies at New York Theological Seminary. He is author of *The Tribes of Yahweh* and *The Hebrew Bible: A Socio-Literary Introduction*, as well as editor of *The Bible and Liberation*.

FRANCES MOORE LAPPÉ is cofounder of the Institute for Food and Development Policy in San Francisco and author of *Diet for a Small Planet* and *Rediscovering America's Values*.

MICHAEL LERNER, a Jewish liberation theologian, is editor of *Tikkun* magazine— a bimonthly Jewish critique of politics, culture, and society—and author of *Surplus Powerlessness*.

AMATA MILLER, IHM, is Economist and Education Co-ordinator of NETWORK: A National Catholic Social Justice Lobby in Washington, D.C. She has a Ph.D. in economics from the University of California, Berkeley, and is Adjunct Associate Professor of Economics at Marygrove College in Detroit. She writes and lectures widely on economic justice issues and has recently contributed to the *New Dictionary of Catholic Social Thought*.

ANN SEIDMAN is Professor of International Development and Social Change at Clark University, Worcester, Massachusetts. She has been a senior researcher at OXFAM and is the author of *Planning for Development in Sub-Saharan Africa*, *The Roots of Crisis in Southern Africa*, and *Outposts of Monopoly Capitalism: Southern Africa in the Changing Global Economy*.

MICHAEL ZWEIG is Associate Professor of Economics at the State University of New York at Stony Brook. He chaired the planning committee for the Conference on Religion, the Economy, and Social Justice (held at Stony Brook in 1984) and is the author of *The Idea of a World University*.